WOMAN REBEL

THE MARGARET SANGER STORY

By
PETER BAGGE
DRAWN + QUARTERLY

COVER AND INTERIOR COLORING BY JOANNE BAGGE.

www.drawnandquarterly.com

First hardcover edition: September 2013.
Printed in Singapore.
10 9 8 7 6 5 4 3 2 1

Library and Archives Canada Cataloguing in Publication
Bagge, Peter, author, artist
    The Woman Rebel : the Margaret Sanger story / Peter Bagge.
ISBN 978-1-77046-126-0 (bound)
    1. Sanger, Margaret, 1879-1966--Comic books, strips, etc. 2.
Women social reformers--United States--Biography--Comic books,
strips, etc. 3. Birth control--United States--History--20th century--
Comic books, strips, etc. 4. Women's rights--United States--History--
20th century--Comic books, strips, etc. 5. Graphic novels. I. Title.

HQ764.S3B33 2013   363.9'6092   C2013-902364-X

Published in the USA by Drawn & Quarterly, a client publisher of
Farrar, Straus and Giroux
Orders: 888.330.8477

Published in Canada by Drawn & Quarterly, a client publisher of
Raincoast Books
Orders: 800.663.5714

ABOUT THE COVER

Margaret Sanger was prohibited from speaking in Boston, MA, throughout the 1920s by Mayor James Curley (the man most responsible for the phrase "Banned in Boston"). Finally, in 1929, the organizers of the iconoclastic Ford Hall Forum conspired with Sanger to devise a way for her to appear at their annual "frolic" while still technically honoring the ban: by having her take center stage wearing a gag, while historian Arthur Schlesinger Sr. (pictured on the left) read a speech she had written on her behalf (the famous civil rights attorney Clarence Darrow, pictured on the right, followed with a speech of his own).

Sanger's speech read in part:

"I care nothing for Free Speech in and by itself. All of us place too much value on the power of the printed word and the power of the spoken word. We read too much. We listen too much. We live too little. We act too little. . . . I speak to you by my actions past and present. I have been gagged, I have been suppressed, I have been arrested, I have been hauled off to jail. Yet every time, more people have listened to me, more have protested, more have lifted their own voices, more have responded with courage and bravery. . . . As a propagandist, I see immense advantages in being gagged. It silences me, but it makes millions of others talk about me, and the cause in which I live."

On PETER BAGGE and MARGARET SANGER

PETER BAGGE IS AN UNDERAPPRECIATED MASTER OF the comics art form and a hero of American comedy. He was born in 1957, at the tail end of a generation whose most vital artists grappled with the ubiquity of a shared junk culture forced into service as an absurd counterpoint to the specter of nuclear annihilation. Many of the best cartoonists in the generation preceding Bagge seized the means of production but kept to existing forms and styles. They self-published comic books that, save for the subversive elements of their content, looked like something you might buy at the corner drugstore. The best of these comics frequently called on the vitality of earlier, almost forgotten forms of satire for their energy and punch. In contrast, Bagge engaged the American character by combining wildly expressive art and painfully insightful, recursive dialogue. A Peter Bagge comic might recall the visual excesses of past humor comics, might even share their basic comedic grammar, but the effect was more about the clash of two different kinds of energy than it was proper historical context. Bagge's best characters dash themselves against the rocks of promise time and time again, revealing to us but never to themselves through reams of declaration how little they're aware of their own heroic nature. They are Sisyphean actors that fall on their faces long before they get to the job of pushing rocks up hills.

In the first of his two great comic book series, *Neat Stuff* (1985–1989), Bagge provides readers with a revolving cast of protagonists that struggle against the limitations of assigned roles and various appetites and vanities that lock them into basic battles for dignity on terms assigned to them as opposed to grasping any idea of a bigger picture or loftier self-definition that might move them past their immediate surroundings. Junior's embrace of his outsized, nightmarish absurdities; Studs Kirby's alternating rejection of and engagement with the minor platform he's been provided and the rudimentary rewards of bare-bones celebrity that come with it; Chet and Bunny Leeway's basic inability to connect with anything in their world outside of each other; the Bradleys' fevered and at times eerily self-aware absorption into roles and relationships defined for them by well-worn myths about family; each of Bagge's *Neat Stuff*–era serials rips into the central

hopelessness of the 1980s and that decade's shattering combination of core economic exploitation, a cowboy actor with his finger on the button, and bland popular art bleached of all personal vitality for the sake of greater market reach.

Peter Bagge's *Hate* began publication in 1990. It would last thirty issues, concluding in 1998, and has since spawned a small number of stories in sequel annuals. Like the decade which it ruled as one of the two or three most important comedic works in any form, much of what *Hate* accomplished recast the cultural despair of the American Century in the poignantly tragic form of an emergent, feckless youth culture lacking the energy to push back. Through characters like Leonard "Stinky" Brown and the amazing, wholly underappreciated Lisa Leavenworth—arguably the overarching narrative's central protagonist—Bagge gave his audience insight into the kind of people who, on an instinctive level, may be wholly aware they're acting out in painfully circumscribed manners dictated by restrictive cultural triggers but simply don't care or can't see another way to satisfy their enormous appetites. Bagge's iconic everyman Buddy Bradley maintains a sense of dignity by simply embracing his own ordinary nature, by reacting to the outsized personalities around him rather than becoming one himself. *Hate* was by far the most self-aware comic of Bagge's career, serving up a large dollop of criticism for the banalities of a world broken down into character types. It is its creator's greatest work.

In addition to setting the occasional story in Buddy Bradley's world, Bagge has taken aim at the moody Lee/Kirby/Ditko Marvel Comics kid-friendly take on the same central identity dilemmas he satirized more directly and with greater poignancy, delved into more extreme character studies closer to his earliest works than to his later ones, made subversive yet strangely straightforward kids comics, crafted science fiction, reported science fact, and forged a significant number of lively first-person essays in comics form for outlets like the libertarian magazine Reason. The cartoonist seems an odd man out right now in a number of ways, an outsized actor set adrift in a cultural landscape he as much as anyone helped create. Successors on the comics page have tended to embrace lurid, more direct extremes rather than sticking to Bagge's strategy of measured, lengthy narratives. Every post-Huxtables TV family to gain any sort of foothold with an audience boasts a significant amount of the Bradleys and their unblinking, endearing horribleness encoded directly into their DNA, even though Bagge seems to receive little credit of this type. It seems like it should be Peter Bagge's world, and it's anything but.

ENTER MARGARET SANGER.

At first the longtime birth control advocate and twentieth-century political celebrity seems an unlikely subject for a Peter Bagge stand-alone graphic novel, even one that clocks in at a mere seventy-two pages (incredibly dense pages though they may be). For one thing, given the horrors of exploitative, life-destroying moral positioning defined by deep gender biases, it hardly seems like hilarity is near at hand. For another, Sanger enjoyed a great deal of agency and real-world success as a result; she was accomplished in measurable ways matched by almost no one Bagge has ever evoked in comics form, even for the brief period of time defined by an essay of a dozen or fewer pages. If the typical Peter Bagge fictional constructs only find a measure of happiness when they embrace their own idiosyncratic appetites and allow themselves to flower in whatever direction the nourishing sun might meet them, Margaret Sanger locked into a different path fairly early on, defined by a collision of social justice and ego. She may have been satisfied with how things turned out in the end, but personal happiness or fulfillment doesn't even seem like it's an issue. In Bagge's comedies his protagonists come to terms with their limitations; Sanger shattered a lot of those placed in front of her and came up with a list of new criteria upon which her life might be judged.

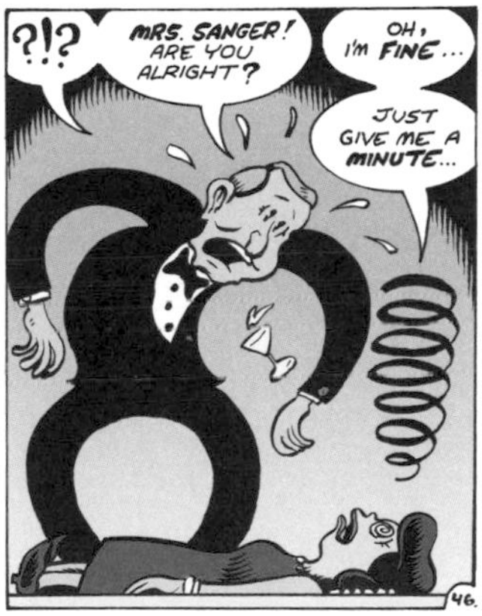
?!?
MRS. SANGER! ARE YOU ALRIGHT?
OH, I'M FINE...
JUST GIVE ME A MINUTE...
46.

What works for *Woman Rebel* and makes what follows not just a fine Peter Bagge comic book narrative but an intriguing character study independent of form is that Bagge treats this wholly unique person as just another person with problems, as someone with an inflated sense of self and a whole list of appetites and specific desires to fulfill on her way from cradle to grave. Bagge portrays Sanger as a comedic protagonist, an upright pile of conflicting wants and needs that is more or less aimed at various issues rather than someone who nobly processes her way through them. Bagge begins by detailing flourishes of personality through conspiratorial asides and digressive thought balloons. Sanger fools a classmate into helping her wash the dishes; she mentally flips her dopey, selfish husband the bird in declaring her intention to pursue free love opportunities once he's away; she sticks her tongue out like a schoolkid when crafting a sarcastic response to the editorial malfeasance of Anthony Comstock. Bagge engages her vanity directly, including even the mostly disastrous late-period Mike Wallace interview that was more about Sanger taking a last walk in the spotlight than it was forwarding any cause. He ends Sanger's story with a scene that might give a film director steeped in crudity pause, and a one-liner at once heartwrenching and brutally hilarious.

What distinguishes Bagge's approach to this specific story is the amount of research he's done and how judiciously he applies what he's learned. Bagge's initial interest in Margaret Sanger came about after he read conflicting reports on what she did and why in a variety of secondary sources touching on related concerns. For as much as *Woman Rebel* is fashioned around any number of comedic comics-medium tropes and an arch visual shorthand, it's also rigorous in a way that reflects Bagge's more recent journalism and the career through-line that is the satirist's desire to get at essential truths. For as much as any Bagge protagonist is hemmed in by social obligation and all-too-human limitations in their imaginative self-conception, Sanger here seems fairly restored from the depredations of those who would use her to make political arguments across an array of perspectives, arguments that don't stand up to insight and scrutiny. It's an act of kindness Bagge does where Margaret Sanger is concerned that he helps restore her wider political legacy even as he pokes fun at some—not all—of the driving forces behind it. Peter Bagge believes in the human condition more than he does the distorting tools of modern media and political opportunism. His Margaret Sanger may sometimes act like a fool in pursuit of her social agenda, but she is her own person. It's the comedians that see the dignity in trampled souls, and Peter Bagge is one of the greats. This is fine work from an excellent cartoonist and I urge you to jump right in.
—Tom Spurgeon

TOM SPURGEON IS THE EDITOR OF THE COMICS REPORTER

WOMAN
REBEL

THE
MARGARET SANGER
STORY

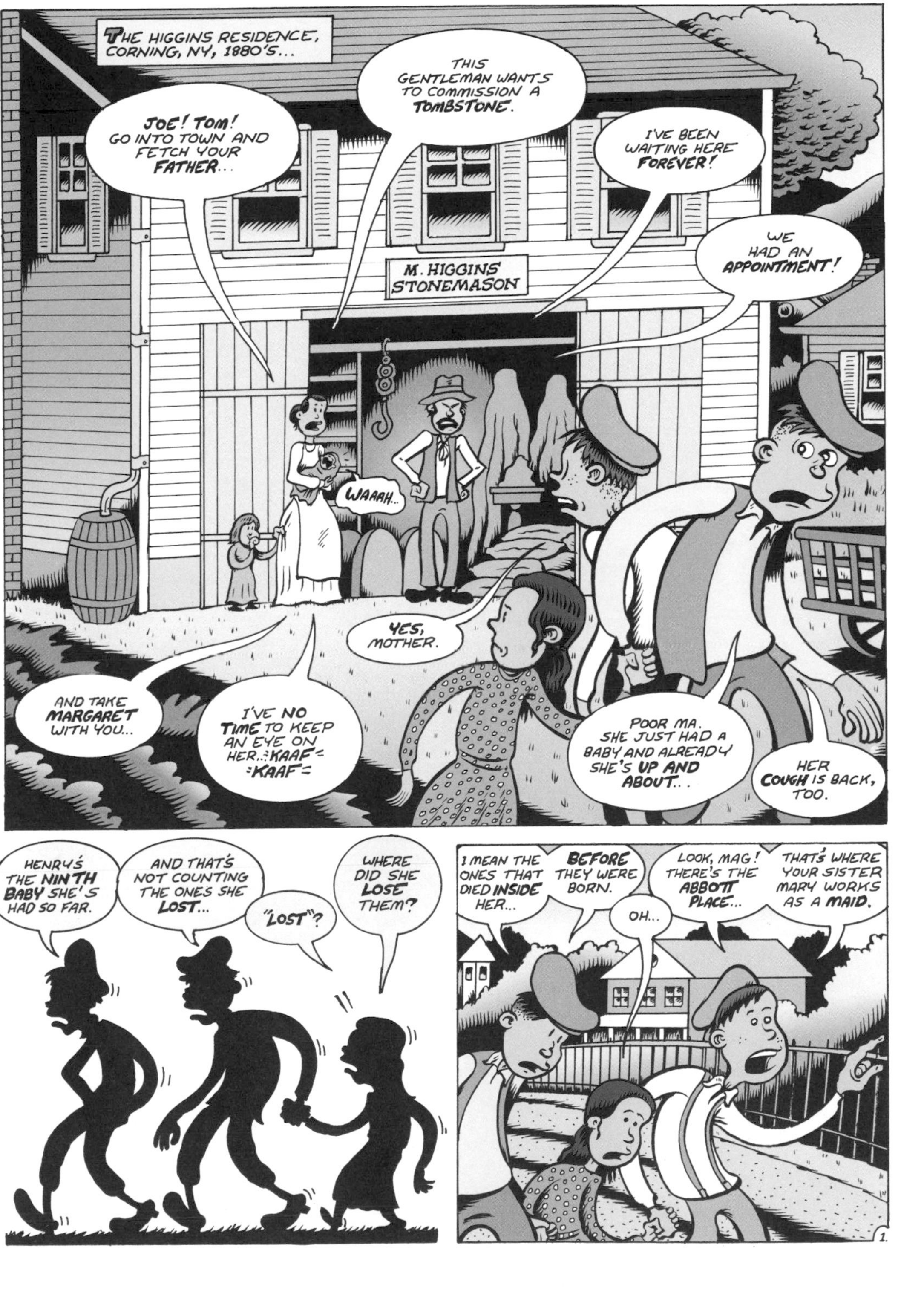
THE HIGGINS RESIDENCE, CORNING, NY, 1880'S...
JOE! TOM! GO INTO TOWN AND FETCH YOUR FATHER...
THIS GENTLEMAN WANTS TO COMMISSION A TOMBSTONE.
I'VE BEEN WAITING HERE FOREVER!
WE HAD AN APPOINTMENT!
M. HIGGINS' STONEMASON
WAAAH...
YES, MOTHER.
AND TAKE MARGARET WITH YOU...
I'VE NO TIME TO KEEP AN EYE ON HER.. =KAAF= =KAAF=
POOR MA. SHE JUST HAD A BABY AND ALREADY SHE'S UP AND ABOUT...
HER COUGH IS BACK, TOO.
HENRY'S THE NINTH BABY SHE'S HAD SO FAR.
AND THAT'S NOT COUNTING THE ONES SHE LOST...
"LOST"?
WHERE DID SHE LOSE THEM?
I MEAN THE ONES THAT DIED INSIDE HER...
BEFORE THEY WERE BORN.
OH...
LOOK, MAG! THERE'S THE ABBOTT PLACE...
THAT'S WHERE YOUR SISTER MARY WORKS AS A MAID.

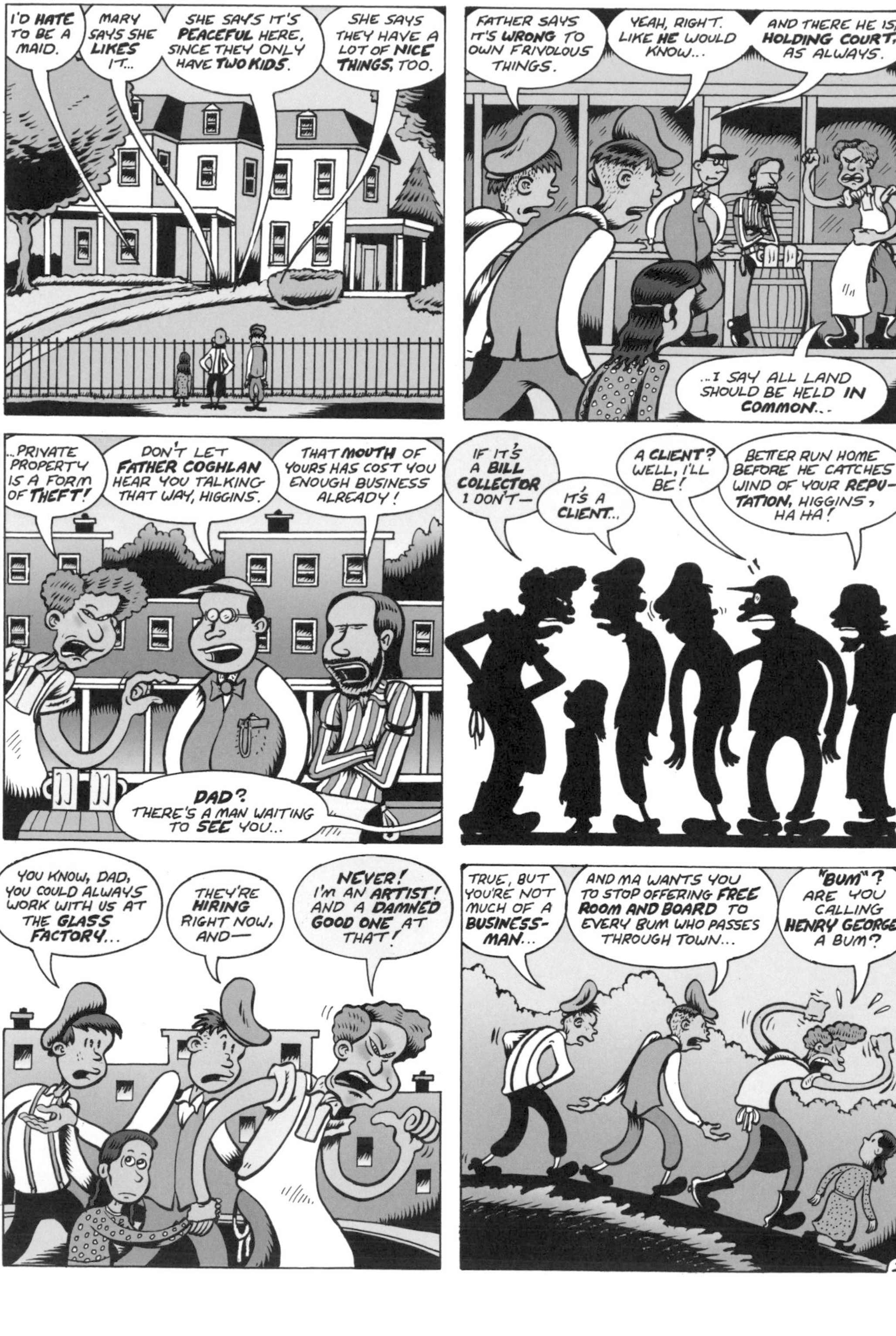
I'D HATE TO BE A MAID.
MARY SAYS SHE LIKES IT...
SHE SAYS IT'S PEACEFUL HERE, SINCE THEY ONLY HAVE TWO KIDS.
SHE SAYS THEY HAVE A LOT OF NICE THINGS, TOO.
FATHER SAYS IT'S WRONG TO OWN FRIVOLOUS THINGS.
YEAH, RIGHT. LIKE HE WOULD KNOW...
AND THERE HE IS, HOLDING COURT, AS ALWAYS.
...I SAY ALL LAND SHOULD BE HELD IN COMMON...
...PRIVATE PROPERTY IS A FORM OF THEFT!
DON'T LET FATHER COGHLAN HEAR YOU TALKING THAT WAY, HIGGINS.
THAT MOUTH OF YOURS HAS COST YOU ENOUGH BUSINESS ALREADY!
DAD? THERE'S A MAN WAITING TO SEE YOU...
IF IT'S A BILL COLLECTOR I DON'T—
IT'S A CLIENT...
A CLIENT? WELL, I'LL BE!
BETTER RUN HOME BEFORE HE CATCHES WIND OF YOUR REPUTATION, HIGGINS, HA HA!
YOU KNOW, DAD, YOU COULD ALWAYS WORK WITH US AT THE GLASS FACTORY...
THEY'RE HIRING RIGHT NOW, AND—
NEVER! I'M AN ARTIST! AND A DAMNED GOOD ONE AT THAT!
TRUE, BUT YOU'RE NOT MUCH OF A BUSINESSMAN...
AND MA WANTS YOU TO STOP OFFERING FREE ROOM AND BOARD TO EVERY BUM WHO PASSES THROUGH TOWN...
"BUM"? ARE YOU CALLING HENRY GEORGE A BUM?
2.

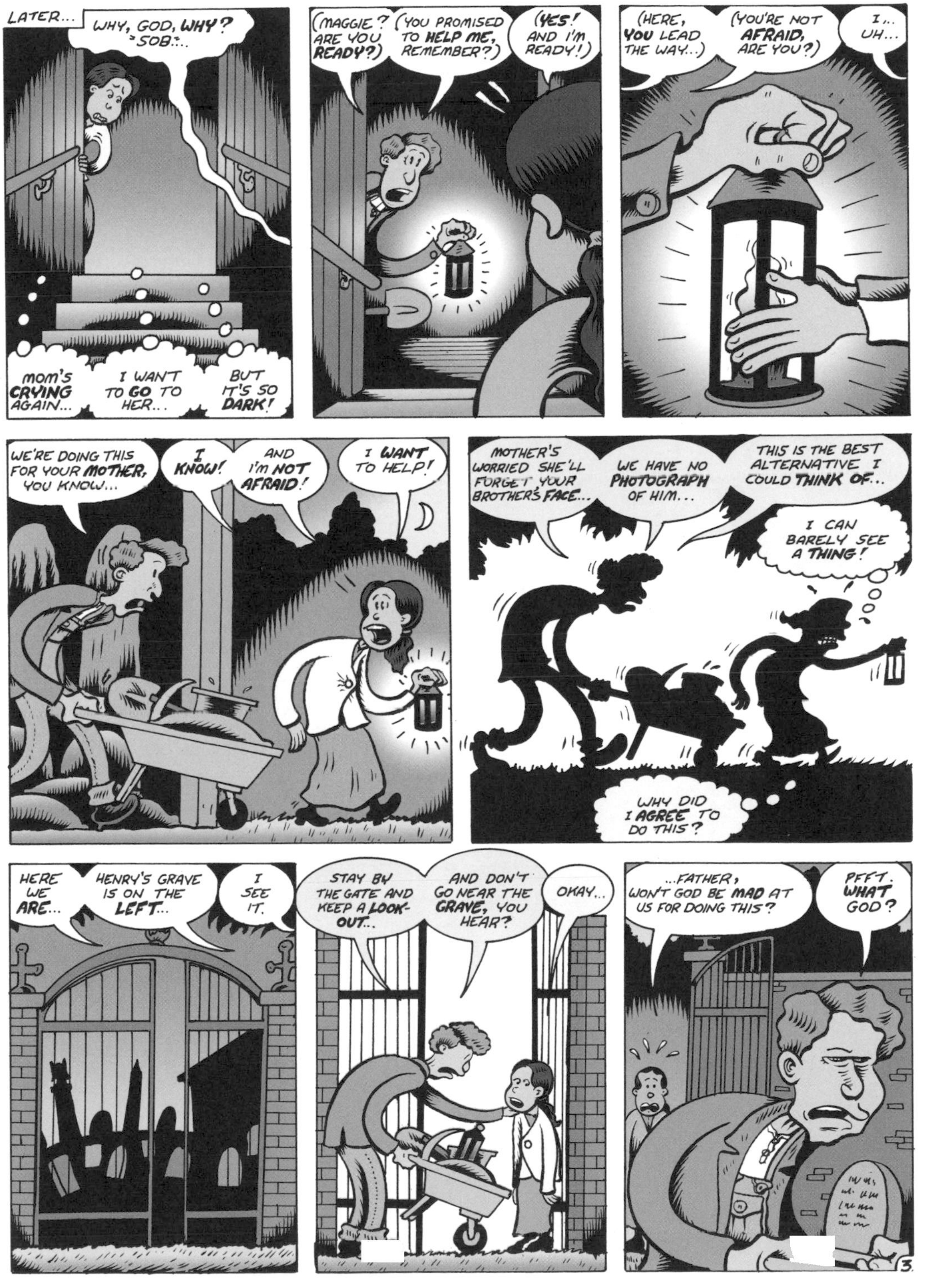
LATER...
WHY, GOD, WHY? SOB...
MOM'S CRYING AGAIN...
I WANT TO GO TO HER...
BUT IT'S SO DARK!
(MAGGIE? ARE YOU READY?)
(YOU PROMISED TO HELP ME, REMEMBER?)
(YES! AND I'M READY!)
(HERE, YOU LEAD THE WAY...)
(YOU'RE NOT AFRAID, ARE YOU?)
I... UH...
WE'RE DOING THIS FOR YOUR MOTHER, YOU KNOW...
I KNOW!
AND I'M NOT AFRAID!
I WANT TO HELP!
MOTHER'S WORRIED SHE'LL FORGET YOUR BROTHER'S FACE...
WE HAVE NO PHOTOGRAPH OF HIM...
THIS IS THE BEST ALTERNATIVE I COULD THINK OF...
I CAN BARELY SEE A THING!
WHY DID I AGREE TO DO THIS?
HERE WE ARE...
HENRY'S GRAVE IS ON THE LEFT...
I SEE IT.
STAY BY THE GATE AND KEEP A LOOK-OUT...
AND DON'T GO NEAR THE GRAVE, YOU HEAR?
OKAY...
...FATHER, WON'T GOD BE MAD AT US FOR DOING THIS?
PFFT. WHAT GOD?

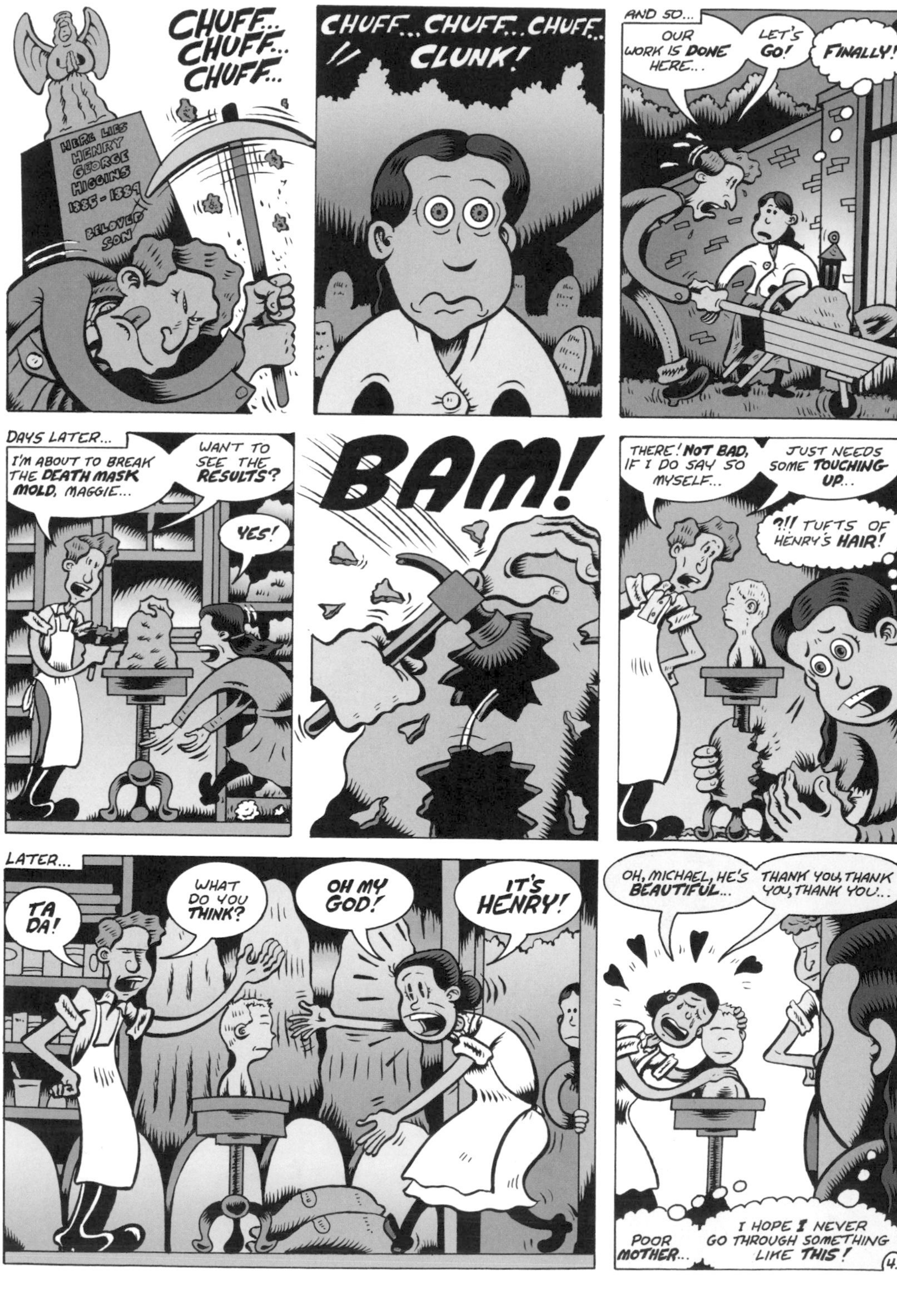
CHUFF... CHUFF... CHUFF...
HERE LIES HENRY GEORGE HIGGINS 1885-1889 BELOVED SON
CHUFF... CHUFF... CHUFF...
CLUNK!
AND SO...
OUR WORK IS DONE HERE...
LET'S GO!
FINALLY!
DAYS LATER...
I'M ABOUT TO BREAK THE DEATH MASK MOLD, MAGGIE...
WANT TO SEE THE RESULTS?
YES!
BAM!
THERE! NOT BAD, IF I DO SAY SO MYSELF...
JUST NEEDS SOME TOUCHING UP...
?!! TUFTS OF HENRY'S HAIR!
LATER...
TA DA!
WHAT DO YOU THINK?
OH MY GOD!
IT'S HENRY!
OH, MICHAEL, HE'S BEAUTIFUL...
THANK YOU, THANK YOU, THANK YOU...
POOR MOTHER...
I HOPE I NEVER GO THROUGH SOMETHING LIKE THIS!

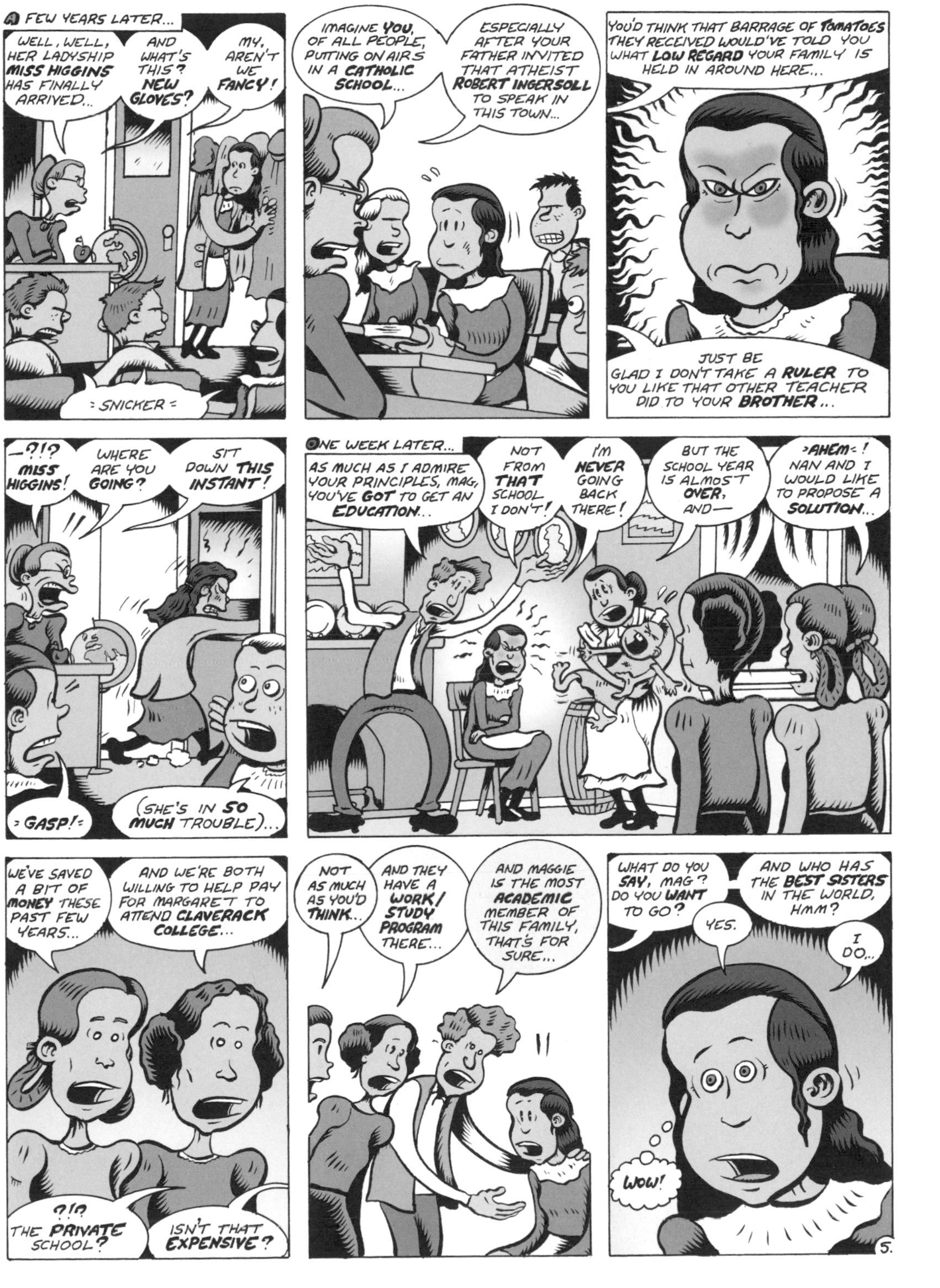

A FEW YEARS LATER...
WELL, WELL, HER LADYSHIP MISS HIGGINS HAS FINALLY ARRIVED...
AND WHAT'S THIS? NEW GLOVES?
MY, AREN'T WE FANCY!
=SNICKER=
IMAGINE YOU, OF ALL PEOPLE, PUTTING ON AIRS IN A CATHOLIC SCHOOL...
ESPECIALLY AFTER YOUR FATHER INVITED THAT ATHEIST ROBERT INGERSOLL TO SPEAK IN THIS TOWN...
YOU'D THINK THAT BARRAGE OF TOMATOES THEY RECEIVED WOULD'VE TOLD YOU WHAT LOW REGARD YOUR FAMILY IS HELD IN AROUND HERE...
JUST BE GLAD I DON'T TAKE A RULER TO YOU LIKE THAT OTHER TEACHER DID TO YOUR BROTHER...
—?!? MISS HIGGINS!
WHERE ARE YOU GOING?
SIT DOWN THIS INSTANT!
=GASP!=
(SHE'S IN SO MUCH TROUBLE)...
ONE WEEK LATER...
AS MUCH AS I ADMIRE YOUR PRINCIPLES, MAG, YOU'VE GOT TO GET AN EDUCATION...
NOT FROM THAT SCHOOL I DON'T!
I'M NEVER GOING BACK THERE!
BUT THE SCHOOL YEAR IS ALMOST OVER, AND—
=AHEM=! NAN AND I WOULD LIKE TO PROPOSE A SOLUTION...
WE'VE SAVED A BIT OF MONEY THESE PAST FEW YEARS...
AND WE'RE BOTH WILLING TO HELP PAY FOR MARGARET TO ATTEND CLAVERACK COLLEGE...
?!? THE PRIVATE SCHOOL?
ISN'T THAT EXPENSIVE?
NOT AS MUCH AS YOU'D THINK...
AND THEY HAVE A WORK/STUDY PROGRAM THERE...
AND MAGGIE IS THE MOST ACADEMIC MEMBER OF THIS FAMILY, THAT'S FOR SURE...
WHAT DO YOU SAY, MAG? DO YOU WANT TO GO?
YES.
AND WHO HAS THE BEST SISTERS IN THE WORLD, HMM?
I DO...
WOW!

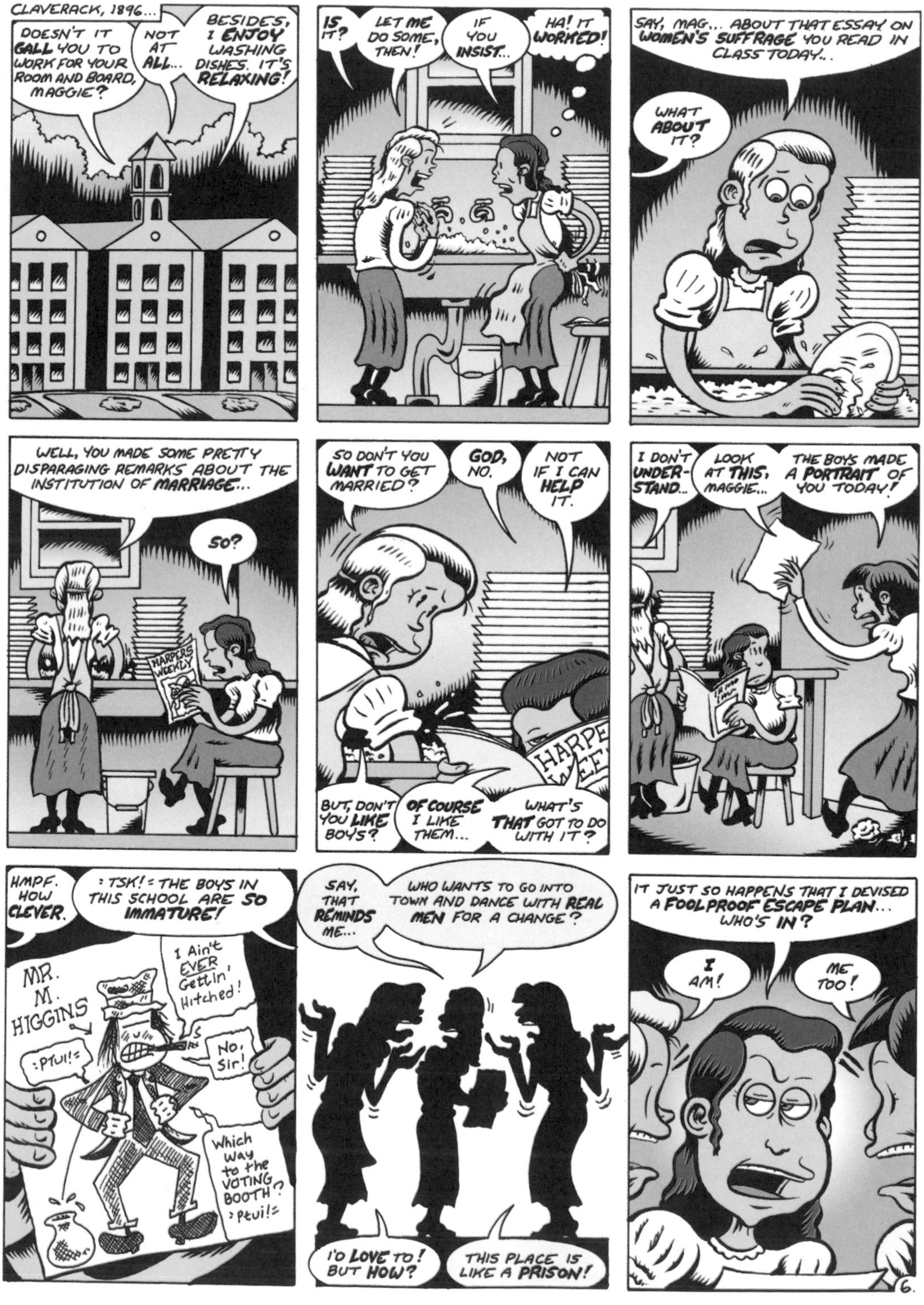
CLAVERACK, 1896...
DOESN'T IT GALL YOU TO WORK FOR YOUR ROOM AND BOARD, MAGGIE?
NOT AT ALL...
BESIDES, I ENJOY WASHING DISHES. IT'S RELAXING!
IS IT?
LET ME DO SOME, THEN!
IF YOU INSIST...
HA! IT WORKED!
SAY, MAG... ABOUT THAT ESSAY ON WOMEN'S SUFFRAGE YOU READ IN CLASS TODAY...
WHAT ABOUT IT?
WELL, YOU MADE SOME PRETTY DISPARAGING REMARKS ABOUT THE INSTITUTION OF MARRIAGE...
SO?
HARPERS WEEKLY
SO DON'T YOU WANT TO GET MARRIED?
GOD, NO.
NOT IF I CAN HELP IT.
BUT, DON'T YOU LIKE BOYS?
OF COURSE I LIKE THEM...
WHAT'S THAT GOT TO DO WITH IT?
I DON'T UNDER-STAND...
LOOK AT THIS, MAGGIE...
THE BOYS MADE A PORTRAIT OF YOU TODAY!
HMPF. HOW CLEVER.
:TSK!: THE BOYS IN THIS SCHOOL ARE SO IMMATURE!
MR. M. HIGGINS
I Ain't EVER Gettin' Hitched!
:PTUI!:
No, Sir!
Which way to the VOTING BOOTH?
:Ptui!:
SAY, THAT REMINDS ME...
WHO WANTS TO GO INTO TOWN AND DANCE WITH REAL MEN FOR A CHANGE?
I'D LOVE TO! BUT HOW?
THIS PLACE IS LIKE A PRISON!
IT JUST SO HAPPENS THAT I DEVISED A FOOLPROOF ESCAPE PLAN... WHO'S IN?
I AM!
ME TOO!

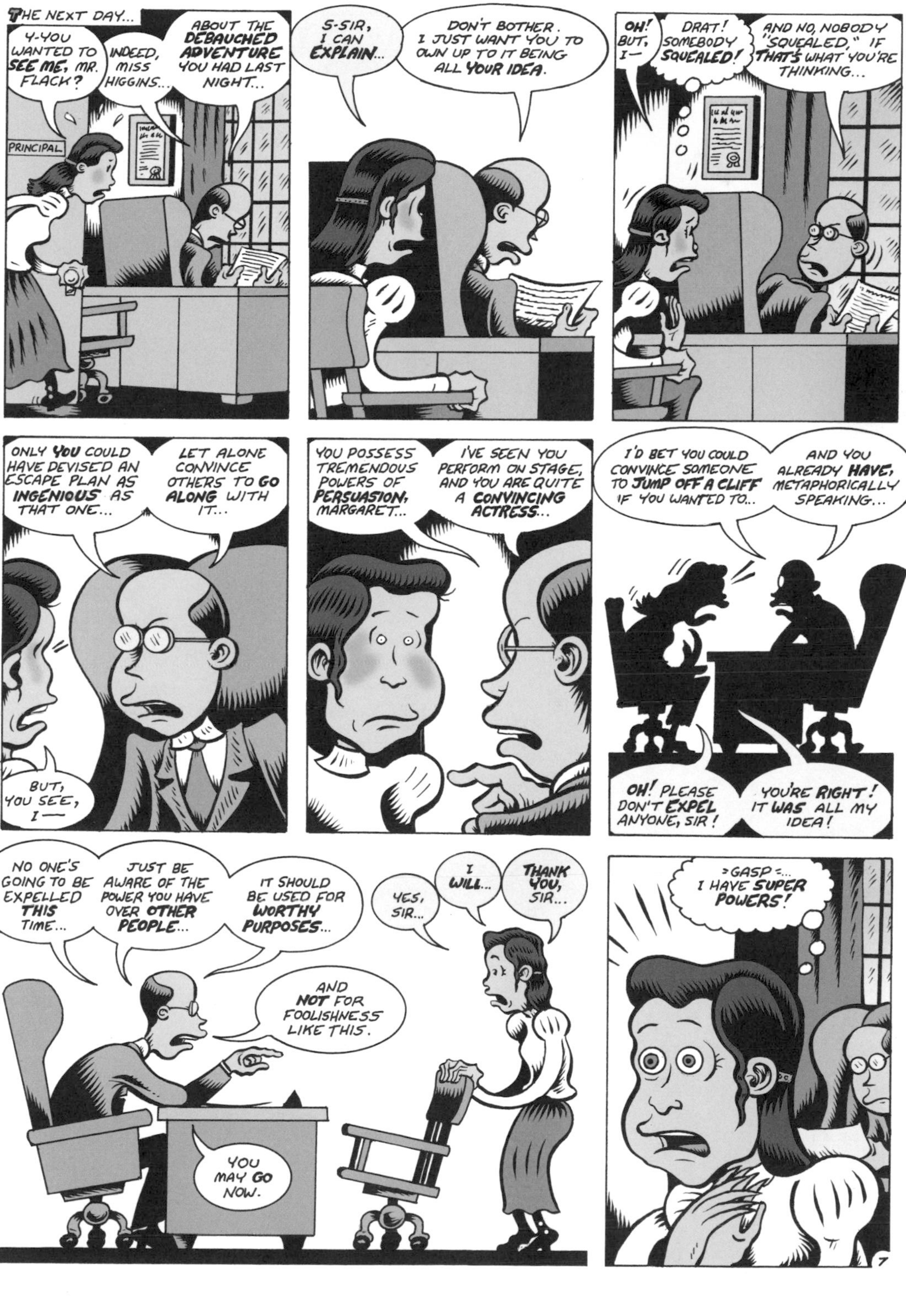
THE NEXT DAY...
Y-YOU WANTED TO SEE ME, MR. FLACK?
INDEED, MISS HIGGINS...
ABOUT THE DEBAUCHED ADVENTURE YOU HAD LAST NIGHT...
PRINCIPAL
S-SIR, I CAN EXPLAIN...
DON'T BOTHER. I JUST WANT YOU TO OWN UP TO IT BEING ALL YOUR IDEA.
OH! BUT, I—
DRAT! SOMEBODY SQUEALED!
AND NO, NOBODY "SQUEALED," IF THAT'S WHAT YOU'RE THINKING...
ONLY YOU COULD HAVE DEVISED AN ESCAPE PLAN AS INGENIOUS AS THAT ONE...
LET ALONE CONVINCE OTHERS TO GO ALONG WITH IT...
BUT, YOU SEE, I—
YOU POSSESS TREMENDOUS POWERS OF PERSUASION, MARGARET...
I'VE SEEN YOU PERFORM ON STAGE, AND YOU ARE QUITE A CONVINCING ACTRESS...
I'D BET YOU COULD CONVINCE SOMEONE TO JUMP OFF A CLIFF IF YOU WANTED TO...
AND YOU ALREADY HAVE, METAPHORICALLY SPEAKING...
OH! PLEASE DON'T EXPEL ANYONE, SIR!
YOU'RE RIGHT! IT WAS ALL MY IDEA!
NO ONE'S GOING TO BE EXPELLED THIS TIME...
JUST BE AWARE OF THE POWER YOU HAVE OVER OTHER PEOPLE...
IT SHOULD BE USED FOR WORTHY PURPOSES...
AND NOT FOR FOOLISHNESS LIKE THIS.
YOU MAY GO NOW.
YES, SIR...
I WILL...
THANK YOU, SIR...
=GASP=... I HAVE SUPER POWERS!

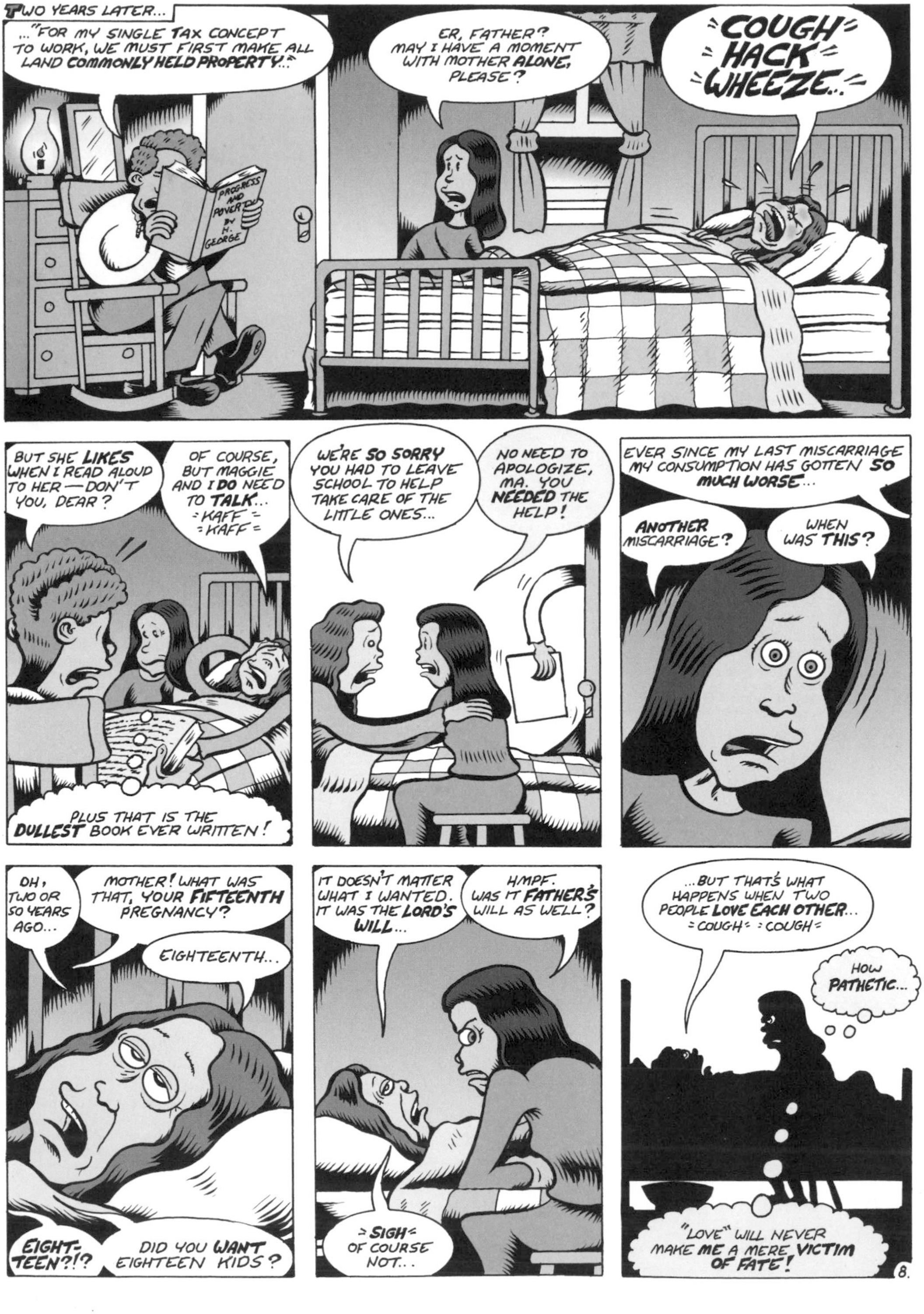
TWO YEARS LATER...
..."FOR MY SINGLE TAX CONCEPT TO WORK, WE MUST FIRST MAKE ALL LAND COMMONLY HELD PROPERTY."...
ER, FATHER? MAY I HAVE A MOMENT WITH MOTHER ALONE, PLEASE?
COUGH HACK WHEEZE...
PROGRESS AND POVERTY BY H. GEORGE
BUT SHE LIKES WHEN I READ ALOUD TO HER — DON'T YOU, DEAR?
OF COURSE, BUT MAGGIE AND I DO NEED TO TALK... KAFF KAFF
PLUS THAT IS THE DULLEST BOOK EVER WRITTEN!
WE'RE SO SORRY YOU HAD TO LEAVE SCHOOL TO HELP TAKE CARE OF THE LITTLE ONES...
NO NEED TO APOLOGIZE, MA. YOU NEEDED THE HELP!
EVER SINCE MY LAST MISCARRIAGE MY CONSUMPTION HAS GOTTEN SO MUCH WORSE...
ANOTHER MISCARRIAGE?
WHEN WAS THIS?
OH, TWO OR SO YEARS AGO...
MOTHER! WHAT WAS THAT, YOUR FIFTEENTH PREGNANCY?
EIGHTEENTH...
EIGHT-TEEN?!?
DID YOU WANT EIGHTEEN KIDS?
IT DOESN'T MATTER WHAT I WANTED. IT WAS THE LORD'S WILL...
HMPF. WAS IT FATHER'S WILL AS WELL?
SIGH OF COURSE NOT...
...BUT THAT'S WHAT HAPPENS WHEN TWO PEOPLE LOVE EACH OTHER... COUGH COUGH
HOW PATHETIC...
"LOVE" WILL NEVER MAKE ME A MERE VICTIM OF FATE!

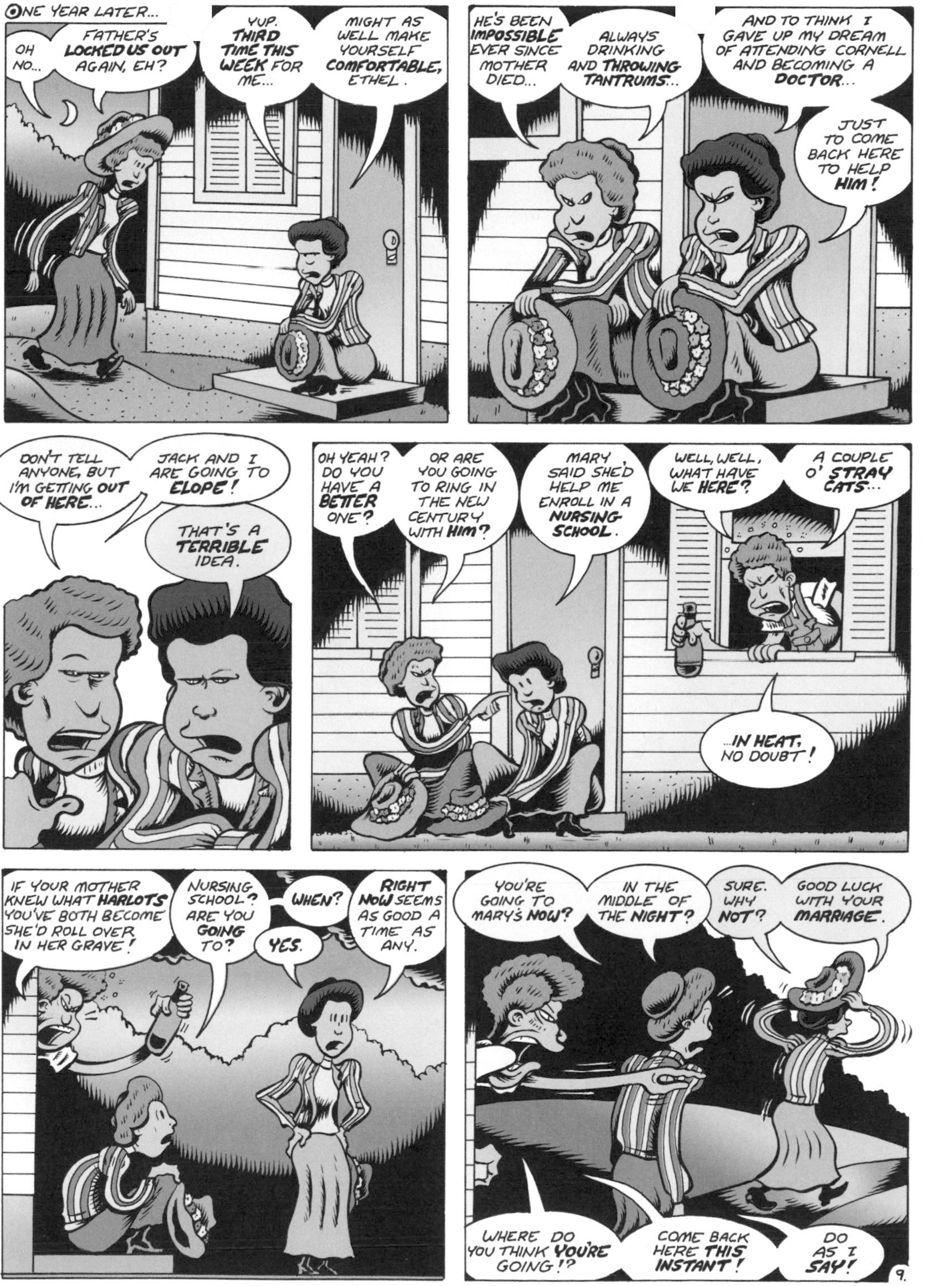
One year later...
Oh no...
Father's **locked us out** again, eh?
Yup. **Third time this week** for me...
Might as well make yourself **comfortable,** Ethel.
He's been **impossible** ever since mother died...
Always drinking and **throwing tantrums**...
And to think I gave up my dream of attending Cornell and becoming a **doctor**...
Just to come back here to help **him!**
Don't tell anyone, but I'm getting **out of here**...
Jack and I are going to **elope!**
That's a **terrible** idea.
Oh yeah? Do you have a **better** one?
Or are you going to ring in the new century with **him?**
Mary said she'd help me enroll in a **nursing school**.
Well, well, what have we **here?**
A couple o' **stray cats**...
...**In heat,** no doubt!
If your mother knew what **harlots** you've both become she'd roll over in her grave!
Nursing school? Are you **going** to?
When?
Yes.
Right now seems as good a time as any.
You're going to Mary's **now?**
In the middle of the **night?**
Sure. Why **not?**
Good luck with your **marriage**.
Where do you think **you're** going!?
Come back here **this instant!**
Do as I **say!**
9.

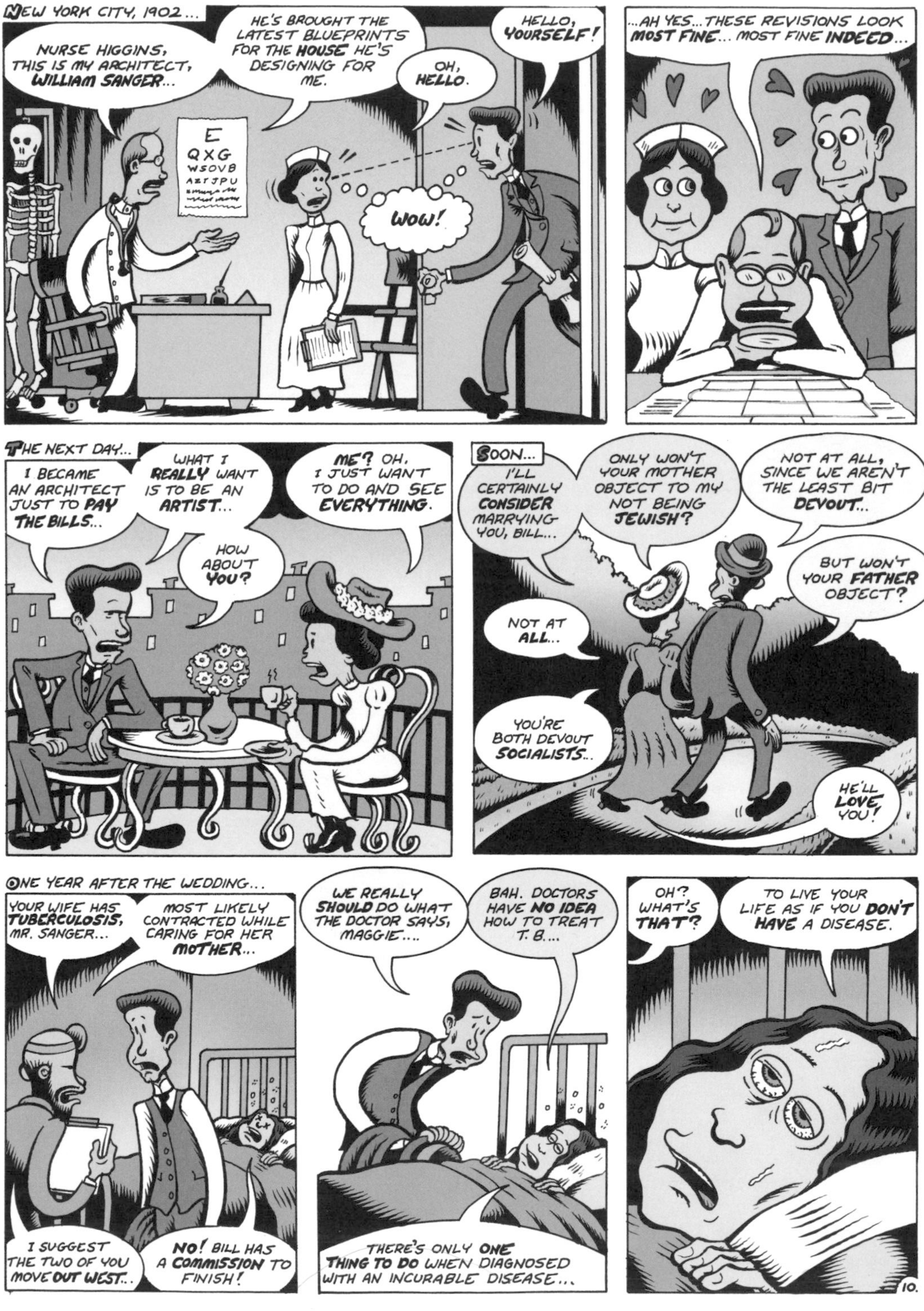
NEW YORK CITY, 1902...
NURSE HIGGINS, THIS IS MY ARCHITECT, WILLIAM SANGER...
HE'S BROUGHT THE LATEST BLUEPRINTS FOR THE HOUSE HE'S DESIGNING FOR ME.
OH, HELLO.
HELLO, YOURSELF!
E QXG WSOVB AZTJPU
WOW!
...AH YES... THESE REVISIONS LOOK MOST FINE... MOST FINE INDEED...
THE NEXT DAY...
I BECAME AN ARCHITECT JUST TO PAY THE BILLS...
WHAT I REALLY WANT IS TO BE AN ARTIST...
HOW ABOUT YOU?
ME? OH, I JUST WANT TO DO AND SEE EVERYTHING.
SOON...
I'LL CERTAINLY CONSIDER MARRYING YOU, BILL...
ONLY WON'T YOUR MOTHER OBJECT TO MY NOT BEING JEWISH?
NOT AT ALL, SINCE WE AREN'T THE LEAST BIT DEVOUT...
BUT WON'T YOUR FATHER OBJECT?
NOT AT ALL...
YOU'RE BOTH DEVOUT SOCIALISTS...
HE'LL LOVE YOU!
ONE YEAR AFTER THE WEDDING...
YOUR WIFE HAS TUBERCULOSIS, MR. SANGER...
MOST LIKELY CONTRACTED WHILE CARING FOR HER MOTHER...
I SUGGEST THE TWO OF YOU MOVE OUT WEST...
NO! BILL HAS A COMMISSION TO FINISH!
WE REALLY SHOULD DO WHAT THE DOCTOR SAYS, MAGGIE....
BAH. DOCTORS HAVE NO IDEA HOW TO TREAT T.B....
THERE'S ONLY ONE THING TO DO WHEN DIAGNOSED WITH AN INCURABLE DISEASE...
OH? WHAT'S THAT?
TO LIVE YOUR LIFE AS IF YOU DON'T HAVE A DISEASE.

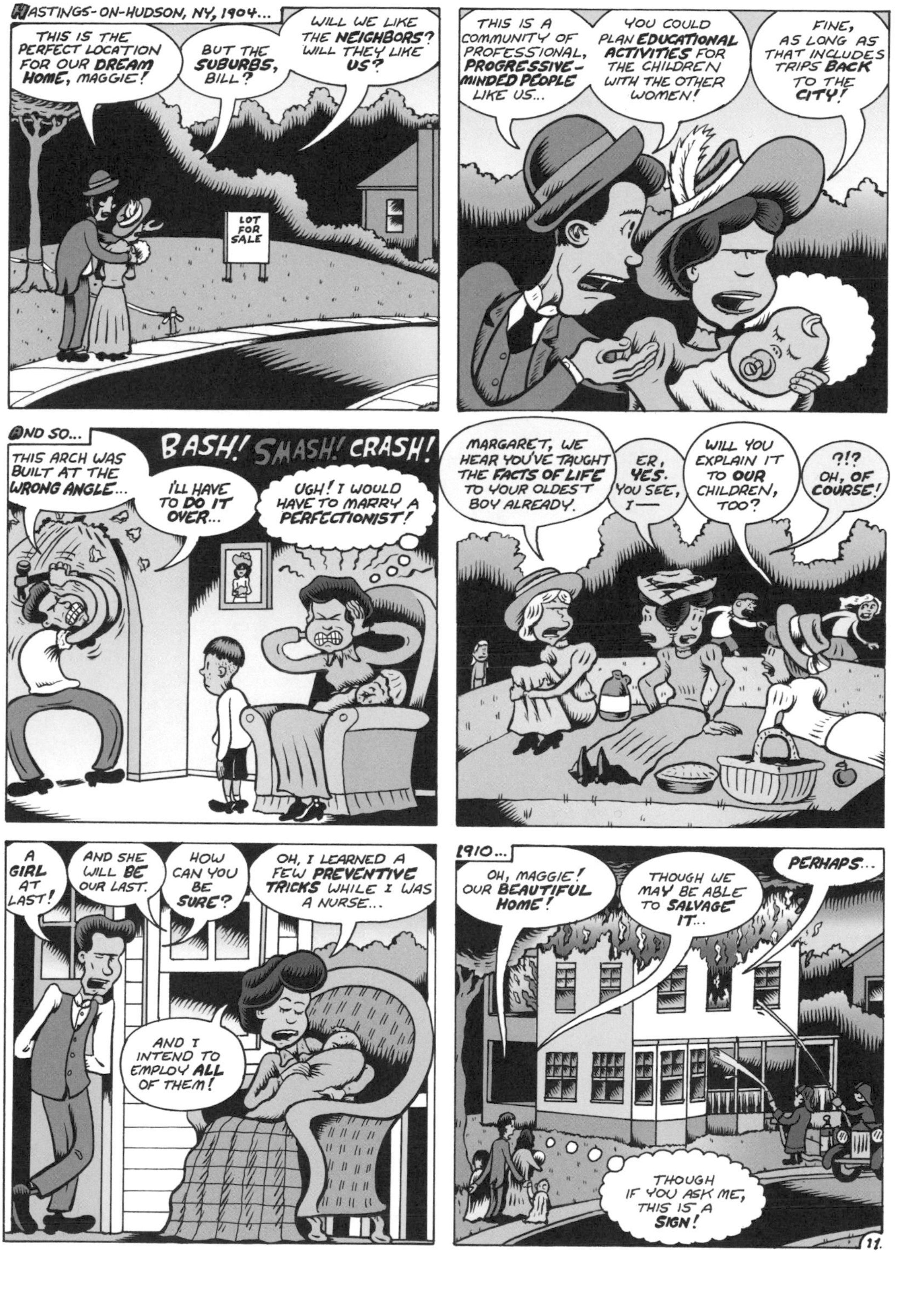
HASTINGS-ON-HUDSON, NY, 1904...
THIS IS THE PERFECT LOCATION FOR OUR DREAM HOME, MAGGIE!
BUT THE SUBURBS, BILL?
WILL WE LIKE THE NEIGHBORS? WILL THEY LIKE US?
LOT FOR SALE
THIS IS A COMMUNITY OF PROFESSIONAL, PROGRESSIVE-MINDED PEOPLE LIKE US...
YOU COULD PLAN EDUCATIONAL ACTIVITIES FOR THE CHILDREN WITH THE OTHER WOMEN!
FINE, AS LONG AS THAT INCLUDES TRIPS BACK TO THE CITY!
AND SO...
BASH! SMASH! CRASH!
THIS ARCH WAS BUILT AT THE WRONG ANGLE...
I'LL HAVE TO DO IT OVER...
UGH! I WOULD HAVE TO MARRY A PERFECTIONIST!
MARGARET, WE HEAR YOU'VE TAUGHT THE FACTS OF LIFE TO YOUR OLDEST BOY ALREADY.
ER, YES. YOU SEE, I—
WILL YOU EXPLAIN IT TO OUR CHILDREN, TOO?
?!? OH, OF COURSE!
A GIRL AT LAST!
AND SHE WILL BE OUR LAST.
HOW CAN YOU BE SURE?
OH, I LEARNED A FEW PREVENTIVE TRICKS WHILE I WAS A NURSE...
AND I INTEND TO EMPLOY ALL OF THEM!
1910...
OH, MAGGIE! OUR BEAUTIFUL HOME!
THOUGH WE MAY BE ABLE TO SALVAGE IT...
PERHAPS...
THOUGH IF YOU ASK ME, THIS IS A SIGN!

NEW YORK CITY, 1912...

I'M ALL FOR YOU RESUMING YOUR **CAREER** AGAIN, MAGGIE...

BUT MUST YOU MAKE HOUSE CALLS ON THE **LOWER EAST SIDE**?

WOULDN'T YOU RATHER BE A **PRIVATE NURSE** FOR SOME OLD RICH GUY?

IT'S THE POOR WHO **NEED ME,** BILL.

WHAT ABOUT **YOUR OWN** HEALTH?

YOU STILL GET T.B. **FLARE-UPS**...

AND THE **AIR** IN THOSE TENEMENTS—

LEAVE HER ALONE, BILL!

SHE'S DOINK A **GOOD** TING...

IT'S A **MITZVAH** IS WHAT IT TIZ!

THANK YOU, MRS. SANGER...

AND THANKS FOR **WATCHING THE KIDS** FOR US AS WELL...

I JUST HOPE YOUR **YIDDISH** ACCENT DOESN'T RUB OFF ON **THEM**!

IT TIZ MY **PLEASURE!**

JUST DON'T BE **LATE**, MAGS...

YOU PROMISED TO ATTEND THE **CÉZANNE EXHIBIT** WITH ME TONIGHT...

AND WE'RE ENROLLING THE KIDS IN THAT **NEW SCHOOL** TOMORROW...

RIGHT, RIGHT, I HAVEN'T **FORGOTTEN**...

NO! MAMA STAY HOME!

MOMMY HAS TO **WORK,** PEGGY.

OTHER MOMMIES DON'T WORK!

YES, WELL, **THIS** ONE DOES...

YOU'LL JUST HAVE TO GET **USED TO IT**...

PEGGY! COME TO **GRANDMA!**

12.

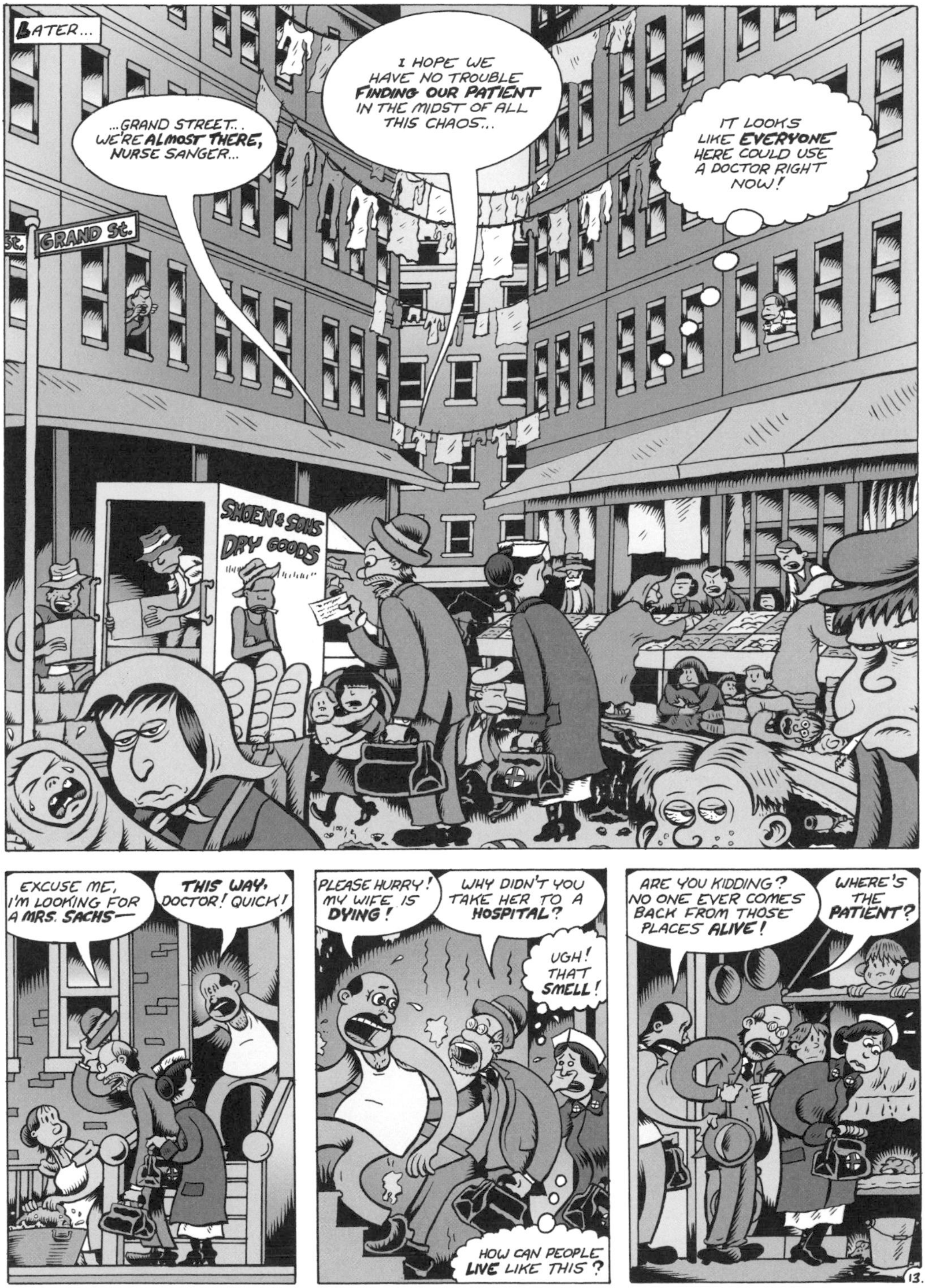
LATER...
...GRAND STREET... WE'RE ALMOST THERE, NURSE SANGER...
I HOPE WE HAVE NO TROUBLE FINDING OUR PATIENT IN THE MIDST OF ALL THIS CHAOS...
IT LOOKS LIKE EVERYONE HERE COULD USE A DOCTOR RIGHT NOW!
GRAND St.
SHOEN & SONS DRY GOODS
EXCUSE ME, I'M LOOKING FOR A MRS. SACHS—
THIS WAY, DOCTOR! QUICK!
PLEASE HURRY! MY WIFE IS DYING!
WHY DIDN'T YOU TAKE HER TO A HOSPITAL?
UGH! THAT SMELL!
HOW CAN PEOPLE LIVE LIKE THIS?
ARE YOU KIDDING? NO ONE EVER COMES BACK FROM THOSE PLACES ALIVE!
WHERE'S THE PATIENT?

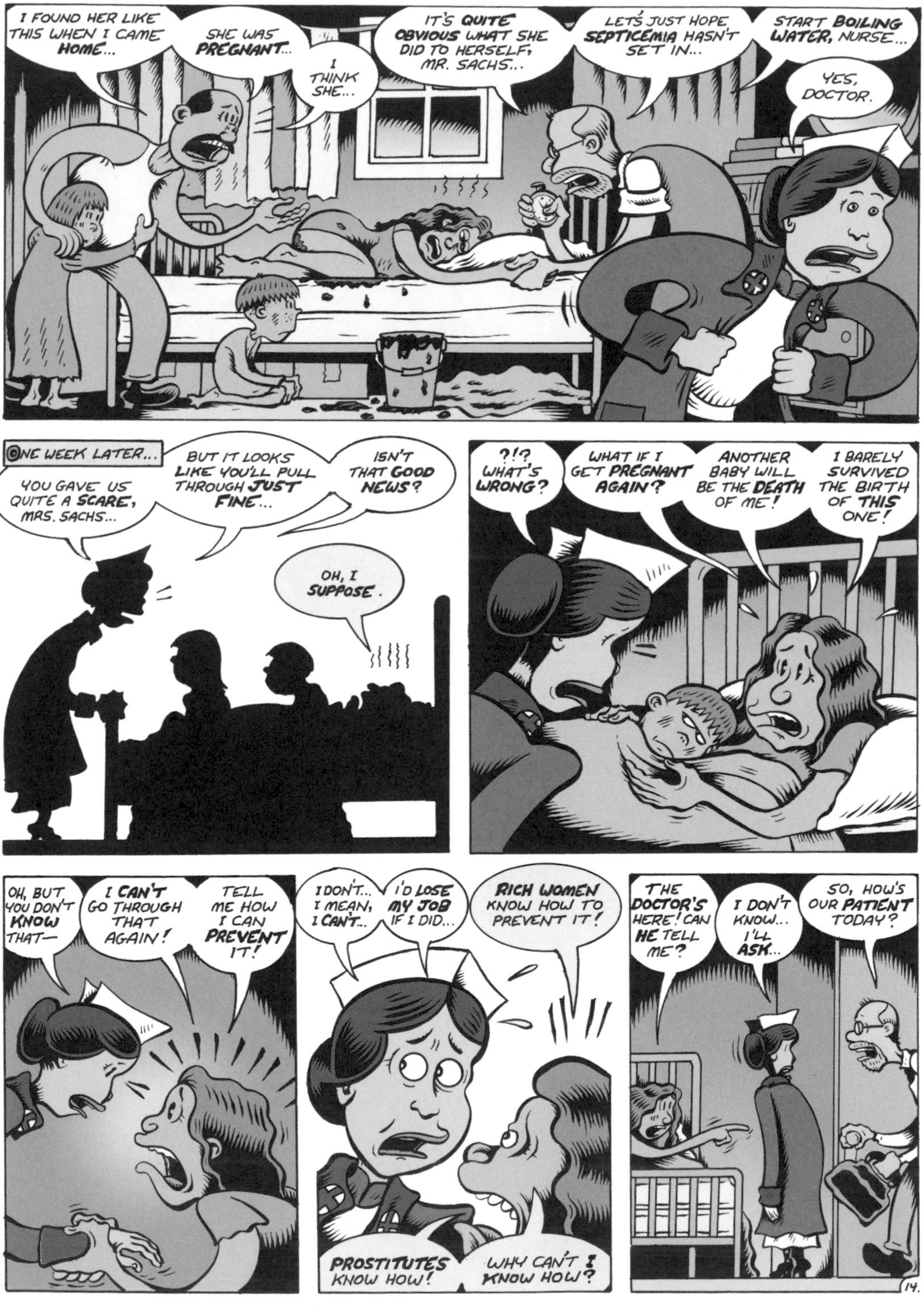
I FOUND HER LIKE THIS WHEN I CAME HOME...
SHE WAS PREGNANT...
I THINK SHE...
IT'S QUITE OBVIOUS WHAT SHE DID TO HERSELF, MR. SACHS...
LET'S JUST HOPE SEPTICEMIA HASN'T SET IN...
START BOILING WATER, NURSE...
YES, DOCTOR.
ONE WEEK LATER...
YOU GAVE US QUITE A SCARE, MRS. SACHS...
BUT IT LOOKS LIKE YOU'LL PULL THROUGH JUST FINE...
ISN'T THAT GOOD NEWS?
OH, I SUPPOSE.
?!? WHAT'S WRONG?
WHAT IF I GET PREGNANT AGAIN?
ANOTHER BABY WILL BE THE DEATH OF ME!
I BARELY SURVIVED THE BIRTH OF THIS ONE!
OH, BUT YOU DON'T KNOW THAT—
I CAN'T GO THROUGH THAT AGAIN!
TELL ME HOW I CAN PREVENT IT!
I DON'T... I MEAN, I CAN'T...
I'D LOSE MY JOB IF I DID...
RICH WOMEN KNOW HOW TO PREVENT IT!
PROSTITUTES KNOW HOW!
WHY CAN'T I KNOW HOW?
THE DOCTOR'S HERE! CAN HE TELL ME?
I DON'T KNOW... I'LL ASK...
SO, HOW'S OUR PATIENT TODAY?

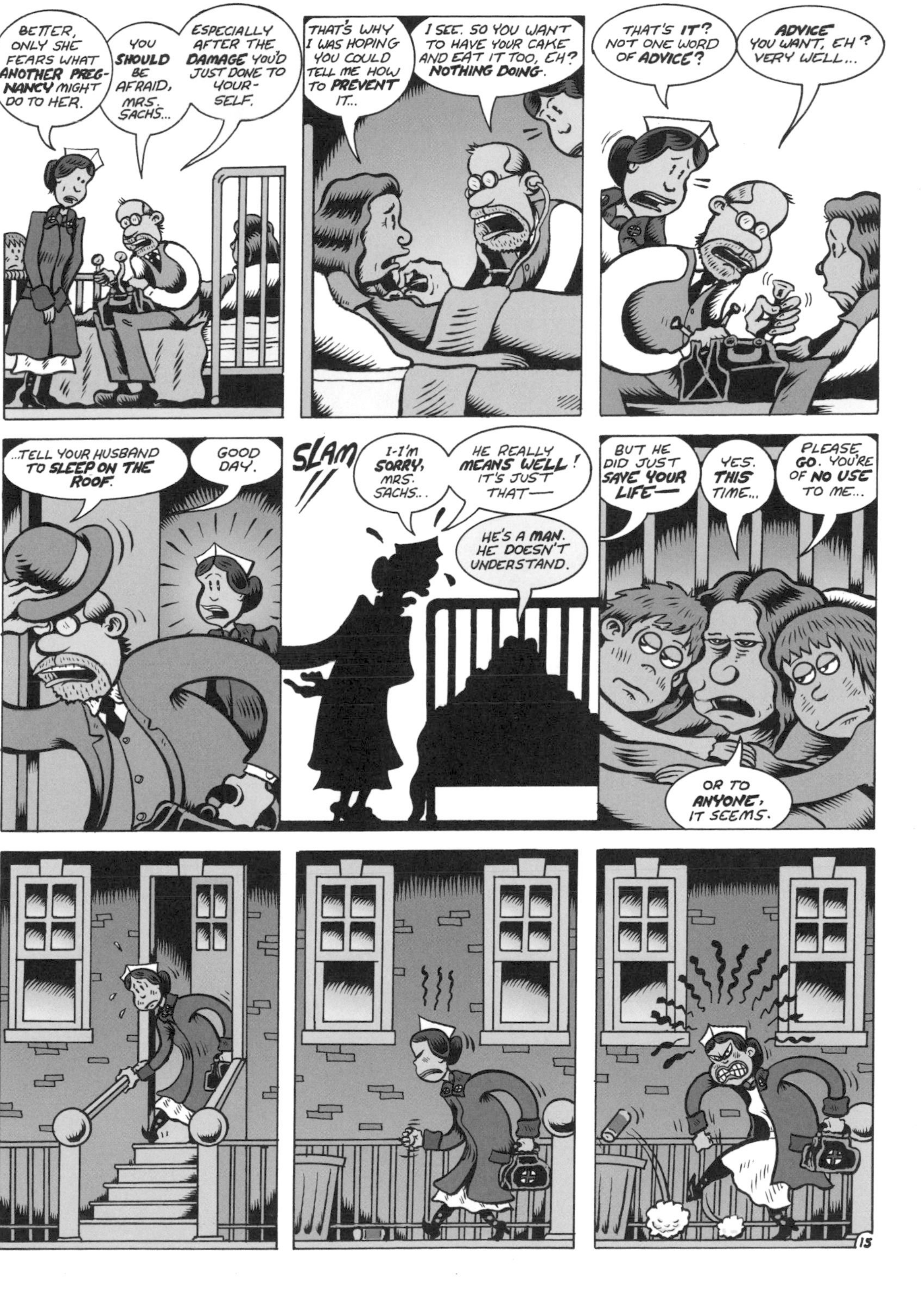
BETTER, ONLY SHE FEARS WHAT ANOTHER PREGNANCY MIGHT DO TO HER.
YOU SHOULD BE AFRAID, MRS. SACHS...
ESPECIALLY AFTER THE DAMAGE YOU'D JUST DONE TO YOURSELF.
THAT'S WHY I WAS HOPING YOU COULD TELL ME HOW TO PREVENT IT...
I SEE. SO YOU WANT TO HAVE YOUR CAKE AND EAT IT TOO, EH? NOTHING DOING.
THAT'S IT? NOT ONE WORD OF ADVICE?
ADVICE YOU WANT, EH? VERY WELL...
...TELL YOUR HUSBAND TO SLEEP ON THE ROOF.
GOOD DAY.
SLAM
I-I'M SORRY, MRS. SACHS...
HE REALLY MEANS WELL! IT'S JUST THAT—
HE'S A MAN. HE DOESN'T UNDERSTAND.
BUT HE DID JUST SAVE YOUR LIFE—
YES. THIS TIME...
PLEASE GO. YOU'RE OF NO USE TO ME...
OR TO ANYONE, IT SEEMS.

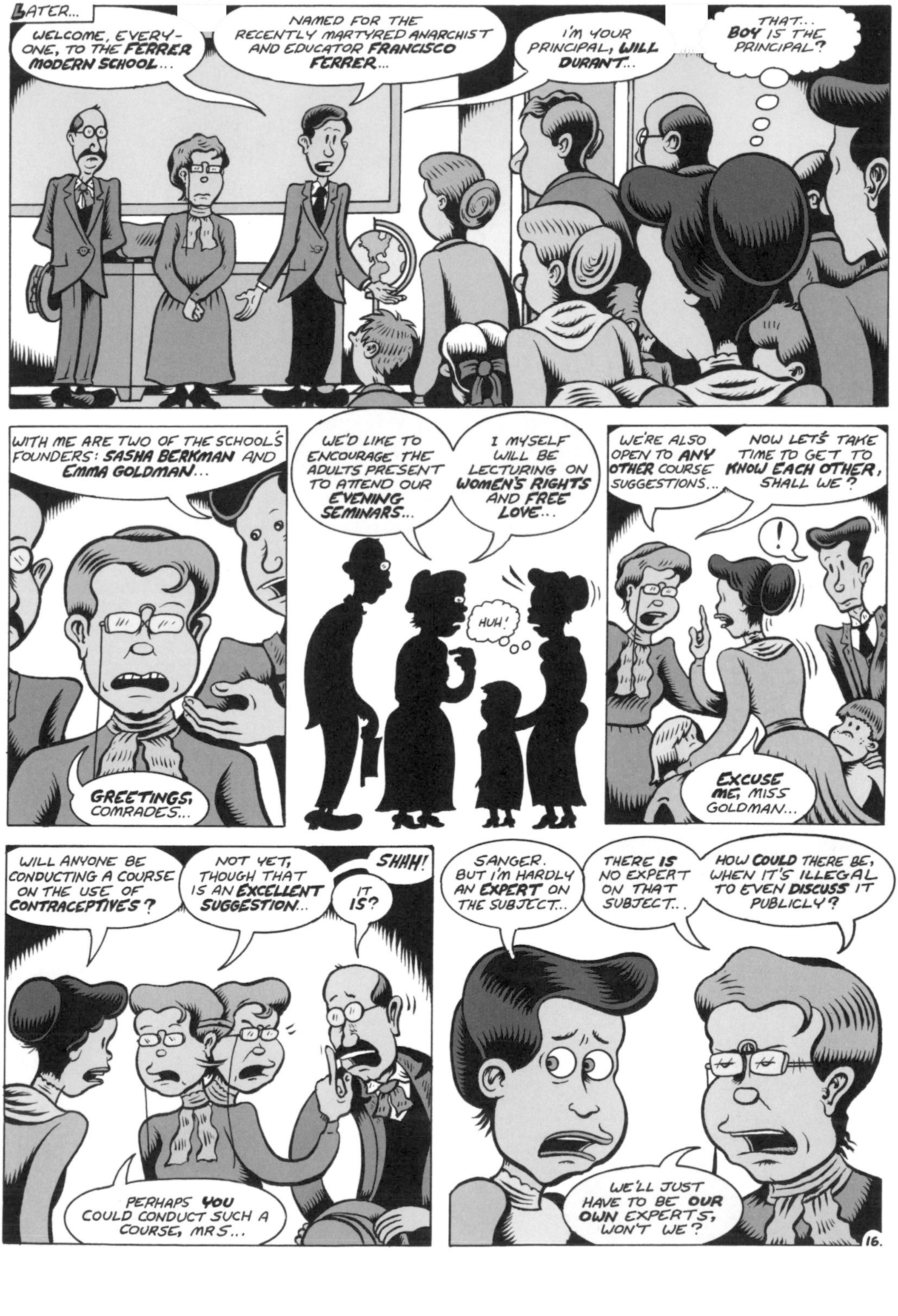
LATER...
WELCOME, EVERYONE, TO THE FERRER MODERN SCHOOL...
NAMED FOR THE RECENTLY MARTYRED ANARCHIST AND EDUCATOR FRANCISCO FERRER...
I'M YOUR PRINCIPAL, WILL DURANT...
THAT... BOY IS THE PRINCIPAL?
WITH ME ARE TWO OF THE SCHOOL'S FOUNDERS: SASHA BERKMAN AND EMMA GOLDMAN...
GREETINGS, COMRADES...
WE'D LIKE TO ENCOURAGE THE ADULTS PRESENT TO ATTEND OUR EVENING SEMINARS...
I MYSELF WILL BE LECTURING ON WOMEN'S RIGHTS AND FREE LOVE...
HUH!
WE'RE ALSO OPEN TO ANY OTHER COURSE SUGGESTIONS...
NOW LET'S TAKE TIME TO GET TO KNOW EACH OTHER, SHALL WE?
!
EXCUSE ME, MISS GOLDMAN...
WILL ANYONE BE CONDUCTING A COURSE ON THE USE OF CONTRACEPTIVES?
NOT YET, THOUGH THAT IS AN EXCELLENT SUGGESTION...
SHHH!
IT IS?
PERHAPS YOU COULD CONDUCT SUCH A COURSE, MRS...
SANGER. BUT I'M HARDLY AN EXPERT ON THE SUBJECT...
THERE IS NO EXPERT ON THAT SUBJECT...
HOW COULD THERE BE, WHEN IT'S ILLEGAL TO EVEN DISCUSS IT PUBLICLY?
WE'LL JUST HAVE TO BE OUR OWN EXPERTS, WON'T WE?
16.

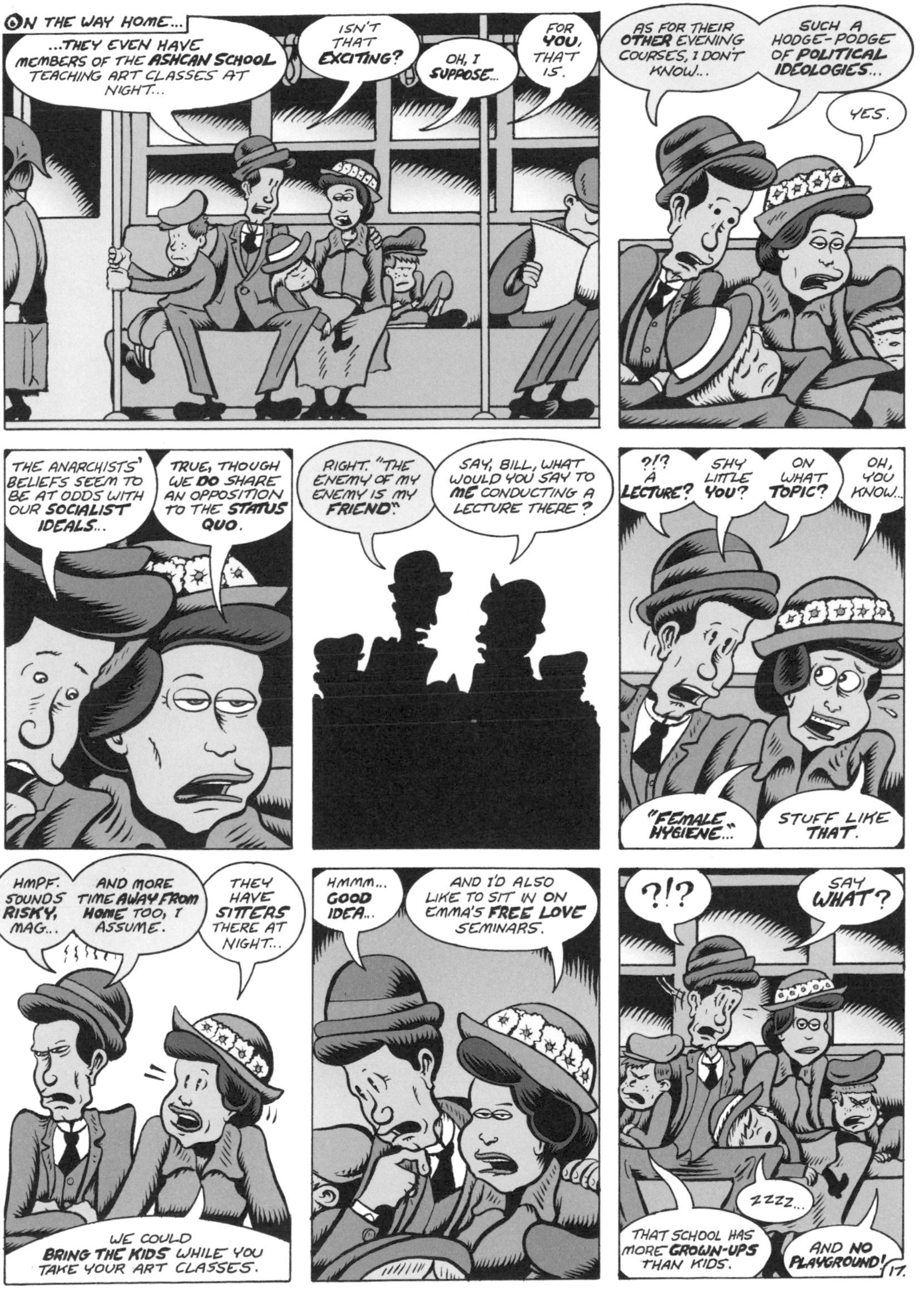
ON THE WAY HOME...
...THEY EVEN HAVE MEMBERS OF THE ASHCAN SCHOOL TEACHING ART CLASSES AT NIGHT...
ISN'T THAT EXCITING?
OH, I SUPPOSE...
FOR YOU, THAT IS.
AS FOR THEIR OTHER EVENING COURSES, I DON'T KNOW...
SUCH A HODGE-PODGE OF POLITICAL IDEOLOGIES...
YES.
THE ANARCHISTS' BELIEFS SEEM TO BE AT ODDS WITH OUR SOCIALIST IDEALS...
TRUE, THOUGH WE DO SHARE AN OPPOSITION TO THE STATUS QUO.
RIGHT. "THE ENEMY OF MY ENEMY IS MY FRIEND".
SAY, BILL, WHAT WOULD YOU SAY TO ME CONDUCTING A LECTURE THERE?
?!? A LECTURE?
SHY LITTLE YOU?
ON WHAT TOPIC?
OH, YOU KNOW...
"FEMALE HYGIENE..."
STUFF LIKE THAT.
HMPF. SOUNDS RISKY, MAG...
AND MORE TIME AWAY FROM HOME TOO, I ASSUME.
THEY HAVE SITTERS THERE AT NIGHT...
WE COULD BRING THE KIDS WHILE YOU TAKE YOUR ART CLASSES.
HMMM... GOOD IDEA...
AND I'D ALSO LIKE TO SIT IN ON EMMA'S FREE LOVE SEMINARS.
?!?
SAY WHAT?
ZZZZ...
THAT SCHOOL HAS MORE GROWN-UPS THAN KIDS.
AND NO PLAYGROUND!

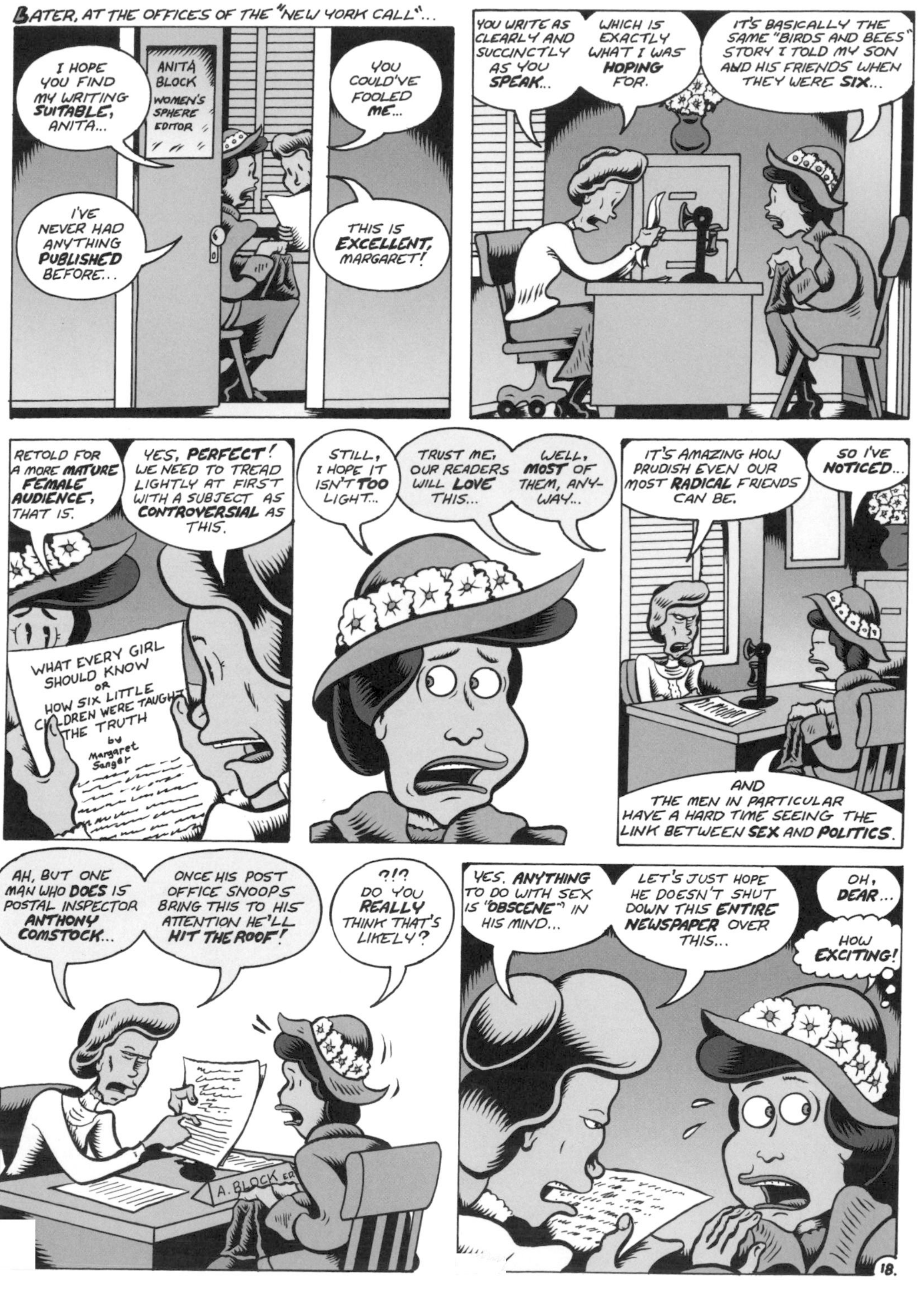
LATER, AT THE OFFICES OF THE "NEW YORK CALL"...
ANITA BLOCK WOMEN'S SPHERE EDITOR
I HOPE YOU FIND MY WRITING SUITABLE, ANITA...
I'VE NEVER HAD ANYTHING PUBLISHED BEFORE...
YOU COULD'VE FOOLED ME...
THIS IS EXCELLENT, MARGARET!
YOU WRITE AS CLEARLY AND SUCCINCTLY AS YOU SPEAK...
WHICH IS EXACTLY WHAT I WAS HOPING FOR.
IT'S BASICALLY THE SAME "BIRDS AND BEES" STORY I TOLD MY SON AND HIS FRIENDS WHEN THEY WERE SIX...
RETOLD FOR A MORE MATURE FEMALE AUDIENCE, THAT IS.
YES, PERFECT! WE NEED TO TREAD LIGHTLY AT FIRST WITH A SUBJECT AS CONTROVERSIAL AS THIS.
WHAT EVERY GIRL SHOULD KNOW OR HOW SIX LITTLE CHILDREN WERE TAUGHT THE TRUTH by Margaret Sanger
STILL, I HOPE IT ISN'T TOO LIGHT...
TRUST ME, OUR READERS WILL LOVE THIS...
WELL, MOST OF THEM, ANY-WAY...
IT'S AMAZING HOW PRUDISH EVEN OUR MOST RADICAL FRIENDS CAN BE.
SO I'VE NOTICED...
AND THE MEN IN PARTICULAR HAVE A HARD TIME SEEING THE LINK BETWEEN SEX AND POLITICS.
AH, BUT ONE MAN WHO DOES IS POSTAL INSPECTOR ANTHONY COMSTOCK...
ONCE HIS POST OFFICE SNOOPS BRING THIS TO HIS ATTENTION HE'LL HIT THE ROOF!
?!? DO YOU REALLY THINK THAT'S LIKELY?
A. BLOCK ED.
YES. ANYTHING TO DO WITH SEX IS "OBSCENE" IN HIS MIND...
LET'S JUST HOPE HE DOESN'T SHUT DOWN THIS ENTIRE NEWSPAPER OVER THIS...
OH, DEAR...
HOW EXCITING!

SIX WEEKS LATER...

MY COLUMN'S BEEN CENSORED?!?

I TOLD YOU THIS WOULD HAPPEN!

IN FACT, I'M SURPRISED IT TOOK THIS LONG!

WHAT WOULD HAPPEN IF WE JUST IGNORED THEM?

WE'D ALL BE ARRESTED, FOR ONE THING...

U.S.P.S

ATTN: A. BLOCK "WOMEN'S SPHERE" ED NEW YORK CALL

OFFICE OF A. COMSTOCK U.S. POSTAL INSPECTOR

Dear Madam,

A column in your section of the N.Y. CALL entitled "What Every Girl Should Know", written by one M. Sanger, has recently come to our attention. The contents of one installment, in particular, dealing with the subject of venereal disease, has been deemed unsuitable for the U.S. mail. Failure to cease and desist from publishing such material may lead to more drastic forms of enforcement on our part.

Thank you for your cooperation. — A. Com──

BAH! I'D LIKE TO SEE THEM TRY...

SPEAK FOR YOURSELF, MARGARET!

PEOPLE'S LIVELIHOODS ARE AT STAKE!

LOOK ON THE BRIGHT SIDE: YOUR SEX ED COLUMN GENERATED A LOT OF INTEREST...

IF WE LAY LOW FOR A WHILE, WE COULD START UP AGAIN WITH A DIFFERENT...

... ER, WHAT ARE YOU DOING?

I'M COMPOSING THIS WEEK'S COLUMN.

MARGARET! HAVEN'T YOU BEEN LISTENING TO A WORD I SAID?

HERE! READ THIS AND TELL ME IF IT'S TOO "OBSCENE" TO PRINT.

...HA! MAG, THIS IS BRILLIANT!

WHAT EVERY GIRL SHOULD KNOW

NOTHING!

BY ORDER OF THE POST OFFICE DEPT.

AND IRONIC TOO, SINCE WHAT THEY'RE DOING IS OBSCENE...

WHAT A RESPONSE THIS WILL GET!

THAT COMSTOCK CHARACTER HAS GOT MY IRISH UP...

HE PICKED A FIGHT WITH THE WRONG LASSIE...

THIS MEANS WAR...

AND I'M GOING TO WIN!

19.

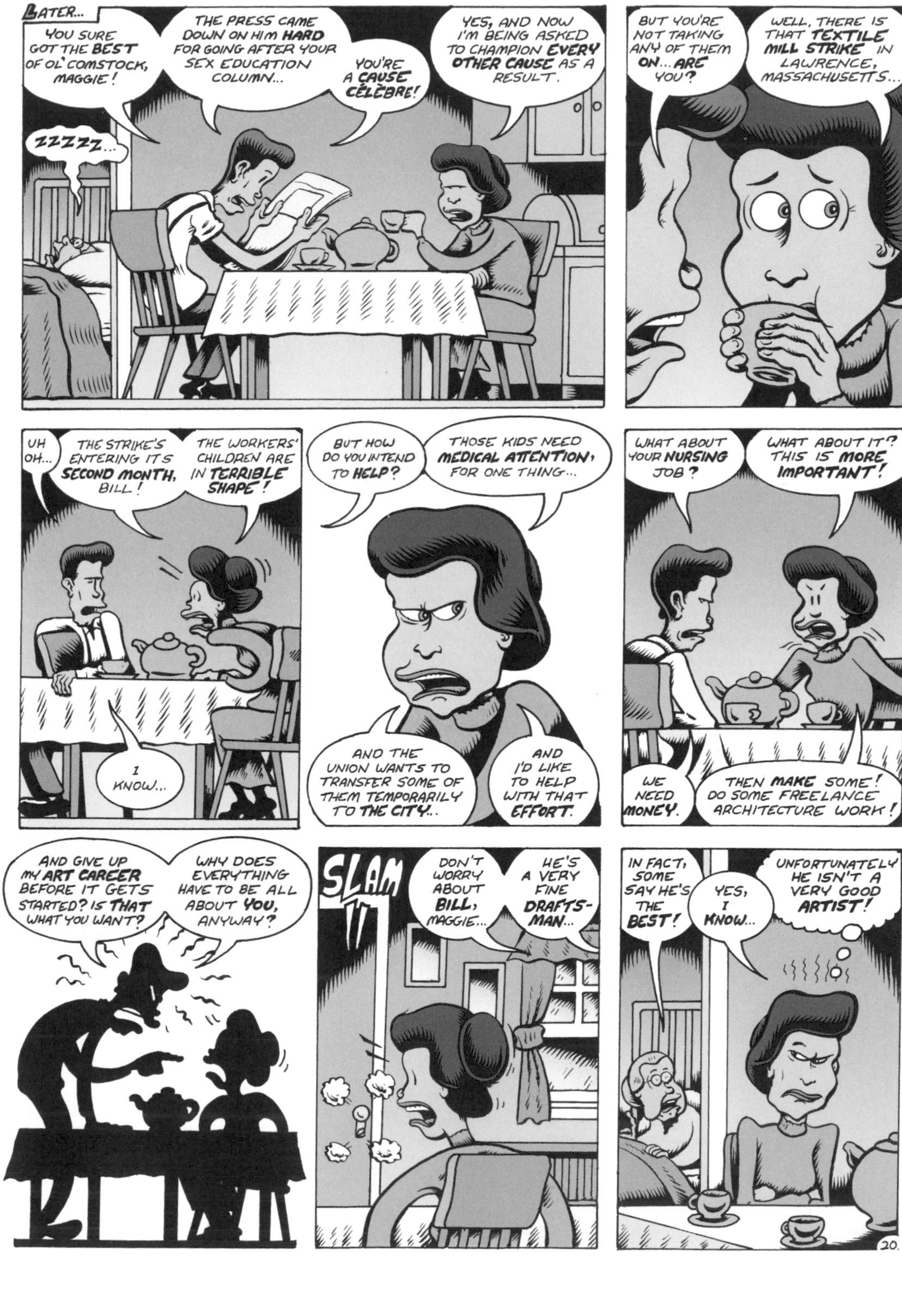
LATER...
YOU SURE GOT THE BEST OF OL' COMSTOCK, MAGGIE!
THE PRESS CAME DOWN ON HIM HARD FOR GOING AFTER YOUR SEX EDUCATION COLUMN...
YOU'RE A CAUSE CÉLÈBRE!
ZZZZZ...
YES, AND NOW I'M BEING ASKED TO CHAMPION EVERY OTHER CAUSE AS A RESULT.
BUT YOU'RE NOT TAKING ANY OF THEM ON... ARE YOU?
WELL, THERE IS THAT TEXTILE MILL STRIKE IN LAWRENCE, MASSACHUSETTS...
UH OH...
THE STRIKE'S ENTERING ITS SECOND MONTH, BILL!
THE WORKERS' CHILDREN ARE IN TERRIBLE SHAPE!
I KNOW...
BUT HOW DO YOU INTEND TO HELP?
THOSE KIDS NEED MEDICAL ATTENTION, FOR ONE THING...
AND THE UNION WANTS TO TRANSFER SOME OF THEM TEMPORARILY TO THE CITY...
AND I'D LIKE TO HELP WITH THAT EFFORT.
WHAT ABOUT YOUR NURSING JOB?
WHAT ABOUT IT? THIS IS MORE IMPORTANT!
WE NEED MONEY.
THEN MAKE SOME! DO SOME FREELANCE ARCHITECTURE WORK!
AND GIVE UP MY ART CAREER BEFORE IT GETS STARTED? IS THAT WHAT YOU WANT?
WHY DOES EVERYTHING HAVE TO BE ALL ABOUT YOU, ANYWAY?
SLAM
DON'T WORRY ABOUT BILL, MAGGIE...
HE'S A VERY FINE DRAFTS-MAN...
IN FACT, SOME SAY HE'S THE BEST!
YES, I KNOW...
UNFORTUNATELY HE ISN'T A VERY GOOD ARTIST!

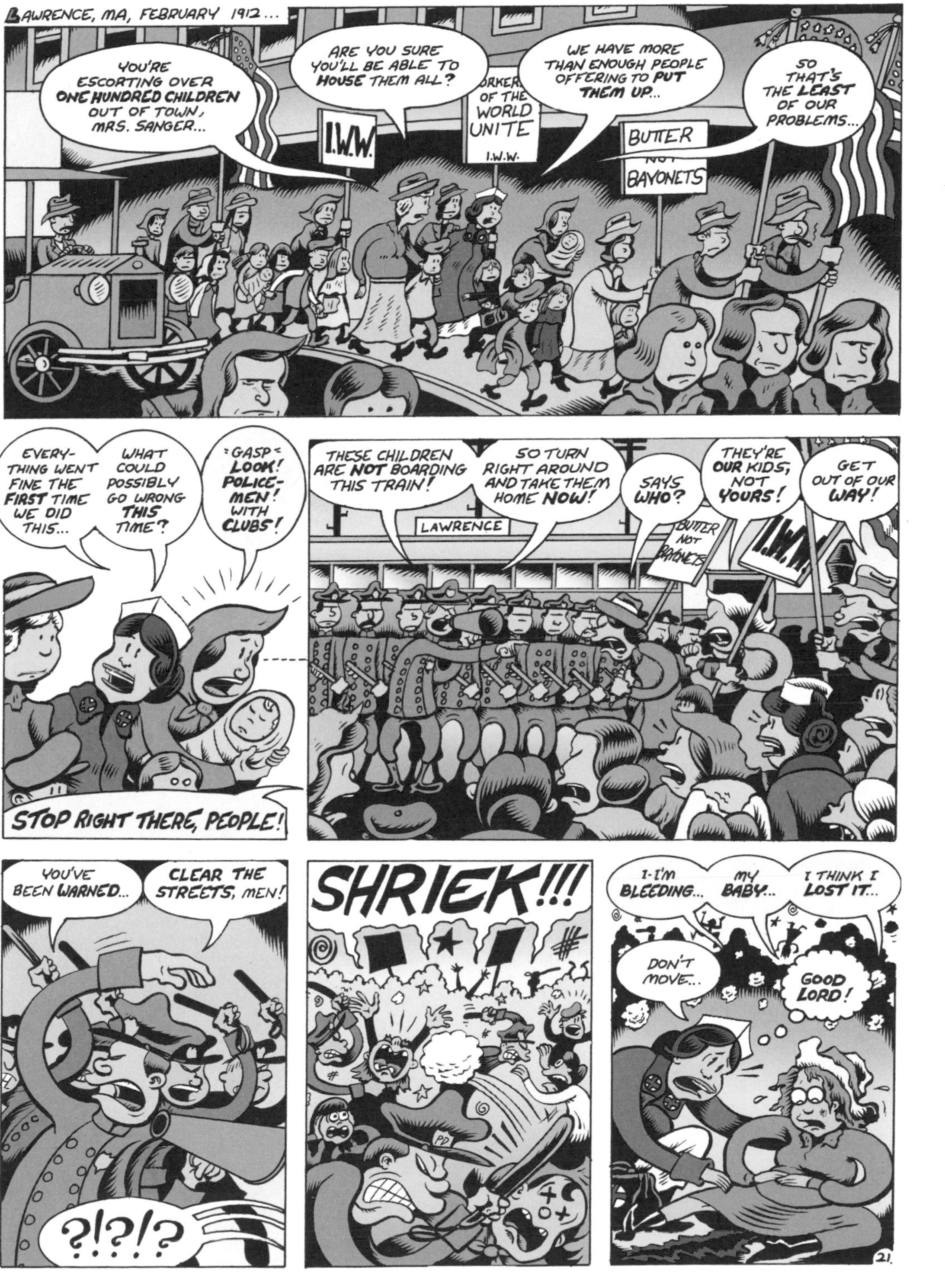
LAWRENCE, MA, FEBRUARY 1912...
YOU'RE ESCORTING OVER ONE HUNDRED CHILDREN OUT OF TOWN, MRS. SANGER...
ARE YOU SURE YOU'LL BE ABLE TO HOUSE THEM ALL?
WE HAVE MORE THAN ENOUGH PEOPLE OFFERING TO PUT THEM UP...
SO THAT'S THE LEAST OF OUR PROBLEMS...
I.W.W.
OF THE WORLD UNITE I.W.W.
BUTTER BAYONETS
EVERY-THING WENT FINE THE FIRST TIME WE DID THIS...
WHAT COULD POSSIBLY GO WRONG THIS TIME?
=GASP= LOOK! POLICE-MEN! WITH CLUBS!
STOP RIGHT THERE, PEOPLE!
THESE CHILDREN ARE NOT BOARDING THIS TRAIN!
SO TURN RIGHT AROUND AND TAKE THEM HOME NOW!
SAYS WHO?
THEY'RE OUR KIDS, NOT YOURS!
GET OUT OF OUR WAY!
LAWRENCE
BUTTER NOT BAYONETS
I.W.W.
YOU'VE BEEN WARNED...
CLEAR THE STREETS, MEN!
?!?!?
SHRIEK!!!
PD
I-I'M BLEEDING...
MY BABY...
I THINK I LOST IT...
DON'T MOVE...
GOOD LORD!

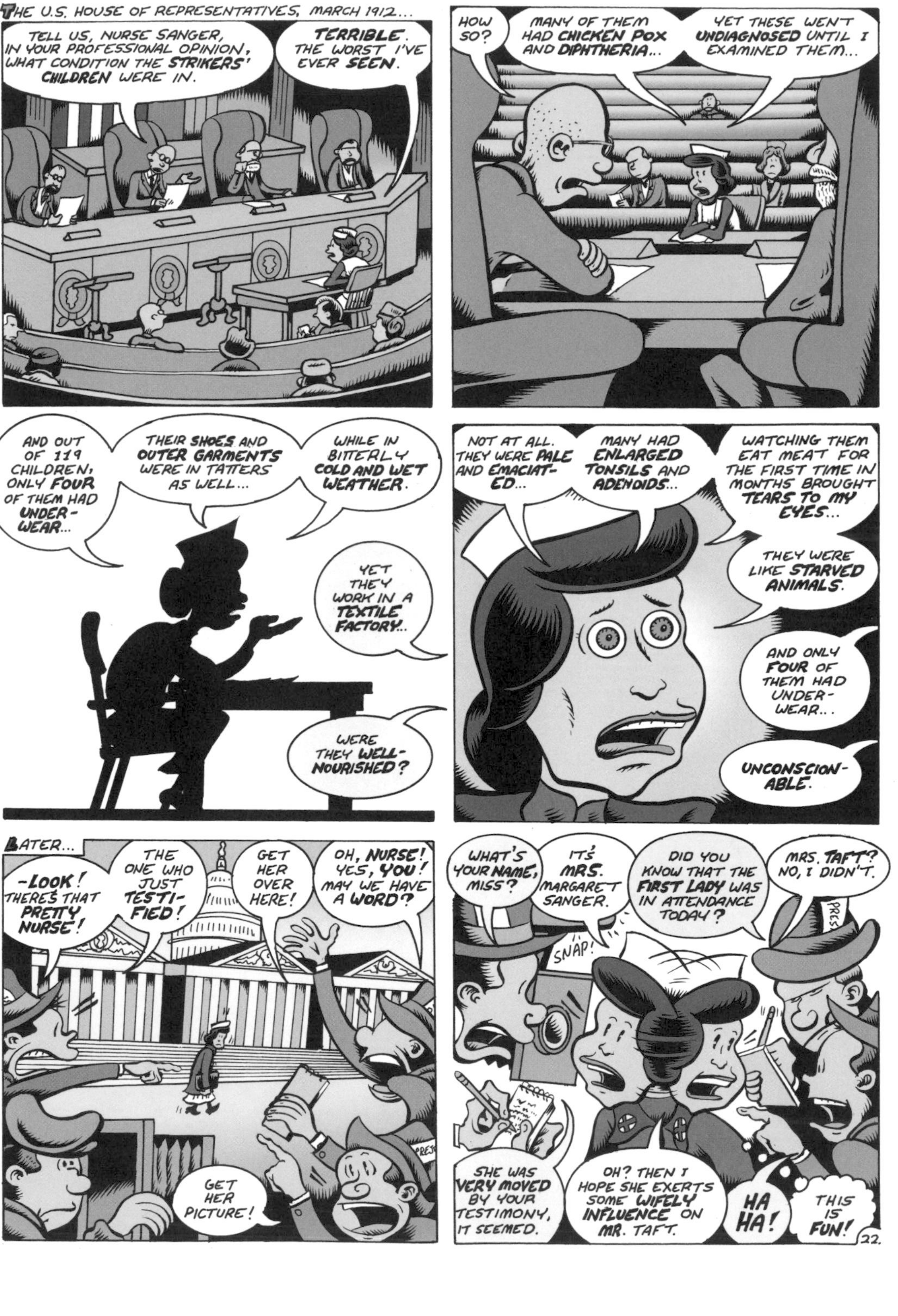
THE U.S. HOUSE OF REPRESENTATIVES, MARCH 1912...
TELL US, NURSE SANGER, IN YOUR PROFESSIONAL OPINION, WHAT CONDITION THE STRIKERS' CHILDREN WERE IN.
TERRIBLE. THE WORST I'VE EVER SEEN.
HOW SO?
MANY OF THEM HAD CHICKEN POX AND DIPHTHERIA...
YET THESE WENT UNDIAGNOSED UNTIL I EXAMINED THEM...
AND OUT OF 119 CHILDREN, ONLY FOUR OF THEM HAD UNDER-WEAR...
THEIR SHOES AND OUTER GARMENTS WERE IN TATTERS AS WELL...
WHILE IN BITTERLY COLD AND WET WEATHER.
YET THEY WORK IN A TEXTILE FACTORY...
WERE THEY WELL-NOURISHED?
NOT AT ALL. THEY WERE PALE AND EMACIAT-ED...
MANY HAD ENLARGED TONSILS AND ADENOIDS...
WATCHING THEM EAT MEAT FOR THE FIRST TIME IN MONTHS BROUGHT TEARS TO MY EYES...
THEY WERE LIKE STARVED ANIMALS.
AND ONLY FOUR OF THEM HAD UNDER-WEAR...
UNCONSCION-ABLE.
LATER...
-LOOK! THERE'S THAT PRETTY NURSE!
THE ONE WHO JUST TESTI-FIED!
GET HER OVER HERE!
OH, NURSE! YES, YOU! MAY WE HAVE A WORD?
GET HER PICTURE!
WHAT'S YOUR NAME, MISS?
IT'S MRS. MARGARET SANGER.
SNAP!
DID YOU KNOW THAT THE FIRST LADY WAS IN ATTENDANCE TODAY?
MRS. TAFT? NO, I DIDN'T.
SHE WAS VERY MOVED BY YOUR TESTIMONY, IT SEEMED.
OH? THEN I HOPE SHE EXERTS SOME WIFELY INFLUENCE ON MR. TAFT.
HA HA!
THIS IS FUN!

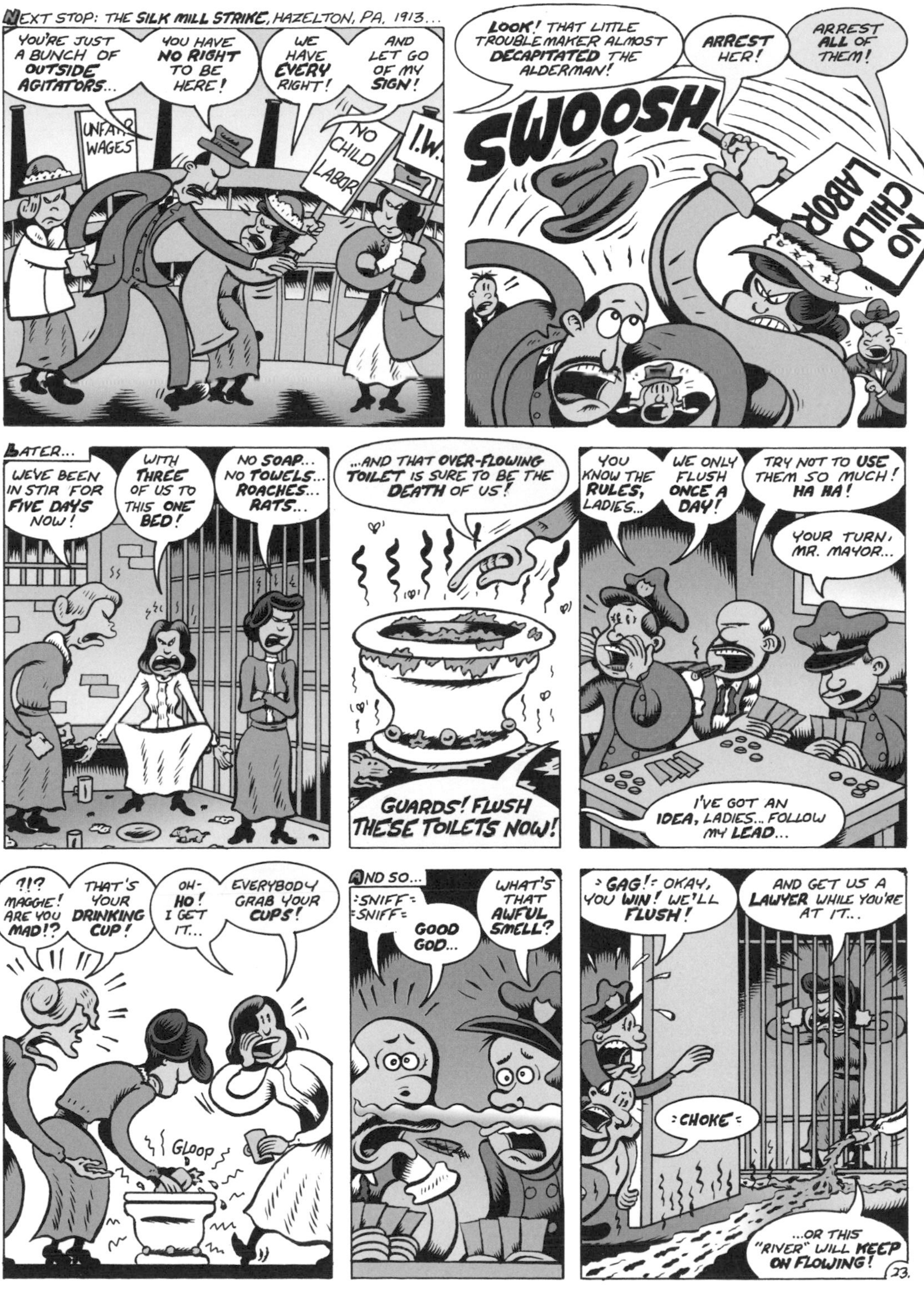
NEXT STOP: THE SILK MILL STRIKE, HAZELTON, PA. 1913...
YOU'RE JUST A BUNCH OF OUTSIDE AGITATORS...
YOU HAVE NO RIGHT TO BE HERE!
WE HAVE EVERY RIGHT!
AND LET GO OF MY SIGN!
UNFAIR WAGES
NO CHILD LABOR
I.W.
LOOK! THAT LITTLE TROUBLEMAKER ALMOST DECAPITATED THE ALDERMAN!
ARREST HER!
ARREST ALL OF THEM!
SWOOSH
NO CHILD LABOR
LATER...
WE'VE BEEN IN STIR FOR FIVE DAYS NOW!
WITH THREE OF US TO THIS ONE BED!
NO SOAP... NO TOWELS... ROACHES... RATS...
...AND THAT OVER-FLOWING TOILET IS SURE TO BE THE DEATH OF US!
GUARDS! FLUSH THESE TOILETS NOW!
YOU KNOW THE RULES, LADIES...
WE ONLY FLUSH ONCE A DAY!
TRY NOT TO USE THEM SO MUCH! HA HA!
YOUR TURN, MR. MAYOR...
I'VE GOT AN IDEA, LADIES... FOLLOW MY LEAD...
?!? MAGGIE! ARE YOU MAD!?
THAT'S YOUR DRINKING CUP!
OH-HO! I GET IT...
EVERYBODY GRAB YOUR CUPS!
GLOOP
AND SO...
=SNIFF= =SNIFF=
GOOD GOD...
WHAT'S THAT AWFUL SMELL?
=GAG!= OKAY, YOU WIN! WE'LL FLUSH!
AND GET US A LAWYER WHILE YOU'RE AT IT...
=CHOKE=
...OR THIS "RIVER" WILL KEEP ON FLOWING!
23.

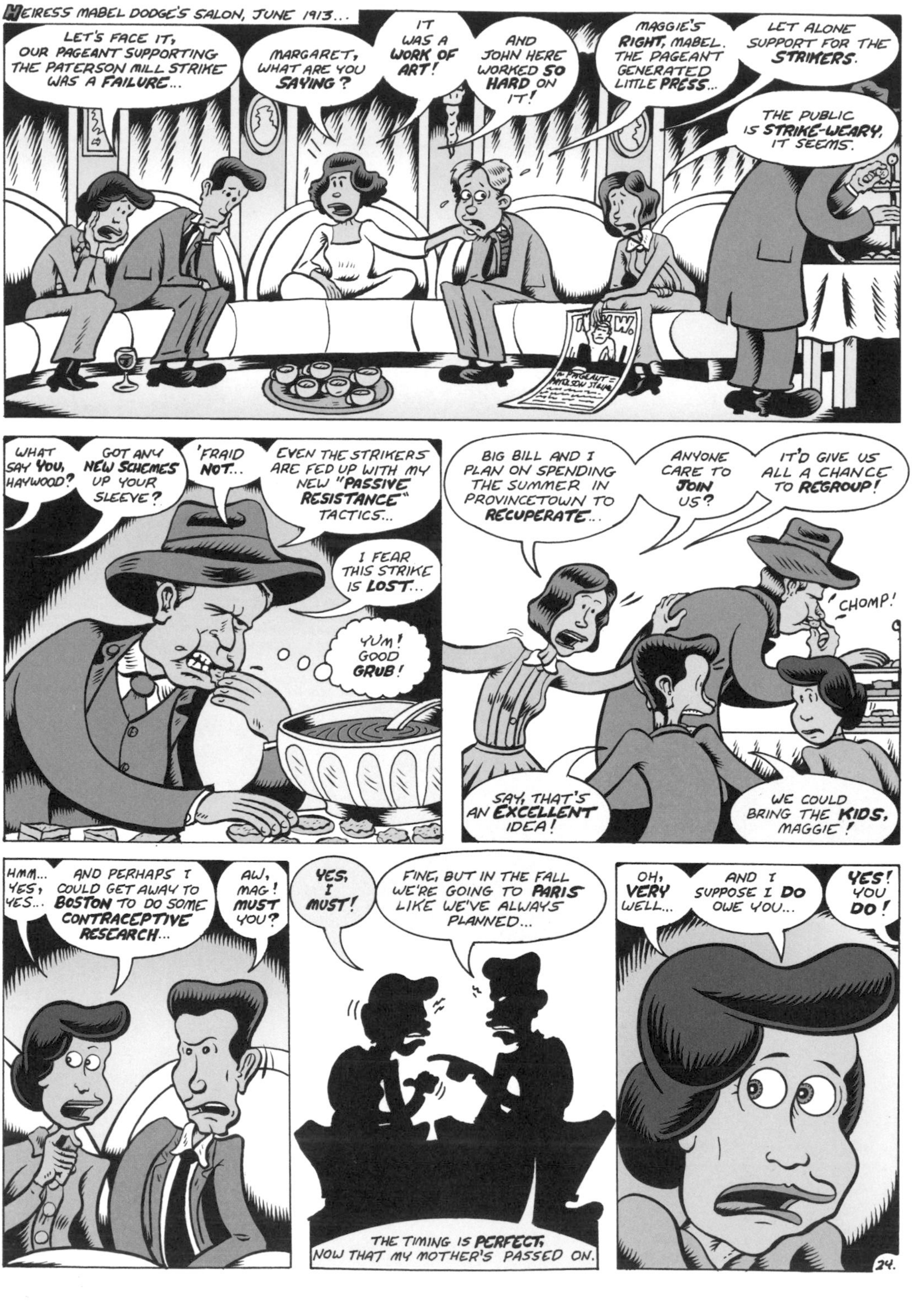
HEIRESS MABEL DODGE'S SALON, JUNE 1913...
LET'S FACE IT, OUR PAGEANT SUPPORTING THE PATERSON MILL STRIKE WAS A FAILURE...
MARGARET, WHAT ARE YOU SAYING?
IT WAS A WORK OF ART!
AND JOHN HERE WORKED SO HARD ON IT!
MAGGIE'S RIGHT, MABEL. THE PAGEANT GENERATED LITTLE PRESS...
LET ALONE SUPPORT FOR THE STRIKERS.
THE PUBLIC IS STRIKE-WEARY, IT SEEMS.
WHAT SAY YOU, HAYWOOD?
GOT ANY NEW SCHEMES UP YOUR SLEEVE?
'FRAID NOT...
EVEN THE STRIKERS ARE FED UP WITH MY NEW "PASSIVE RESISTANCE" TACTICS...
I FEAR THIS STRIKE IS LOST...
YUM! GOOD GRUB!
BIG BILL AND I PLAN ON SPENDING THE SUMMER IN PROVINCETOWN TO RECUPERATE...
ANYONE CARE TO JOIN US?
IT'D GIVE US ALL A CHANCE TO REGROUP!
CHOMP!
SAY, THAT'S AN EXCELLENT IDEA!
WE COULD BRING THE KIDS, MAGGIE!
HMM... YES, YES...
AND PERHAPS I COULD GET AWAY TO BOSTON TO DO SOME CONTRACEPTIVE RESEARCH...
AW, MAG! MUST YOU?
YES, I MUST!
FINE, BUT IN THE FALL WE'RE GOING TO PARIS LIKE WE'VE ALWAYS PLANNED...
THE TIMING IS PERFECT, NOW THAT MY MOTHER'S PASSED ON.
OH, VERY WELL...
AND I SUPPOSE I DO OWE YOU...
YES! YOU DO!
24.

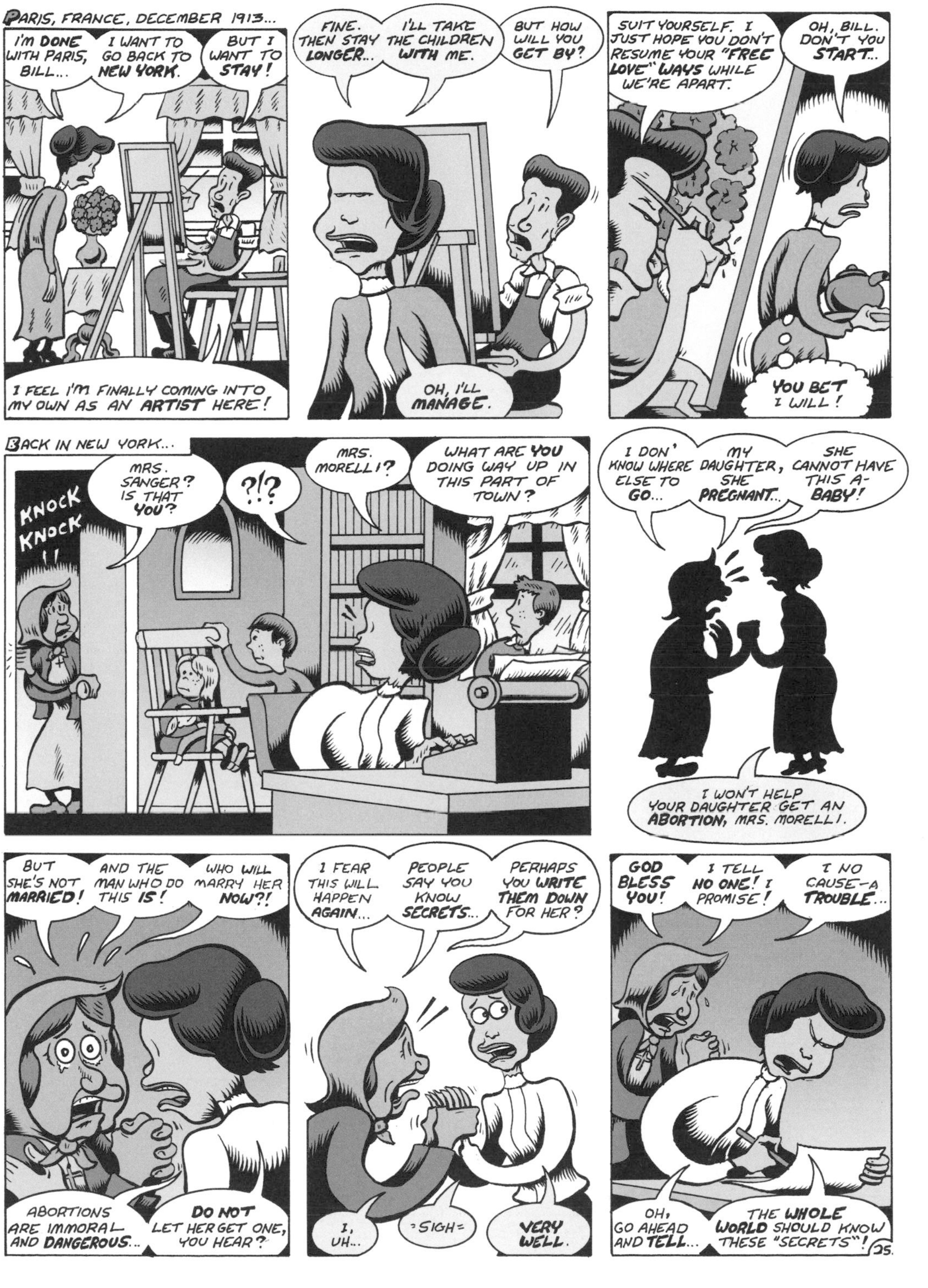
PARIS, FRANCE, DECEMBER 1913...
I'M DONE WITH PARIS, BILL...
I WANT TO GO BACK TO NEW YORK.
BUT I WANT TO STAY!
I FEEL I'M FINALLY COMING INTO MY OWN AS AN ARTIST HERE!
FINE. THEN STAY LONGER...
I'LL TAKE THE CHILDREN WITH ME.
BUT HOW WILL YOU GET BY?
OH, I'LL MANAGE.
SUIT YOURSELF. I JUST HOPE YOU DON'T RESUME YOUR "FREE LOVE" WAYS WHILE WE'RE APART.
OH, BILL. DON'T YOU START...
YOU BET I WILL!
BACK IN NEW YORK...
KNOCK KNOCK
MRS. SANGER? IS THAT YOU?
?!?
MRS. MORELLI?
WHAT ARE YOU DOING WAY UP IN THIS PART OF TOWN?
I DON' KNOW WHERE ELSE TO GO...
MY DAUGHTER, SHE PREGNANT...
SHE CANNOT HAVE THIS A-BABY!
I WON'T HELP YOUR DAUGHTER GET AN ABORTION, MRS. MORELLI.
BUT SHE'S NOT MARRIED!
AND THE MAN WHO DO THIS IS!
WHO WILL MARRY HER NOW?!
ABORTIONS ARE IMMORAL AND DANGEROUS...
DO NOT LET HER GET ONE, YOU HEAR?
I FEAR THIS WILL HAPPEN AGAIN...
PEOPLE SAY YOU KNOW SECRETS...
PERHAPS YOU WRITE THEM DOWN FOR HER?
I, UH...
=SIGH=
VERY WELL.
GOD BLESS YOU!
I TELL NO ONE! I PROMISE!
I NO CAUSE-A TROUBLE...
OH, GO AHEAD AND TELL...
THE WHOLE WORLD SHOULD KNOW THESE "SECRETS"!

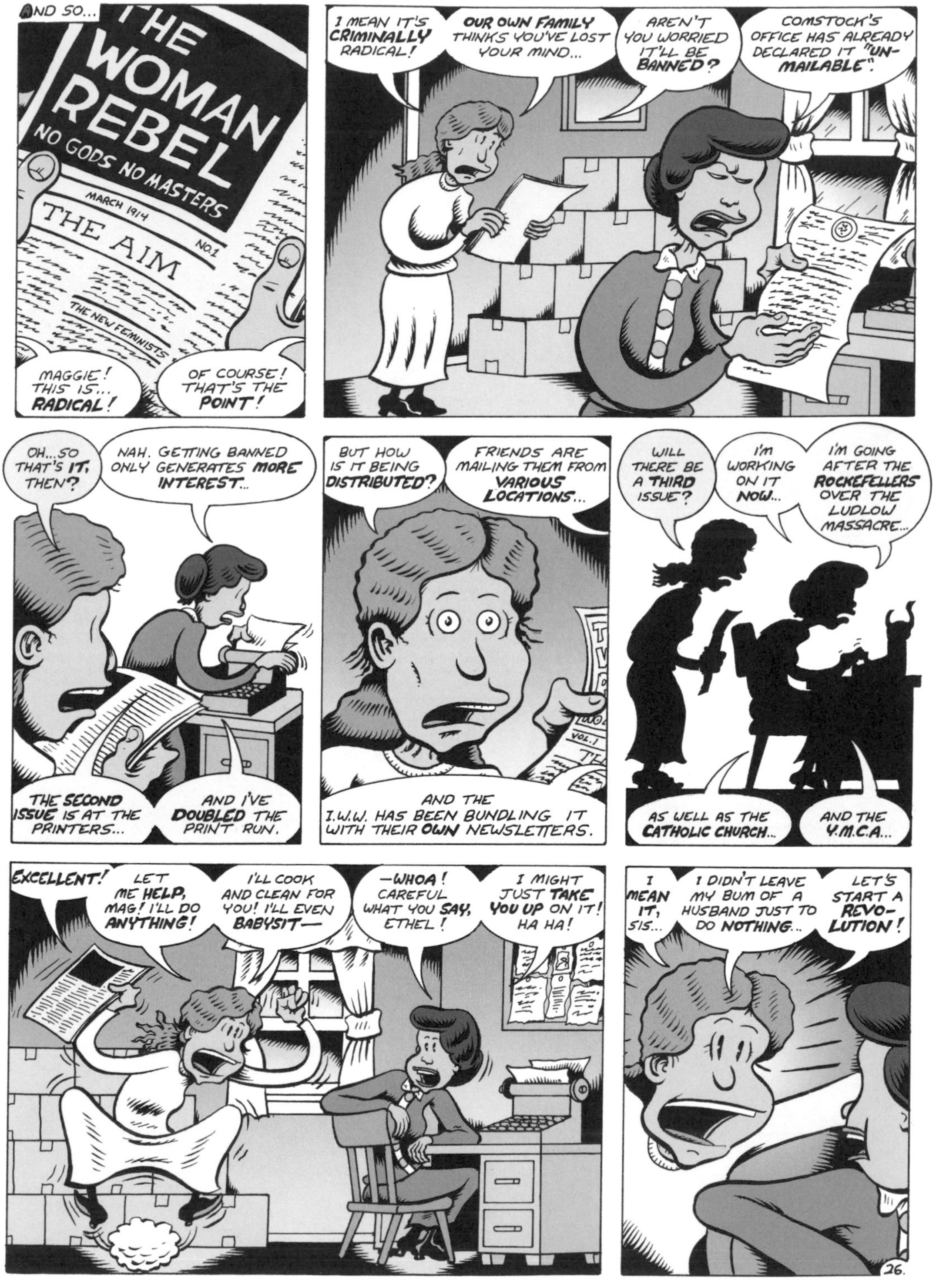
AND SO...
THE WOMAN REBEL
NO GODS NO MASTERS
MARCH 1914
NO.1
THE AIM
THE NEW FEMINISTS
MAGGIE! THIS IS... RADICAL!
OF COURSE! THAT'S THE POINT!
I MEAN IT'S CRIMINALLY RADICAL!
OUR OWN FAMILY THINKS YOU'VE LOST YOUR MIND...
AREN'T YOU WORRIED IT'LL BE BANNED?
COMSTOCK'S OFFICE HAS ALREADY DECLARED IT "UN-MAILABLE".
OH... SO THAT'S IT, THEN?
NAH. GETTING BANNED ONLY GENERATES MORE INTEREST...
THE SECOND ISSUE IS AT THE PRINTERS...
AND I'VE DOUBLED THE PRINT RUN.
BUT HOW IS IT BEING DISTRIBUTED?
FRIENDS ARE MAILING THEM FROM VARIOUS LOCATIONS...
AND THE I.W.W. HAS BEEN BUNDLING IT WITH THEIR OWN NEWSLETTERS.
WILL THERE BE A THIRD ISSUE?
I'M WORKING ON IT NOW...
I'M GOING AFTER THE ROCKEFELLERS OVER THE LUDLOW MASSACRE...
AS WELL AS THE CATHOLIC CHURCH...
AND THE Y.M.C.A...
EXCELLENT!
LET ME HELP, MAG! I'LL DO ANYTHING!
I'LL COOK AND CLEAN FOR YOU! I'LL EVEN BABYSIT—
—WHOA! CAREFUL WHAT YOU SAY, ETHEL!
I MIGHT JUST TAKE YOU UP ON IT! HA HA!
I MEAN IT, SIS...
I DIDN'T LEAVE MY BUM OF A HUSBAND JUST TO DO NOTHING...
LET'S START A REVO-LUTION!

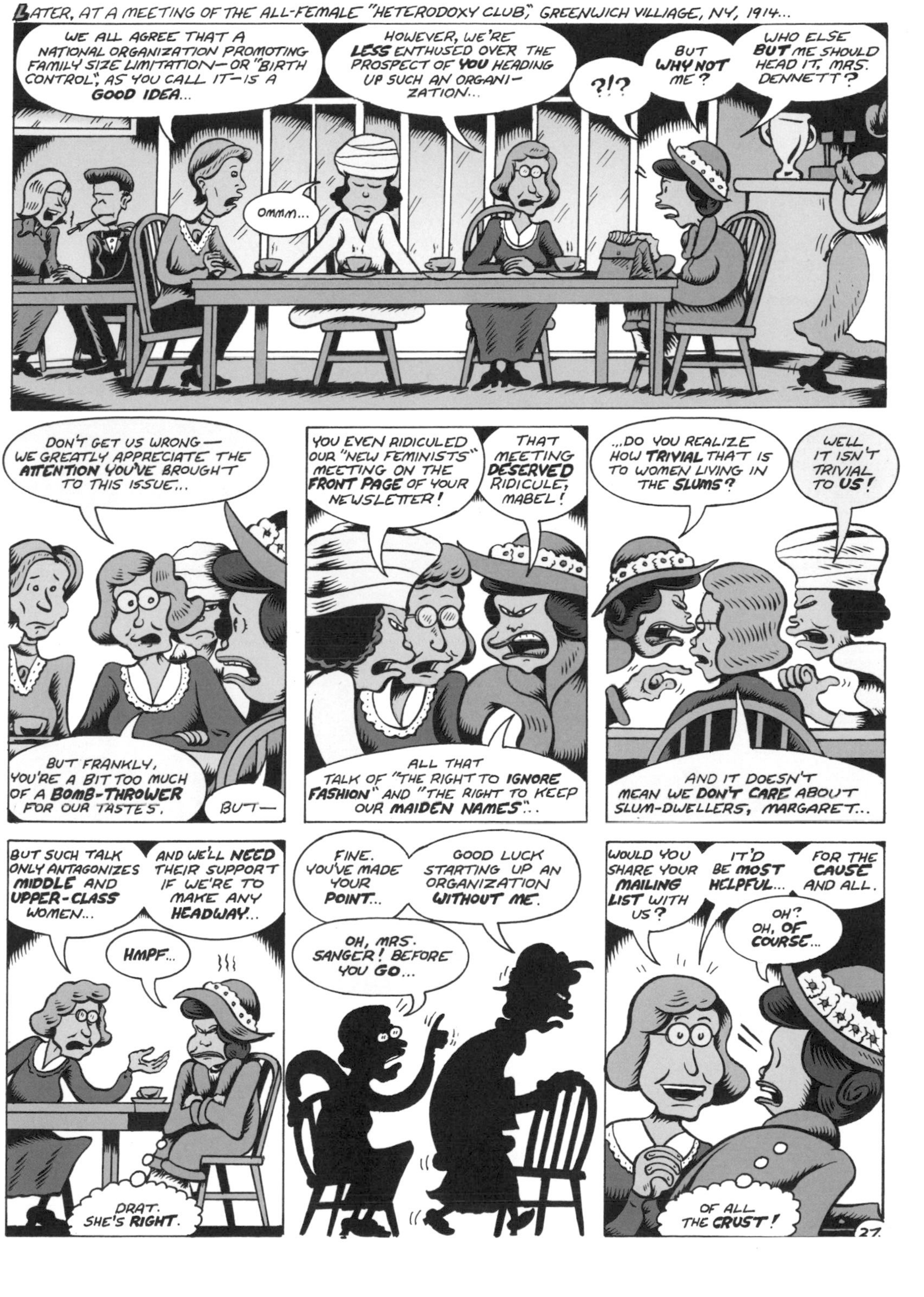
LATER, AT A MEETING OF THE ALL-FEMALE "HETERODOXY CLUB," GREENWICH VILLIAGE, NY, 1914...
WE ALL AGREE THAT A NATIONAL ORGANIZATION PROMOTING FAMILY SIZE LIMITATION—OR "BIRTH CONTROL", AS YOU CALL IT—IS A GOOD IDEA...
OMMM...
HOWEVER, WE'RE LESS ENTHUSED OVER THE PROSPECT OF YOU HEADING UP SUCH AN ORGANI-ZATION...
?!?
BUT WHY NOT ME?
WHO ELSE BUT ME SHOULD HEAD IT, MRS. DENNETT?
DON'T GET US WRONG— WE GREATLY APPRECIATE THE ATTENTION YOU'VE BROUGHT TO THIS ISSUE...
BUT FRANKLY, YOU'RE A BIT TOO MUCH OF A BOMB-THROWER FOR OUR TASTES.
BUT—
YOU EVEN RIDICULED OUR "NEW FEMINISTS" MEETING ON THE FRONT PAGE OF YOUR NEWSLETTER!
THAT MEETING DESERVED RIDICULE, MABEL!
ALL THAT TALK OF "THE RIGHT TO IGNORE FASHION" AND "THE RIGHT TO KEEP OUR MAIDEN NAMES"...
...DO YOU REALIZE HOW TRIVIAL THAT IS TO WOMEN LIVING IN THE SLUMS?
WELL, IT ISN'T TRIVIAL TO US!
AND IT DOESN'T MEAN WE DON'T CARE ABOUT SLUM-DWELLERS, MARGARET...
BUT SUCH TALK ONLY ANTAGONIZES MIDDLE AND UPPER-CLASS WOMEN...
AND WE'LL NEED THEIR SUPPORT IF WE'RE TO MAKE ANY HEADWAY...
HMPF...
DRAT. SHE'S RIGHT.
FINE. YOU'VE MADE YOUR POINT...
GOOD LUCK STARTING UP AN ORGANIZATION WITHOUT ME.
OH, MRS. SANGER! BEFORE YOU GO...
WOULD YOU SHARE YOUR MAILING LIST WITH US?
IT'D BE MOST HELPFUL...
FOR THE CAUSE AND ALL.
OH? OH, OF COURSE...
OF ALL THE CRUST!
27

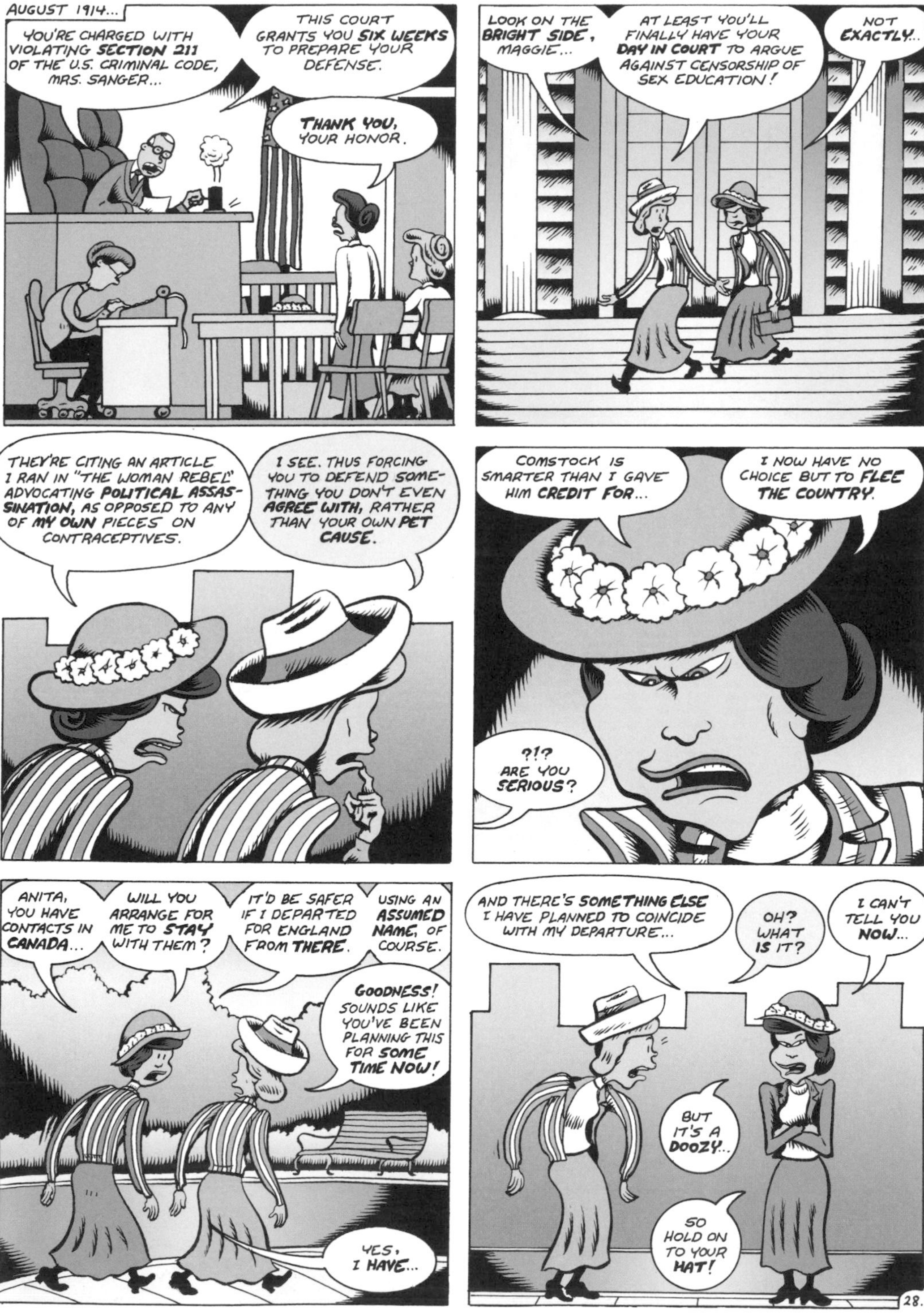

AUGUST 1914...
YOU'RE CHARGED WITH VIOLATING SECTION 211 OF THE U.S. CRIMINAL CODE, MRS. SANGER...
THIS COURT GRANTS YOU SIX WEEKS TO PREPARE YOUR DEFENSE.
THANK YOU, YOUR HONOR.
LOOK ON THE BRIGHT SIDE, MAGGIE...
AT LEAST YOU'LL FINALLY HAVE YOUR DAY IN COURT TO ARGUE AGAINST CENSORSHIP OF SEX EDUCATION!
NOT EXACTLY...
THEY'RE CITING AN ARTICLE I RAN IN "THE WOMAN REBEL" ADVOCATING POLITICAL ASSASSINATION, AS OPPOSED TO ANY OF MY OWN PIECES ON CONTRACEPTIVES.
I SEE. THUS FORCING YOU TO DEFEND SOMETHING YOU DON'T EVEN AGREE WITH, RATHER THAN YOUR OWN PET CAUSE.
COMSTOCK IS SMARTER THAN I GAVE HIM CREDIT FOR...
I NOW HAVE NO CHOICE BUT TO FLEE THE COUNTRY.
?!? ARE YOU SERIOUS?
ANITA, YOU HAVE CONTACTS IN CANADA...
WILL YOU ARRANGE FOR ME TO STAY WITH THEM?
IT'D BE SAFER IF I DEPARTED FOR ENGLAND FROM THERE.
USING AN ASSUMED NAME, OF COURSE.
GOODNESS! SOUNDS LIKE YOU'VE BEEN PLANNING THIS FOR SOME TIME NOW!
YES, I HAVE...
AND THERE'S SOMETHING ELSE I HAVE PLANNED TO COINCIDE WITH MY DEPARTURE...
OH? WHAT IS IT?
I CAN'T TELL YOU NOW...
BUT IT'S A DOOZY...
SO HOLD ON TO YOUR HAT!

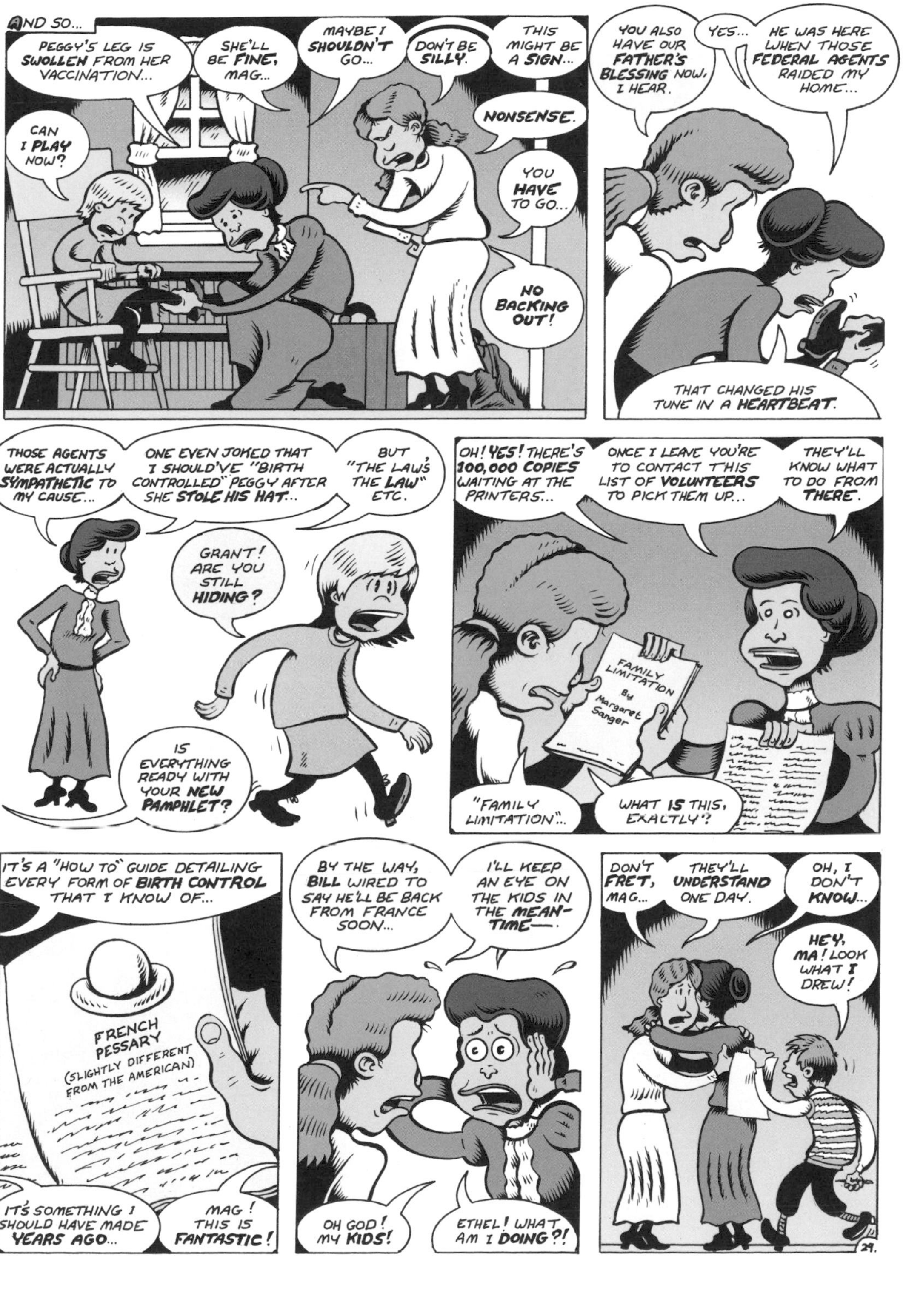
AND SO...
PEGGY'S LEG IS SWOLLEN FROM HER VACCINATION...
SHE'LL BE FINE, MAG...
CAN I PLAY NOW?
MAYBE I SHOULDN'T GO...
DON'T BE SILLY.
THIS MIGHT BE A SIGN...
NONSENSE.
YOU HAVE TO GO...
NO BACKING OUT!
YOU ALSO HAVE OUR FATHER'S BLESSING NOW, I HEAR.
YES...
HE WAS HERE WHEN THOSE FEDERAL AGENTS RAIDED MY HOME...
THAT CHANGED HIS TUNE IN A HEARTBEAT.
THOSE AGENTS WERE ACTUALLY SYMPATHETIC TO MY CAUSE...
ONE EVEN JOKED THAT I SHOULD'VE "BIRTH CONTROLLED" PEGGY AFTER SHE STOLE HIS HAT...
BUT "THE LAW'S THE LAW" ETC.
GRANT! ARE YOU STILL HIDING?
IS EVERYTHING READY WITH YOUR NEW PAMPHLET?
OH! YES! THERE'S 100,000 COPIES WAITING AT THE PRINTERS...
ONCE I LEAVE YOU'RE TO CONTACT THIS LIST OF VOLUNTEERS TO PICK THEM UP...
THEY'LL KNOW WHAT TO DO FROM THERE.
FAMILY LIMITATION By Margaret Sanger
"FAMILY LIMITATION"...
WHAT IS THIS, EXACTLY?
IT'S A "HOW TO" GUIDE DETAILING EVERY FORM OF BIRTH CONTROL THAT I KNOW OF...
FRENCH PESSARY
(SLIGHTLY DIFFERENT FROM THE AMERICAN)
IT'S SOMETHING I SHOULD HAVE MADE YEARS AGO...
MAG! THIS IS FANTASTIC!
BY THE WAY, BILL WIRED TO SAY HE'LL BE BACK FROM FRANCE SOON...
I'LL KEEP AN EYE ON THE KIDS IN THE MEAN-TIME—
OH GOD! MY KIDS!
ETHEL! WHAT AM I DOING?!
DON'T FRET, MAG...
THEY'LL UNDERSTAND ONE DAY.
OH, I DON'T KNOW...
HEY, MA! LOOK WHAT I DREW!

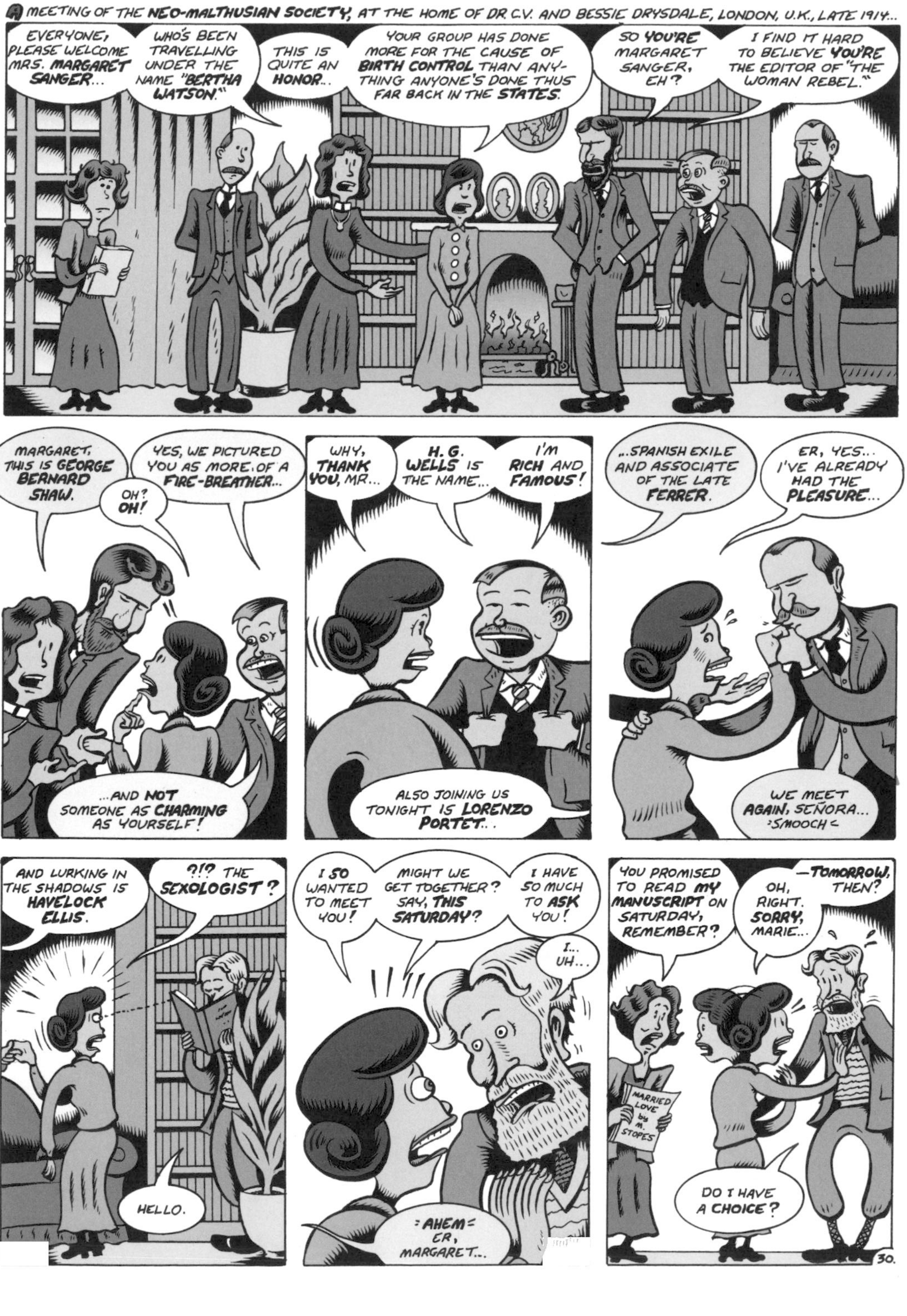
A MEETING OF THE NEO-MALTHUSIAN SOCIETY, AT THE HOME OF DR. C.V. AND BESSIE DRYSDALE, LONDON, U.K., LATE 1914...
EVERYONE, PLEASE WELCOME MRS. MARGARET SANGER...
WHO'S BEEN TRAVELLING UNDER THE NAME "BERTHA WATSON."
THIS IS QUITE AN HONOR...
YOUR GROUP HAS DONE MORE FOR THE CAUSE OF BIRTH CONTROL THAN ANYTHING ANYONE'S DONE THUS FAR BACK IN THE STATES.
SO YOU'RE MARGARET SANGER, EH?
I FIND IT HARD TO BELIEVE YOU'RE THE EDITOR OF "THE WOMAN REBEL."
MARGARET, THIS IS GEORGE BERNARD SHAW.
YES, WE PICTURED YOU AS MORE OF A FIRE-BREATHER...
OH? OH!
...AND NOT SOMEONE AS CHARMING AS YOURSELF!
WHY, THANK YOU, MR...
H. G. WELLS IS THE NAME...
I'M RICH AND FAMOUS!
ALSO JOINING US TONIGHT IS LORENZO PORTET...
...SPANISH EXILE AND ASSOCIATE OF THE LATE FERRER.
ER, YES... I'VE ALREADY HAD THE PLEASURE...
WE MEET AGAIN, SEÑORA...
:SMOOCH:
AND LURKING IN THE SHADOWS IS HAVELOCK ELLIS.
?!? THE SEXOLOGIST?
HELLO.
I SO WANTED TO MEET YOU!
MIGHT WE GET TOGETHER? SAY, THIS SATURDAY?
I HAVE SO MUCH TO ASK YOU!
I... UH...
:AHEM: ER, MARGARET...
YOU PROMISED TO READ MY MANUSCRIPT ON SATURDAY, REMEMBER?
OH, RIGHT. SORRY, MARIE...
—TOMORROW, THEN?
MARRIED LOVE by M. STOPES
DO I HAVE A CHOICE?

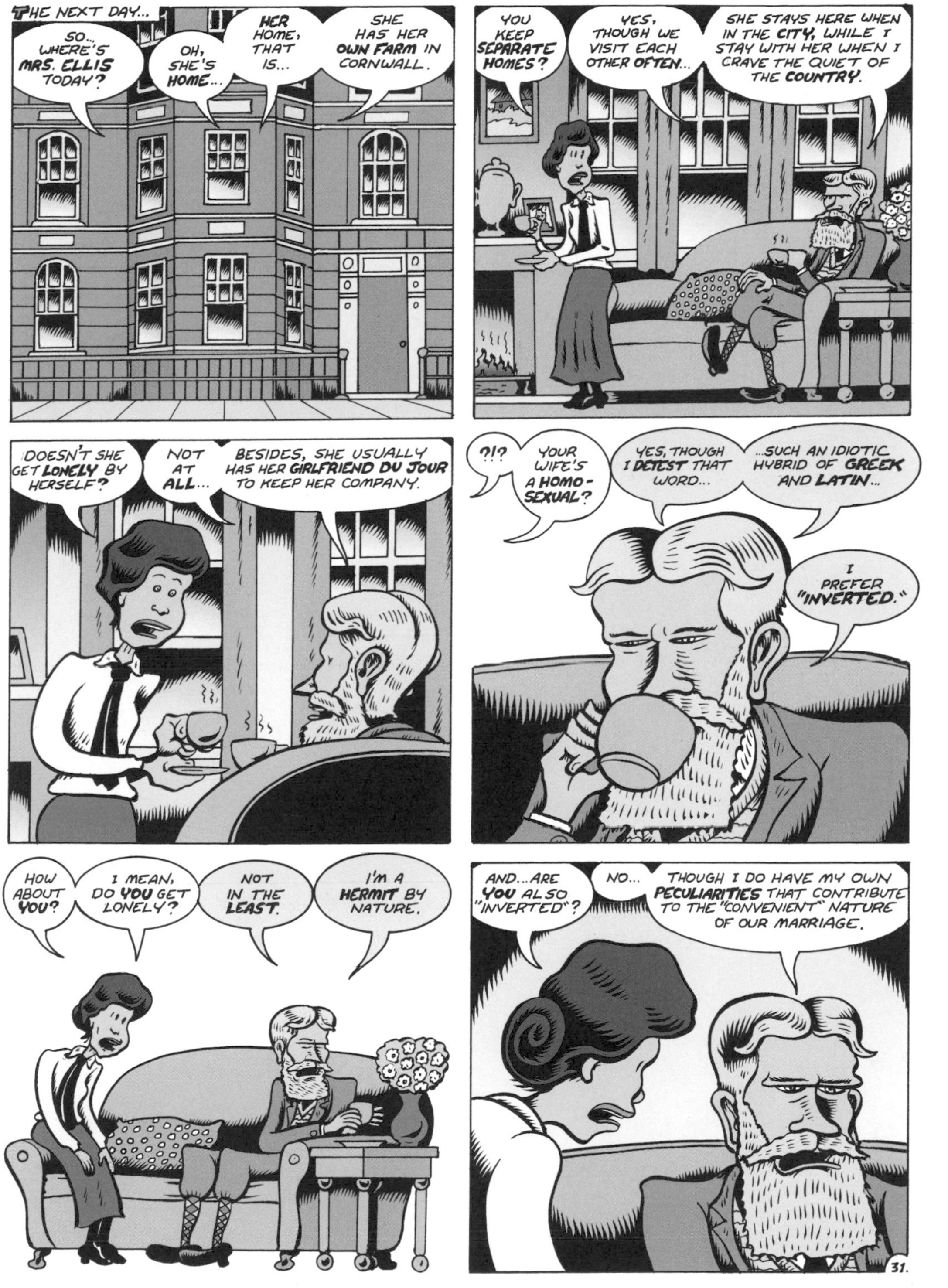
THE NEXT DAY...
SO... WHERE'S MRS. ELLIS TODAY?
OH, SHE'S HOME...
HER HOME, THAT IS...
SHE HAS HER OWN FARM IN CORNWALL.
YOU KEEP SEPARATE HOMES?
YES, THOUGH WE VISIT EACH OTHER OFTEN...
SHE STAYS HERE WHEN IN THE CITY, WHILE I STAY WITH HER WHEN I CRAVE THE QUIET OF THE COUNTRY.
DOESN'T SHE GET LONELY BY HERSELF?
NOT AT ALL...
BESIDES, SHE USUALLY HAS HER GIRLFRIEND DU JOUR TO KEEP HER COMPANY.
?!?
YOUR WIFE'S A HOMO-SEXUAL?
YES, THOUGH I DETEST THAT WORD...
...SUCH AN IDIOTIC HYBRID OF GREEK AND LATIN...
I PREFER "INVERTED."
HOW ABOUT YOU?
I MEAN, DO YOU GET LONELY?
NOT IN THE LEAST.
I'M A HERMIT BY NATURE.
AND...ARE YOU ALSO "INVERTED"?
NO...
THOUGH I DO HAVE MY OWN PECULIARITIES THAT CONTRIBUTE TO THE "CONVENIENT" NATURE OF OUR MARRIAGE.

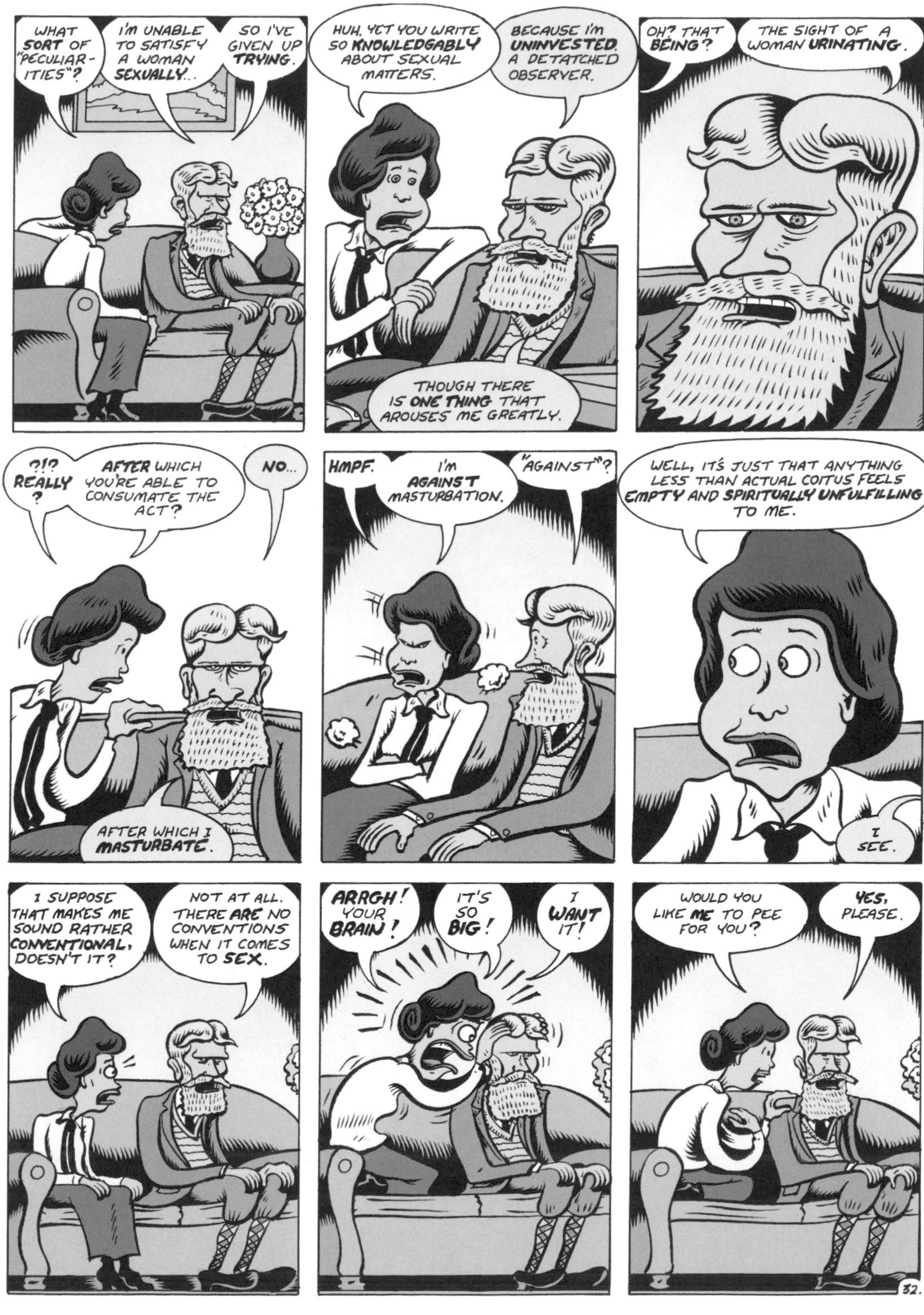
WHAT SORT OF "PECULIAR-ITIES"?
I'M UNABLE TO SATISFY A WOMAN SEXUALLY...
SO I'VE GIVEN UP TRYING.
HUH. YET YOU WRITE SO KNOWLEDGABLY ABOUT SEXUAL MATTERS.
BECAUSE I'M UNINVESTED. A DETATCHED OBSERVER.
THOUGH THERE IS ONE THING THAT AROUSES ME GREATLY.
OH? THAT BEING?
THE SIGHT OF A WOMAN URINATING.
?!? REALLY?
AFTER WHICH YOU'RE ABLE TO CONSUMATE THE ACT?
NO...
AFTER WHICH I MASTURBATE.
HMPF.
I'M AGAINST MASTURBATION.
"AGAINST"?
WELL, IT'S JUST THAT ANYTHING LESS THAN ACTUAL COITUS FEELS EMPTY AND SPIRITUALLY UNFULFILLING TO ME.
I SEE.
I SUPPOSE THAT MAKES ME SOUND RATHER CONVENTIONAL, DOESN'T IT?
NOT AT ALL. THERE ARE NO CONVENTIONS WHEN IT COMES TO SEX.
ARRGH! YOUR BRAIN!
IT'S SO BIG!
I WANT IT!
WOULD YOU LIKE ME TO PEE FOR YOU?
YES, PLEASE.

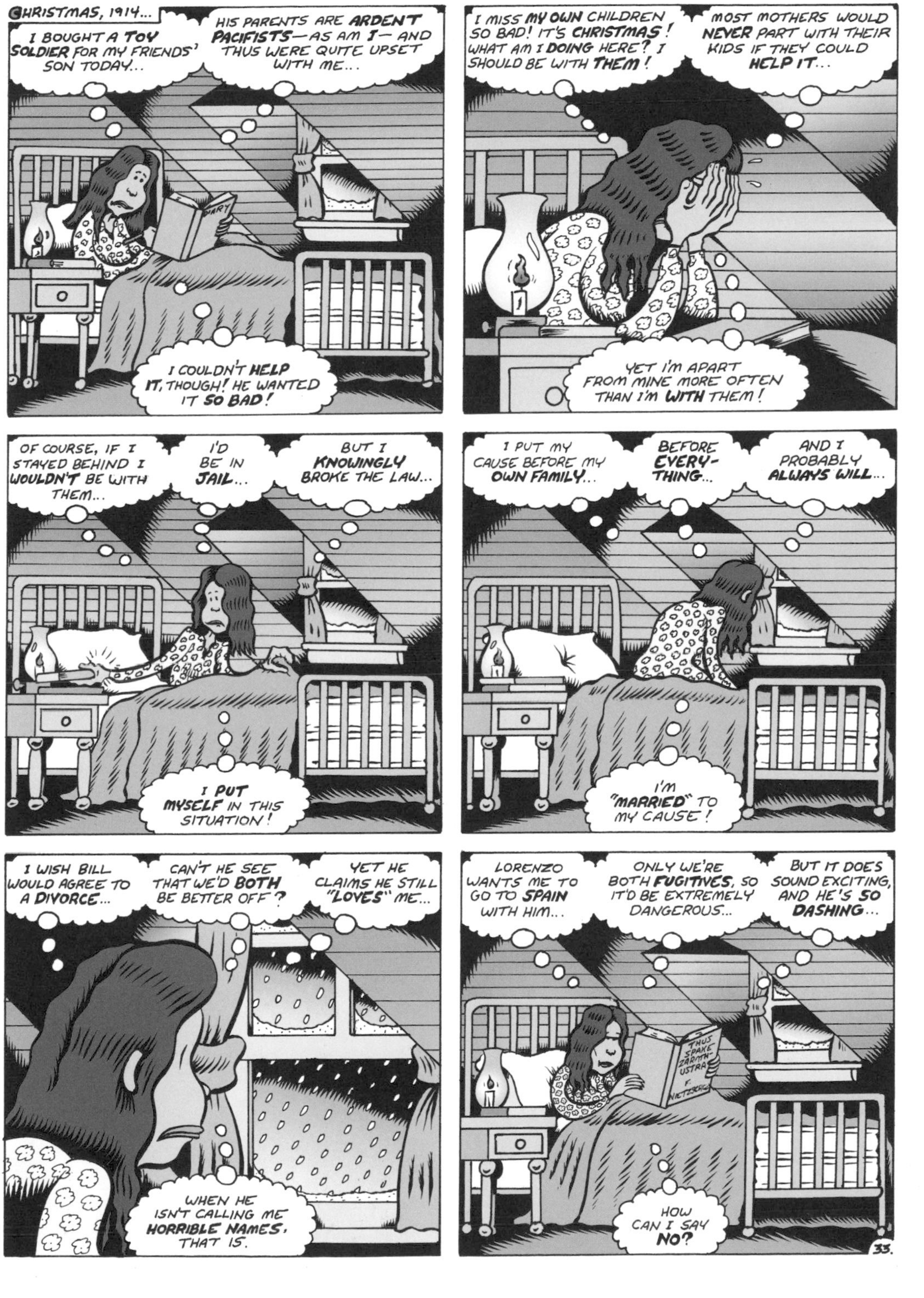
CHRISTMAS, 1914...
I BOUGHT A TOY SOLDIER FOR MY FRIENDS' SON TODAY...
HIS PARENTS ARE ARDENT PACIFISTS—AS AM I— AND THUS WERE QUITE UPSET WITH ME...
MARY
I COULDN'T HELP IT, THOUGH! HE WANTED IT SO BAD!
I MISS MY OWN CHILDREN SO BAD! IT'S CHRISTMAS! WHAT AM I DOING HERE? I SHOULD BE WITH THEM!
MOST MOTHERS WOULD NEVER PART WITH THEIR KIDS IF THEY COULD HELP IT...
YET I'M APART FROM MINE MORE OFTEN THAN I'M WITH THEM!
OF COURSE, IF I STAYED BEHIND I WOULDN'T BE WITH THEM...
I'D BE IN JAIL...
BUT I KNOWINGLY BROKE THE LAW...
I PUT MYSELF IN THIS SITUATION!
I PUT MY CAUSE BEFORE MY OWN FAMILY...
BEFORE EVERY-THING...
AND I PROBABLY ALWAYS WILL...
I'M "MARRIED" TO MY CAUSE!
I WISH BILL WOULD AGREE TO A DIVORCE...
CAN'T HE SEE THAT WE'D BOTH BE BETTER OFF?
YET HE CLAIMS HE STILL "LOVES" ME...
WHEN HE ISN'T CALLING ME HORRIBLE NAMES, THAT IS.
LORENZO WANTS ME TO GO TO SPAIN WITH HIM...
ONLY WE'RE BOTH FUGITIVES, SO IT'D BE EXTREMELY DANGEROUS...
BUT IT DOES SOUND EXCITING, AND HE'S SO DASHING...
THUS SPAKE ZARATH-USTRA F. NIETZSCHE
HOW CAN I SAY NO?

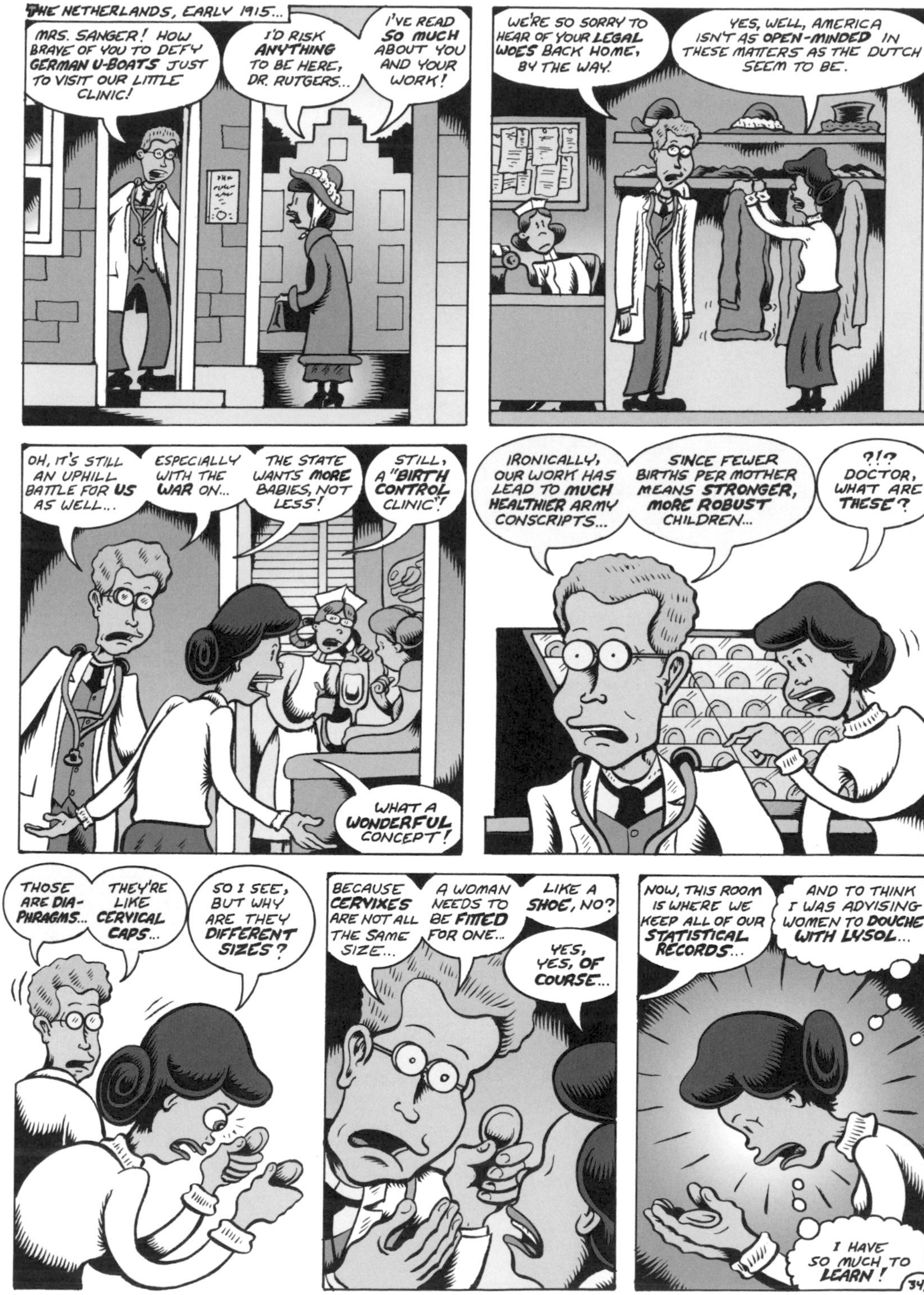
THE NETHERLANDS, EARLY 1915...
MRS. SANGER! HOW BRAVE OF YOU TO DEFY GERMAN U-BOATS JUST TO VISIT OUR LITTLE CLINIC!
I'D RISK ANYTHING TO BE HERE, DR. RUTGERS...
I'VE READ SO MUCH ABOUT YOU AND YOUR WORK!
WE'RE SO SORRY TO HEAR OF YOUR LEGAL WOES BACK HOME, BY THE WAY.
YES, WELL, AMERICA ISN'T AS OPEN-MINDED IN THESE MATTERS AS THE DUTCH SEEM TO BE.
OH, IT'S STILL AN UPHILL BATTLE FOR US AS WELL...
ESPECIALLY WITH THE WAR ON...
THE STATE WANTS MORE BABIES, NOT LESS!
STILL, A "BIRTH CONTROL CLINIC"!
WHAT A WONDERFUL CONCEPT!
IRONICALLY, OUR WORK HAS LEAD TO MUCH HEALTHIER ARMY CONSCRIPTS...
SINCE FEWER BIRTHS PER MOTHER MEANS STRONGER, MORE ROBUST CHILDREN...
?!? DOCTOR, WHAT ARE THESE?
THOSE ARE DIA-PHRAGMS...
THEY'RE LIKE CERVICAL CAPS...
SO I SEE, BUT WHY ARE THEY DIFFERENT SIZES?
BECAUSE CERVIXES ARE NOT ALL THE SAME SIZE...
A WOMAN NEEDS TO BE FITTED FOR ONE...
LIKE A SHOE, NO?
YES, YES, OF COURSE...
NOW, THIS ROOM IS WHERE WE KEEP ALL OF OUR STATISTICAL RECORDS...
AND TO THINK I WAS ADVISING WOMEN TO DOUCHE WITH LYSOL...
I HAVE SO MUCH TO LEARN!

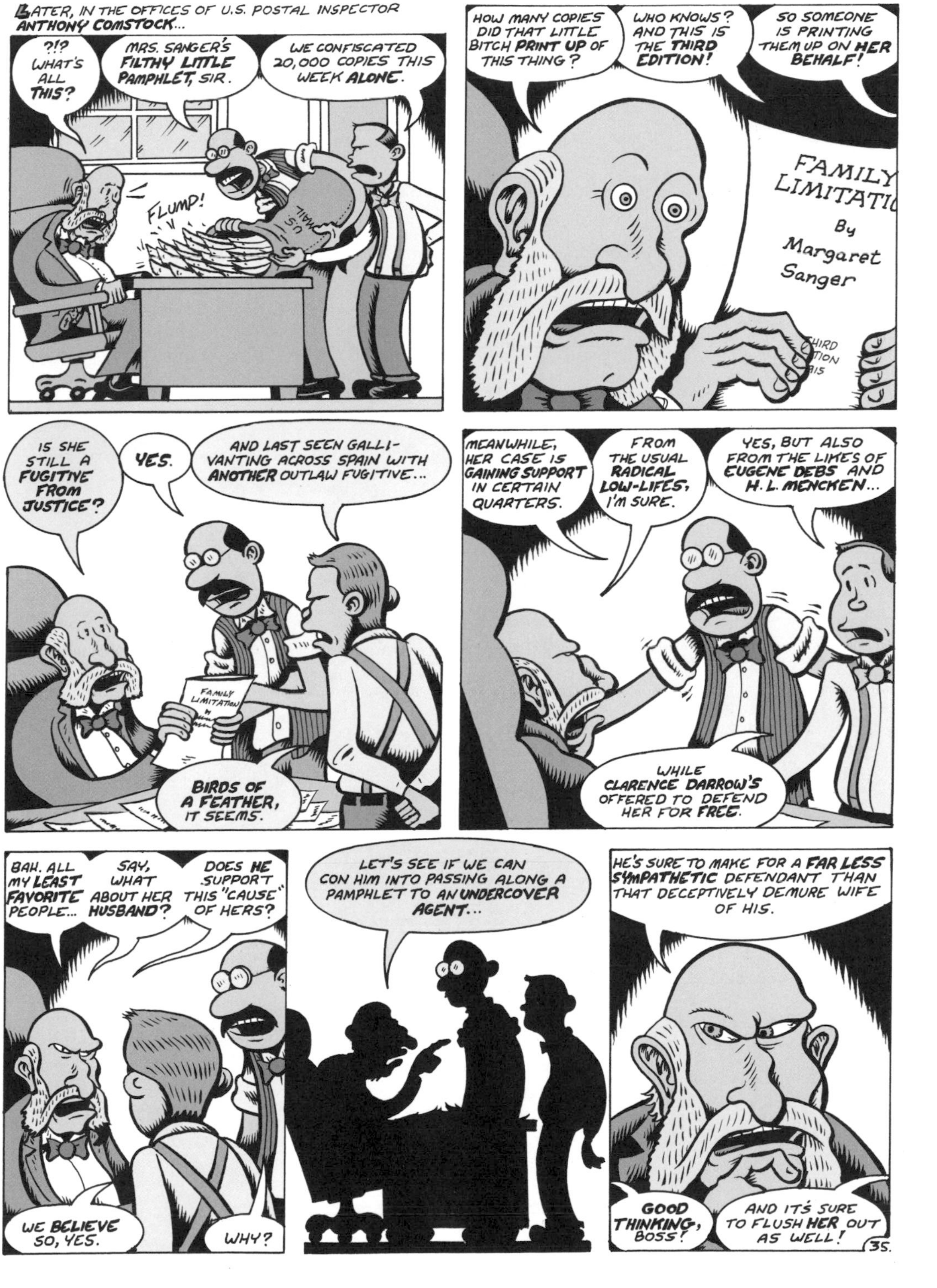
LATER, IN THE OFFICES OF U.S. POSTAL INSPECTOR ANTHONY COMSTOCK...
?!? WHAT'S ALL THIS?
MRS. SANGER'S FILTHY LITTLE PAMPHLET, SIR.
WE CONFISCATED 20,000 COPIES THIS WEEK ALONE.
FLUMP!
U.S. MAIL
HOW MANY COPIES DID THAT LITTLE BITCH PRINT UP OF THIS THING?
WHO KNOWS? AND THIS IS THE THIRD EDITION!
SO SOMEONE IS PRINTING THEM UP ON HER BEHALF!
FAMILY
LIMITATIO
By
Margaret
Sanger
IS SHE STILL A FUGITIVE FROM JUSTICE?
YES.
AND LAST SEEN GALLIVANTING ACROSS SPAIN WITH ANOTHER OUTLAW FUGITIVE...
FAMILY LIMITATION
BIRDS OF A FEATHER, IT SEEMS.
MEANWHILE, HER CASE IS GAINING SUPPORT IN CERTAIN QUARTERS.
FROM THE USUAL RADICAL LOW-LIFES, I'M SURE.
YES, BUT ALSO FROM THE LIKES OF EUGENE DEBS AND H.L. MENCKEN...
WHILE CLARENCE DARROW'S OFFERED TO DEFEND HER FOR FREE.
BAH. ALL MY LEAST FAVORITE PEOPLE...
SAY, WHAT ABOUT HER HUSBAND?
DOES HE SUPPORT THIS "CAUSE" OF HERS?
WE BELIEVE SO, YES.
WHY?
LET'S SEE IF WE CAN CON HIM INTO PASSING ALONG A PAMPHLET TO AN UNDERCOVER AGENT...
HE'S SURE TO MAKE FOR A FAR LESS SYMPATHETIC DEFENDANT THAN THAT DECEPTIVELY DEMURE WIFE OF HIS.
GOOD THINKING, BOSS!
AND IT'S SURE TO FLUSH HER OUT AS WELL!

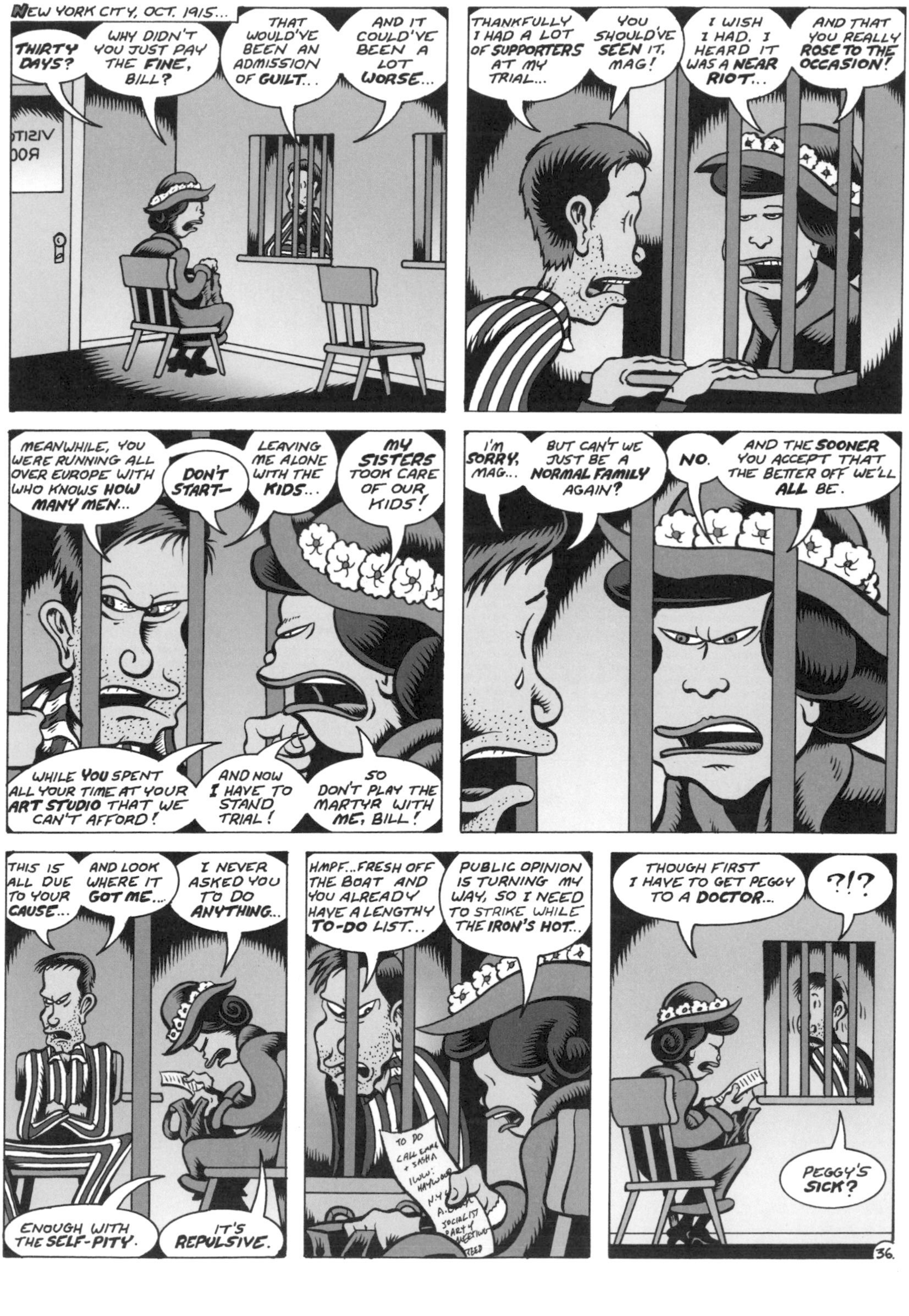
NEW YORK CITY, OCT. 1915...
THIRTY DAYS?
WHY DIDN'T YOU JUST PAY THE FINE, BILL?
THAT WOULD'VE BEEN AN ADMISSION OF GUILT...
AND IT COULD'VE BEEN A LOT WORSE...
VISITO ROO
THANKFULLY I HAD A LOT OF SUPPORTERS AT MY TRIAL...
YOU SHOULD'VE SEEN IT, MAG!
I WISH I HAD. I HEARD IT WAS A NEAR RIOT...
AND THAT YOU REALLY ROSE TO THE OCCASION!
MEANWHILE, YOU WERE RUNNING ALL OVER EUROPE WITH WHO KNOWS HOW MANY MEN...
DON'T START–
LEAVING ME ALONE WITH THE KIDS...
MY SISTERS TOOK CARE OF OUR KIDS!
WHILE YOU SPENT ALL YOUR TIME AT YOUR ART STUDIO THAT WE CAN'T AFFORD!
AND NOW I HAVE TO STAND TRIAL!
SO DON'T PLAY THE MARTYR WITH ME, BILL!
I'M SORRY, MAG...
BUT CAN'T WE JUST BE A NORMAL FAMILY AGAIN?
NO.
AND THE SOONER YOU ACCEPT THAT THE BETTER OFF WE'LL ALL BE.
THIS IS ALL DUE TO YOUR CAUSE...
AND LOOK WHERE IT GOT ME...
I NEVER ASKED YOU TO DO ANYTHING...
ENOUGH WITH THE SELF-PITY.
IT'S REPULSIVE.
HMPF... FRESH OFF THE BOAT AND YOU ALREADY HAVE A LENGTHY TO-DO LIST...
PUBLIC OPINION IS TURNING MY WAY, SO I NEED TO STRIKE WHILE THE IRON'S HOT...
TO DO
CALL EMMA + SASHA
IWW: HAYWOOD
SOCIALIST PARTY MEETING
THOUGH FIRST I HAVE TO GET PEGGY TO A DOCTOR...
?!?
PEGGY'S SICK?

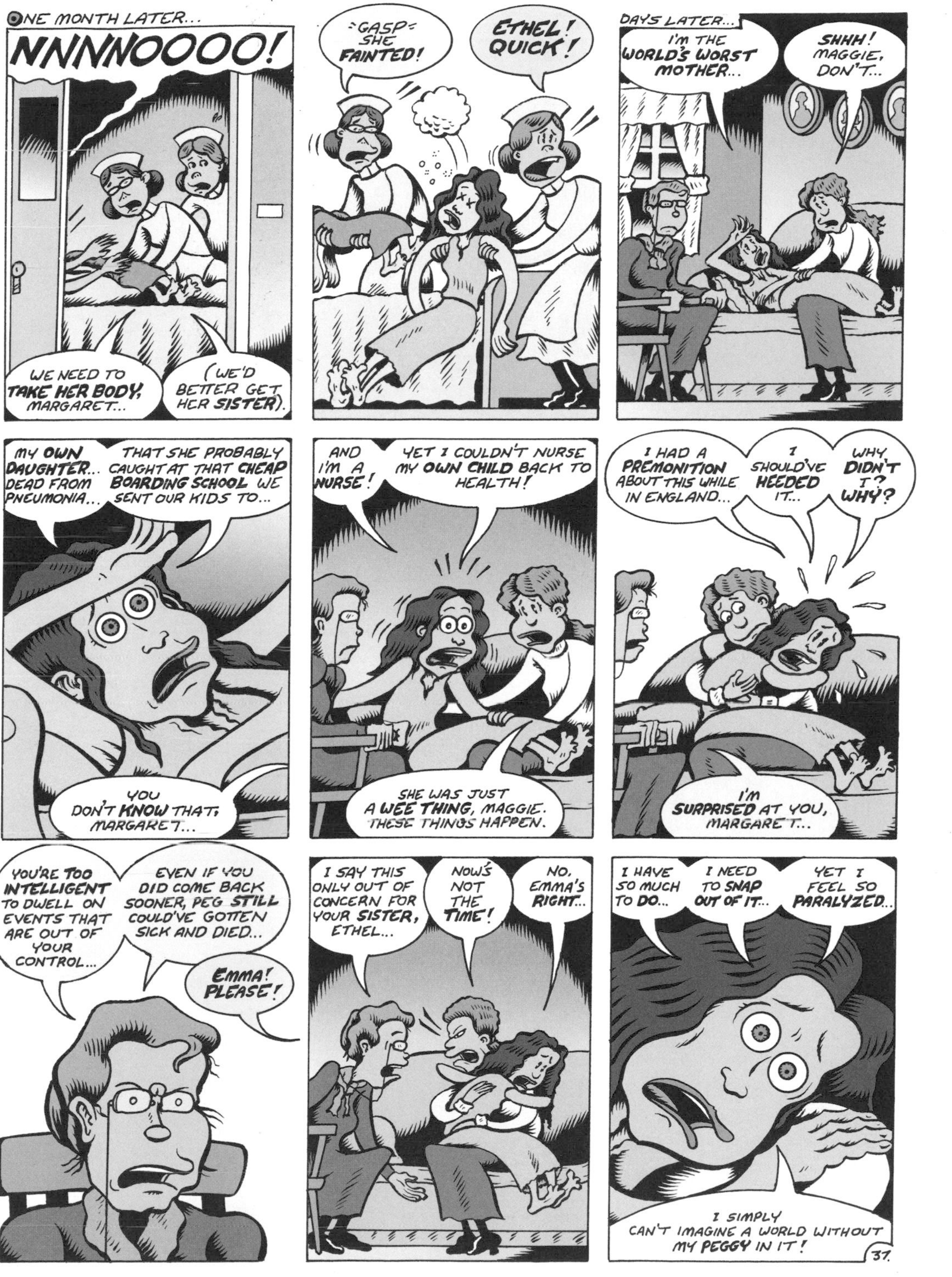
ONE MONTH LATER...
NNNNOOOO!
WE NEED TO TAKE HER BODY, MARGARET...
(WE'D BETTER GET HER SISTER).
=GASP= SHE FAINTED!
ETHEL! QUICK!
DAYS LATER...
I'M THE WORLD'S WORST MOTHER...
SHHH! MAGGIE, DON'T...
MY OWN DAUGHTER... DEAD FROM PNEUMONIA...
THAT SHE PROBABLY CAUGHT AT THAT CHEAP BOARDING SCHOOL WE SENT OUR KIDS TO...
YOU DON'T KNOW THAT, MARGARET...
AND I'M A NURSE!
YET I COULDN'T NURSE MY OWN CHILD BACK TO HEALTH!
SHE WAS JUST A WEE THING, MAGGIE. THESE THINGS HAPPEN.
I HAD A PREMONITION ABOUT THIS WHILE IN ENGLAND...
I SHOULD'VE HEEDED IT...
WHY DIDN'T I? WHY?
I'M SURPRISED AT YOU, MARGARET...
YOU'RE TOO INTELLIGENT TO DWELL ON EVENTS THAT ARE OUT OF YOUR CONTROL...
EVEN IF YOU DID COME BACK SOONER, PEG STILL COULD'VE GOTTEN SICK AND DIED...
EMMA! PLEASE!
I SAY THIS ONLY OUT OF CONCERN FOR YOUR SISTER, ETHEL...
NOW'S NOT THE TIME!
NO, EMMA'S RIGHT...
I HAVE SO MUCH TO DO...
I NEED TO SNAP OUT OF IT...
YET I FEEL SO PARALYZED...
I SIMPLY CAN'T IMAGINE A WORLD WITHOUT MY PEGGY IN IT!

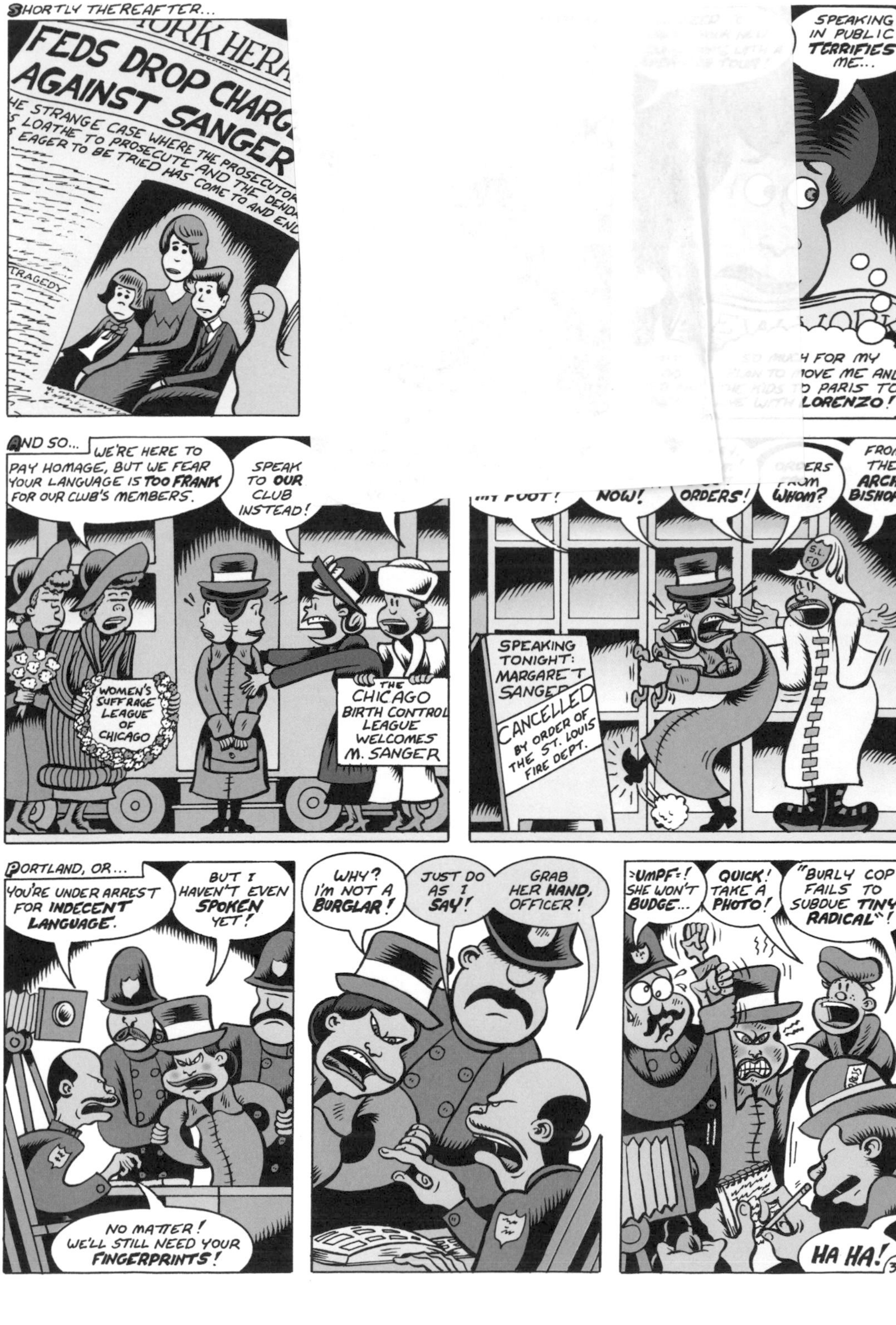
SHORTLY THEREAFTER...
YORK HERA
FEDS DROP CHARG
AGAINST SANGER
HE STRANGE CASE WHERE THE PROSECUTOR
S LOATHE TO PROSECUTE AND THE DEFEND
S EAGER TO BE TRIED HAS COME TO AN END
TRAGEDY
SPEAKING IN PUBLIC TERRIFIES ME...
SO MUCH FOR MY
TO MOVE ME AND
KIDS TO PARIS TO
WITH LORENZO!
AND SO...
WE'RE HERE TO PAY HOMAGE, BUT WE FEAR YOUR LANGUAGE IS TOO FRANK FOR OUR CLUB'S MEMBERS.
SPEAK TO OUR CLUB INSTEAD!
WOMEN'S SUFFRAGE LEAGUE OF CHICAGO
THE CHICAGO BIRTH CONTROL LEAGUE WELCOMES M. SANGER
MY FOOT!
NOW!
ORDERS!
ORDERS FROM WHOM?
FROM THE ARCH-BISHOP!
S.L. F.D.
SPEAKING TONIGHT: MARGARET SANGER
CANCELLED BY ORDER OF THE ST. LOUIS FIRE DEPT.
PORTLAND, OR...
YOU'RE UNDER ARREST FOR INDECENT LANGUAGE.
BUT I HAVEN'T EVEN SPOKEN YET!
NO MATTER! WE'LL STILL NEED YOUR FINGERPRINTS!
WHY? I'M NOT A BURGLAR!
JUST DO AS I SAY!
GRAB HER HAND, OFFICER!
UMPF! SHE WON'T BUDGE...
QUICK! TAKE A PHOTO!
"BURLY COP FAILS TO SUBDUE TINY RADICAL"!
HA HA!

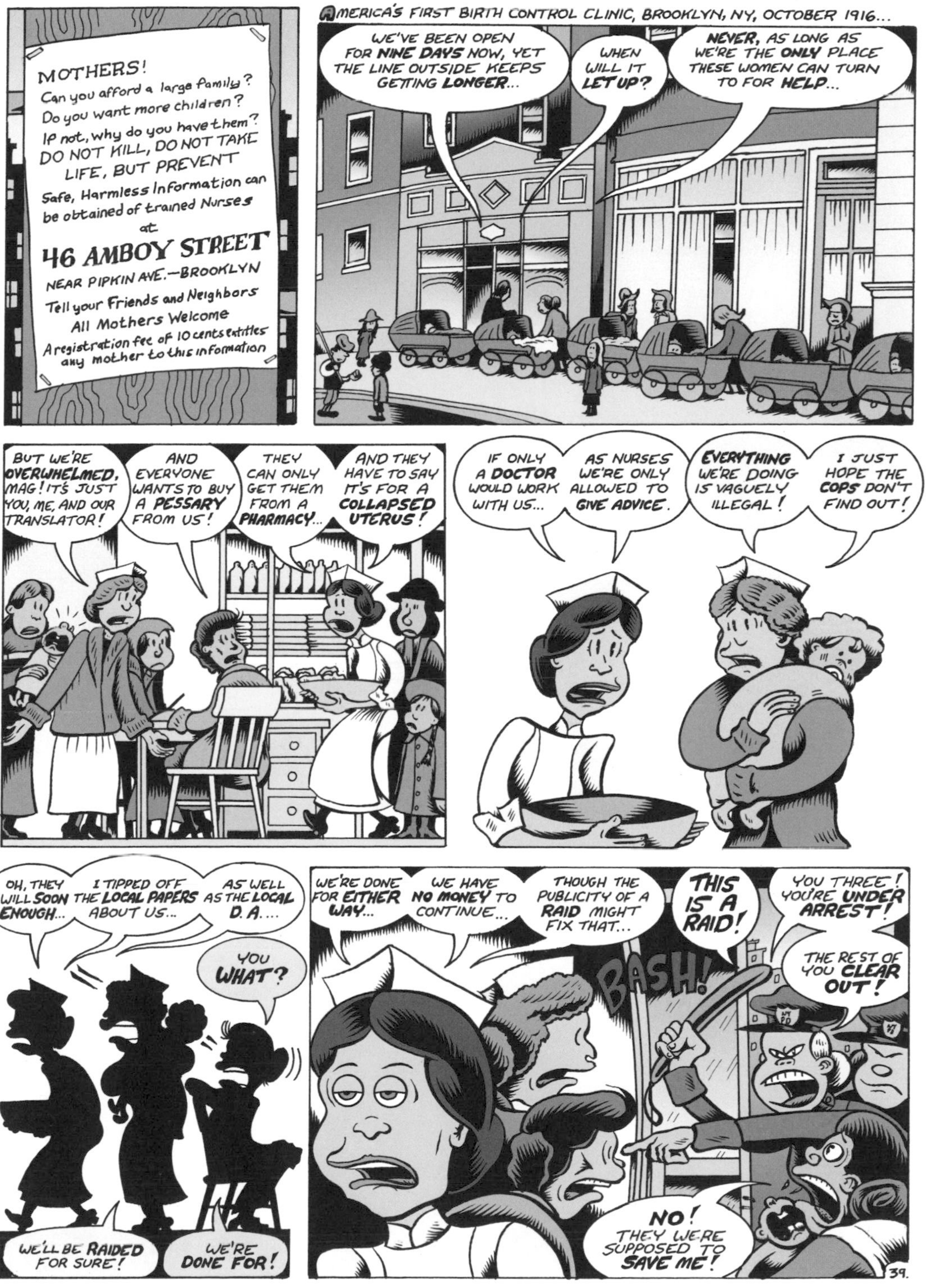
MOTHERS!
Can you afford a large family?
Do you want more children?
If not, why do you have them?
DO NOT KILL, DO NOT TAKE LIFE, BUT PREVENT
Safe, Harmless Information can be obtained of trained Nurses
at
46 AMBOY STREET
NEAR PIPKIN AVE.—BROOKLYN
Tell your Friends and Neighbors
All Mothers Welcome
A registration fee of 10 cents entitles any mother to this information
AMERICA'S FIRST BIRTH CONTROL CLINIC, BROOKLYN, NY, OCTOBER 1916...
WE'VE BEEN OPEN FOR NINE DAYS NOW, YET THE LINE OUTSIDE KEEPS GETTING LONGER...
WHEN WILL IT LET UP?
NEVER, AS LONG AS WE'RE THE ONLY PLACE THESE WOMEN CAN TURN TO FOR HELP...
BUT WE'RE OVERWHELMED, MAG! IT'S JUST YOU, ME, AND OUR TRANSLATOR!
AND EVERYONE WANTS TO BUY A PESSARY FROM US!
THEY CAN ONLY GET THEM FROM A PHARMACY...
AND THEY HAVE TO SAY IT'S FOR A COLLAPSED UTERUS!
IF ONLY A DOCTOR WOULD WORK WITH US...
AS NURSES WE'RE ONLY ALLOWED TO GIVE ADVICE.
EVERYTHING WE'RE DOING IS VAGUELY ILLEGAL!
I JUST HOPE THE COPS DON'T FIND OUT!
OH, THEY WILL SOON ENOUGH...
I TIPPED OFF THE LOCAL PAPERS ABOUT US...
AS WELL AS THE LOCAL D.A....
YOU WHAT?
WE'LL BE RAIDED FOR SURE!
WE'RE DONE FOR!
WE'RE DONE FOR EITHER WAY...
WE HAVE NO MONEY TO CONTINUE...
THOUGH THE PUBLICITY OF A RAID MIGHT FIX THAT...
THIS IS A RAID!
YOU THREE! YOU'RE UNDER ARREST!
THE REST OF YOU CLEAR OUT!
BASH!
NO! THEY WERE SUPPOSED TO SAVE ME!

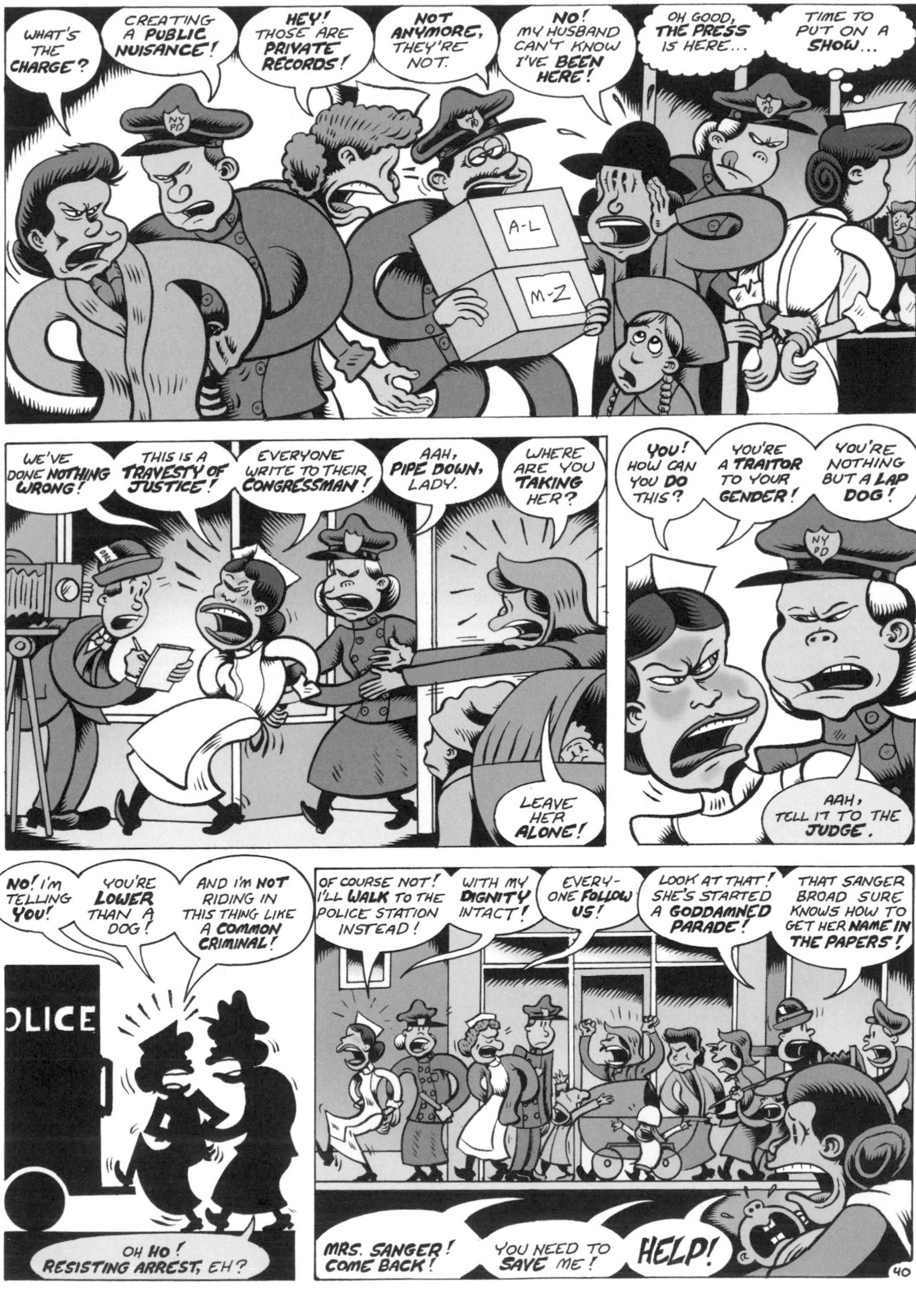
WHAT'S THE CHARGE?
CREATING A PUBLIC NUISANCE!
HEY! THOSE ARE PRIVATE RECORDS!
NOT ANYMORE, THEY'RE NOT.
NO! MY HUSBAND CAN'T KNOW I'VE BEEN HERE!
OH GOOD, THE PRESS IS HERE...
TIME TO PUT ON A SHOW...
A-L
M-Z
WE'VE DONE NOTHING WRONG!
THIS IS A TRAVESTY OF JUSTICE!
EVERYONE WRITE TO THEIR CONGRESSMAN!
AAH, PIPE DOWN, LADY.
WHERE ARE YOU TAKING HER?
LEAVE HER ALONE!
YOU! HOW CAN YOU DO THIS?
YOU'RE A TRAITOR TO YOUR GENDER!
YOU'RE NOTHING BUT A LAP DOG!
AAH, TELL IT TO THE JUDGE.
NO! I'M TELLING YOU!
YOU'RE LOWER THAN A DOG!
AND I'M NOT RIDING IN THIS THING LIKE A COMMON CRIMINAL!
OLICE
OH HO! RESISTING ARREST, EH?
OF COURSE NOT! I'LL WALK TO THE POLICE STATION INSTEAD!
WITH MY DIGNITY INTACT!
EVERY-ONE FOLLOW US!
LOOK AT THAT! SHE'S STARTED A GODDAMNED PARADE!
THAT SANGER BROAD SURE KNOWS HOW TO GET HER NAME IN THE PAPERS!
MRS. SANGER! COME BACK!
YOU NEED TO SAVE ME!
HELP!

LATER, AT THE D.A.'S OFFICE...

AS YOU KNOW, YOUR SISTER HASN'T EATEN IN **FOUR DAYS**...

YES, AND **GOOD FOR HER!**

...AND SHE ALSO REFUSES TO **DRINK**.

OH **NO**...

SO WE HAVE NO CHOICE BUT TO **FORCE FEED** HER.

FORCE FEED? WHY, THAT'S **TORTURE!**

IT **IS** A BRUTAL PROCESS...

BUT SHE'D BE **DEAD** OTHERWISE.

OH DEAR... **POOR ETHEL**...

I'LL HAVE YOU KNOW THAT ETHEL'S HUNGER STRIKE HAS GENERATED A **LOT OF SYMPATHETIC PRESS**...

THERE'S EVEN A PROTEST MEETING IN HER HONOR AT **CARNEGIE HALL** TONIGHT...

SO YOU'D BE WISE TO **DROP ALL CHARGES** AGAINST ETHEL BYRNE AND MRS. SANGER IMMEDIATELY!

THAT'S WHY I ASKED YOU BOTH **HERE**, MR. GOLDSTEIN...

WE'RE WILLING TO DROP THE CHARGES AGAINST MRS. BYRNE ON **ONE CONDITION**...

THAT YOUR CLIENT ASSURES US HER HUNGER STRIKE NEVER FLOUTS THE LAW IN THIS MANNER **EVER AGAIN**...

AND WHAT DO YOU OFFER MY CLIENT **IN RETURN**?

SHE STILL HAS TO STAND TRIAL, BUT IF CONVICTED I'LL PUSH FOR A **LIGHT SENTENCE**.

UNACCEPTABLE!

I ACCEPT.

BAM

WHAT? DARLING, **NO!**

HOW SOON CAN YOU **RELEASE** MY SISTER?

"DARLING"?

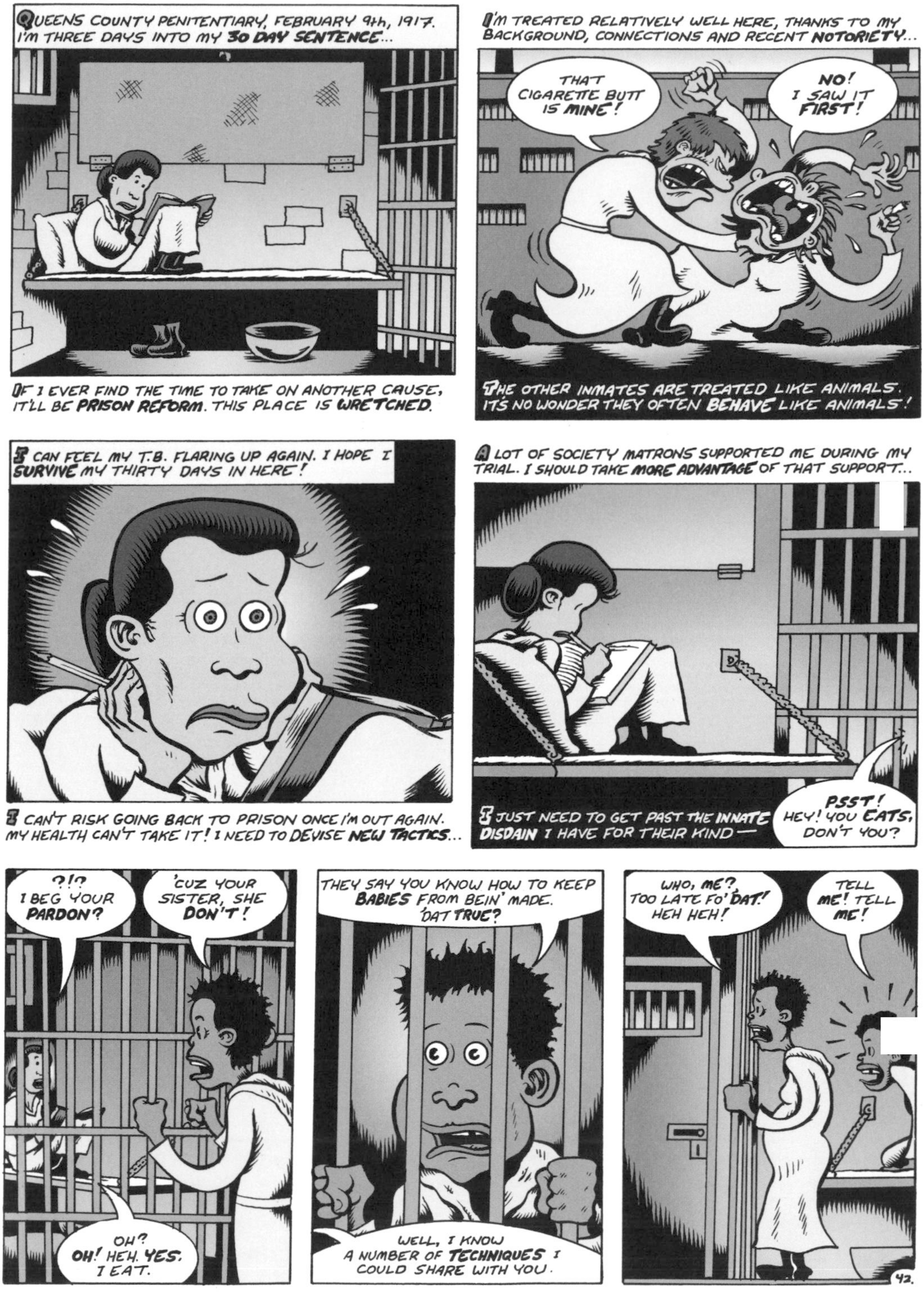
QUEENS COUNTY PENITENTIARY, FEBRUARY 9th, 1917. I'M THREE DAYS INTO MY 30 DAY SENTENCE...
IF I EVER FIND THE TIME TO TAKE ON ANOTHER CAUSE, IT'LL BE PRISON REFORM. THIS PLACE IS WRETCHED.
I'M TREATED RELATIVELY WELL HERE, THANKS TO MY BACKGROUND, CONNECTIONS AND RECENT NOTORIETY...
THAT CIGARETTE BUTT IS MINE!
NO! I SAW IT FIRST!
THE OTHER INMATES ARE TREATED LIKE ANIMALS. IT'S NO WONDER THEY OFTEN BEHAVE LIKE ANIMALS!
I CAN FEEL MY T.B. FLARING UP AGAIN. I HOPE I SURVIVE MY THIRTY DAYS IN HERE!
I CAN'T RISK GOING BACK TO PRISON ONCE I'M OUT AGAIN. MY HEALTH CAN'T TAKE IT! I NEED TO DEVISE NEW TACTICS...
A LOT OF SOCIETY MATRONS SUPPORTED ME DURING MY TRIAL. I SHOULD TAKE MORE ADVANTAGE OF THAT SUPPORT...
I JUST NEED TO GET PAST THE INNATE DISDAIN I HAVE FOR THEIR KIND—
PSST! HEY! YOU EATS, DON'T YOU?
?!? I BEG YOUR PARDON?
'CUZ YOUR SISTER, SHE DON'T!
OH? OH! HEH. YES. I EAT.
THEY SAY YOU KNOW HOW TO KEEP BABIES FROM BEIN' MADE. 'DAT TRUE?
WELL, I KNOW A NUMBER OF TECHNIQUES I COULD SHARE WITH YOU.
WHO, ME? TOO LATE FO' DAT! HEH HEH!
TELL ME! TELL ME!
42.

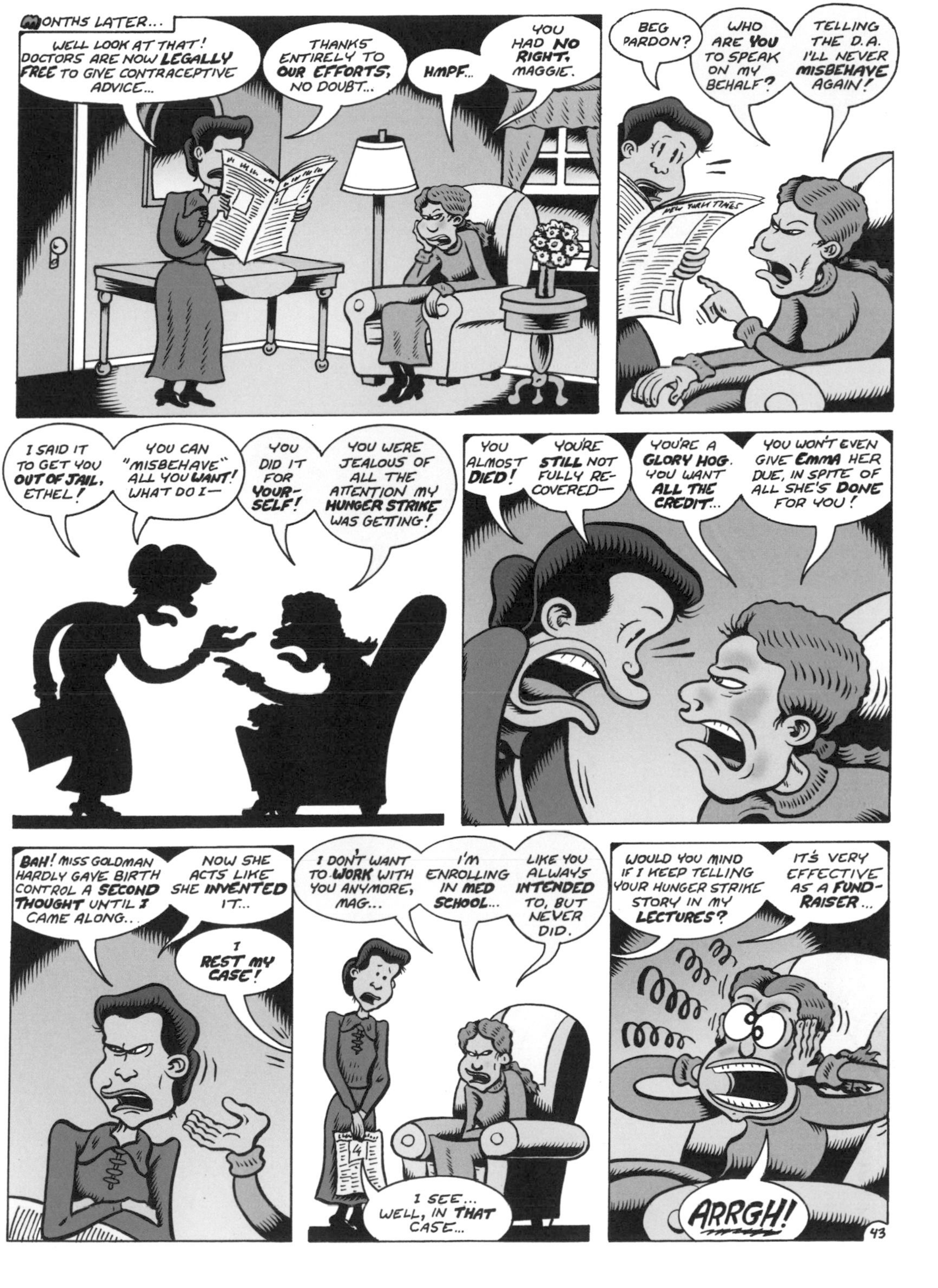
MONTHS LATER...
WELL LOOK AT THAT! DOCTORS ARE NOW LEGALLY FREE TO GIVE CONTRACEPTIVE ADVICE...
THANKS ENTIRELY TO OUR EFFORTS, NO DOUBT...
HMPF...
YOU HAD NO RIGHT, MAGGIE.
BEG PARDON?
WHO ARE YOU TO SPEAK ON MY BEHALF?
TELLING THE D.A. I'LL NEVER MISBEHAVE AGAIN!
I SAID IT TO GET YOU OUT OF JAIL, ETHEL!
YOU CAN "MISBEHAVE" ALL YOU WANT! WHAT DO I—
YOU DID IT FOR YOURSELF!
YOU WERE JEALOUS OF ALL THE ATTENTION MY HUNGER STRIKE WAS GETTING!
YOU ALMOST DIED!
YOU'RE STILL NOT FULLY RE-COVERED—
YOU'RE A GLORY HOG. YOU WANT ALL THE CREDIT...
YOU WON'T EVEN GIVE EMMA HER DUE, IN SPITE OF ALL SHE'S DONE FOR YOU!
BAH! MISS GOLDMAN HARDLY GAVE BIRTH CONTROL A SECOND THOUGHT UNTIL I CAME ALONG...
NOW SHE ACTS LIKE SHE INVENTED IT...
I REST MY CASE!
I DON'T WANT TO WORK WITH YOU ANYMORE, MAG...
I'M ENROLLING IN MED SCHOOL...
LIKE YOU ALWAYS INTENDED TO, BUT NEVER DID.
I SEE... WELL, IN THAT CASE...
WOULD YOU MIND IF I KEEP TELLING YOUR HUNGER STRIKE STORY IN MY LECTURES?
IT'S VERY EFFECTIVE AS A FUND-RAISER...
ARRGH!

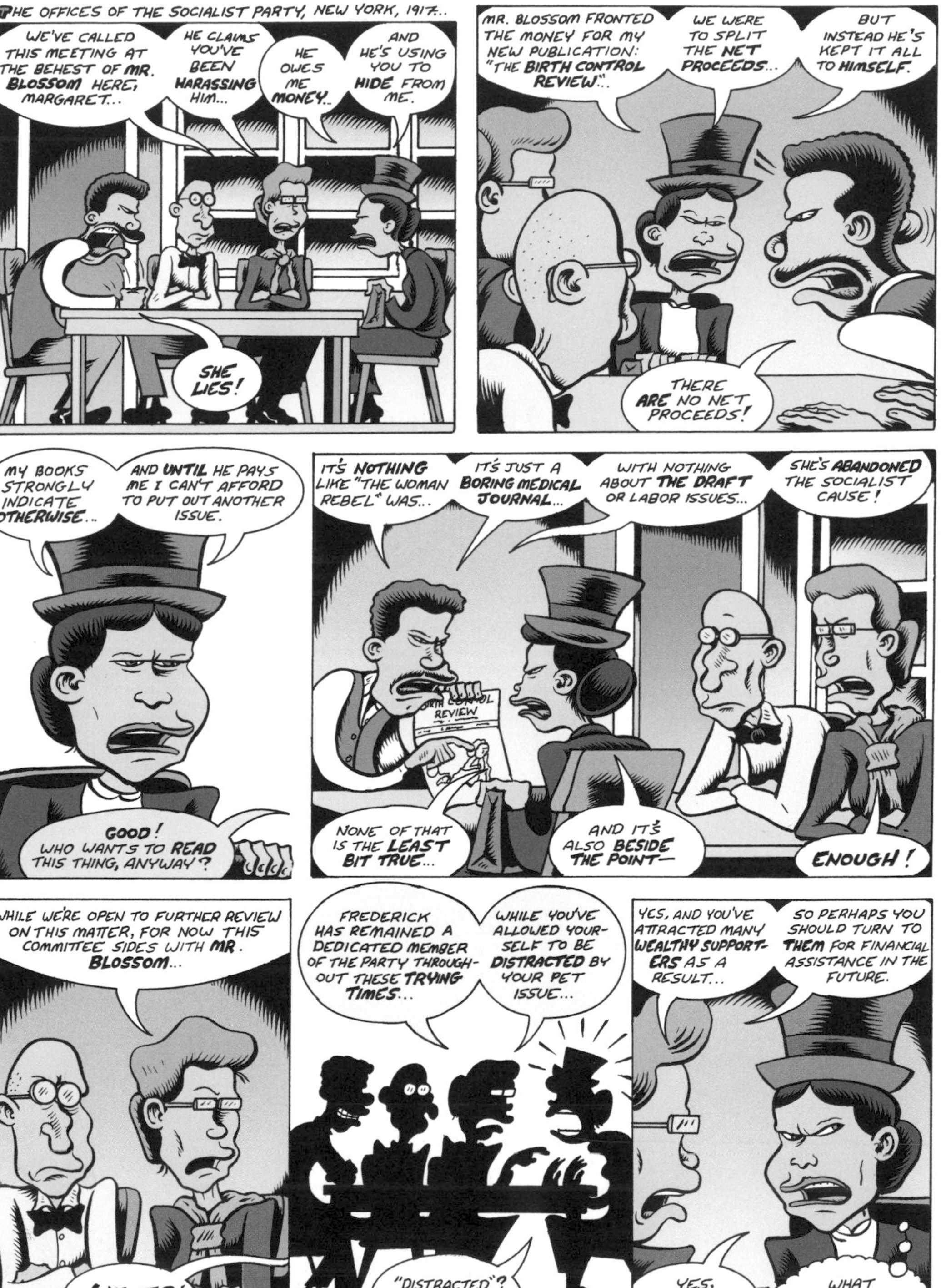
THE OFFICES OF THE SOCIALIST PARTY, NEW YORK, 1917...
WE'VE CALLED THIS MEETING AT THE BEHEST OF MR. BLOSSOM HERE, MARGARET...
HE CLAIMS YOU'VE BEEN HARASSING HIM...
HE OWES ME MONEY...
AND HE'S USING YOU TO HIDE FROM ME.
SHE LIES!
MR. BLOSSOM FRONTED THE MONEY FOR MY NEW PUBLICATION: "THE BIRTH CONTROL REVIEW"...
WE WERE TO SPLIT THE NET PROCEEDS...
BUT INSTEAD HE'S KEPT IT ALL TO HIMSELF.
THERE ARE NO NET PROCEEDS!
MY BOOKS STRONGLY INDICATE OTHERWISE...
AND UNTIL HE PAYS ME I CAN'T AFFORD TO PUT OUT ANOTHER ISSUE.
GOOD! WHO WANTS TO READ THIS THING, ANYWAY?
IT'S NOTHING LIKE "THE WOMAN REBEL" WAS...
IT'S JUST A BORING MEDICAL JOURNAL...
WITH NOTHING ABOUT THE DRAFT OR LABOR ISSUES...
SHE'S ABANDONED THE SOCIALIST CAUSE!
BIRTH CONTROL REVIEW
NONE OF THAT IS THE LEAST BIT TRUE...
AND IT'S ALSO BESIDE THE POINT—
ENOUGH!
WHILE WE'RE OPEN TO FURTHER REVIEW ON THIS MATTER, FOR NOW THIS COMMITTEE SIDES WITH MR. BLOSSOM...
WHAT?! BUT, I—
FREDERICK HAS REMAINED A DEDICATED MEMBER OF THE PARTY THROUGH-OUT THESE TRYING TIMES...
WHILE YOU'VE ALLOWED YOUR-SELF TO BE DISTRACTED BY YOUR PET ISSUE...
"DISTRACTED"? I WAS IN PRISON!
YES, AND YOU'VE ATTRACTED MANY WEALTHY SUPPORT-ERS AS A RESULT...
SO PERHAPS YOU SHOULD TURN TO THEM FOR FINANCIAL ASSISTANCE IN THE FUTURE.
YES, PERHAPS I SHOULD!
WHAT A BUNCH OF PHONIES!

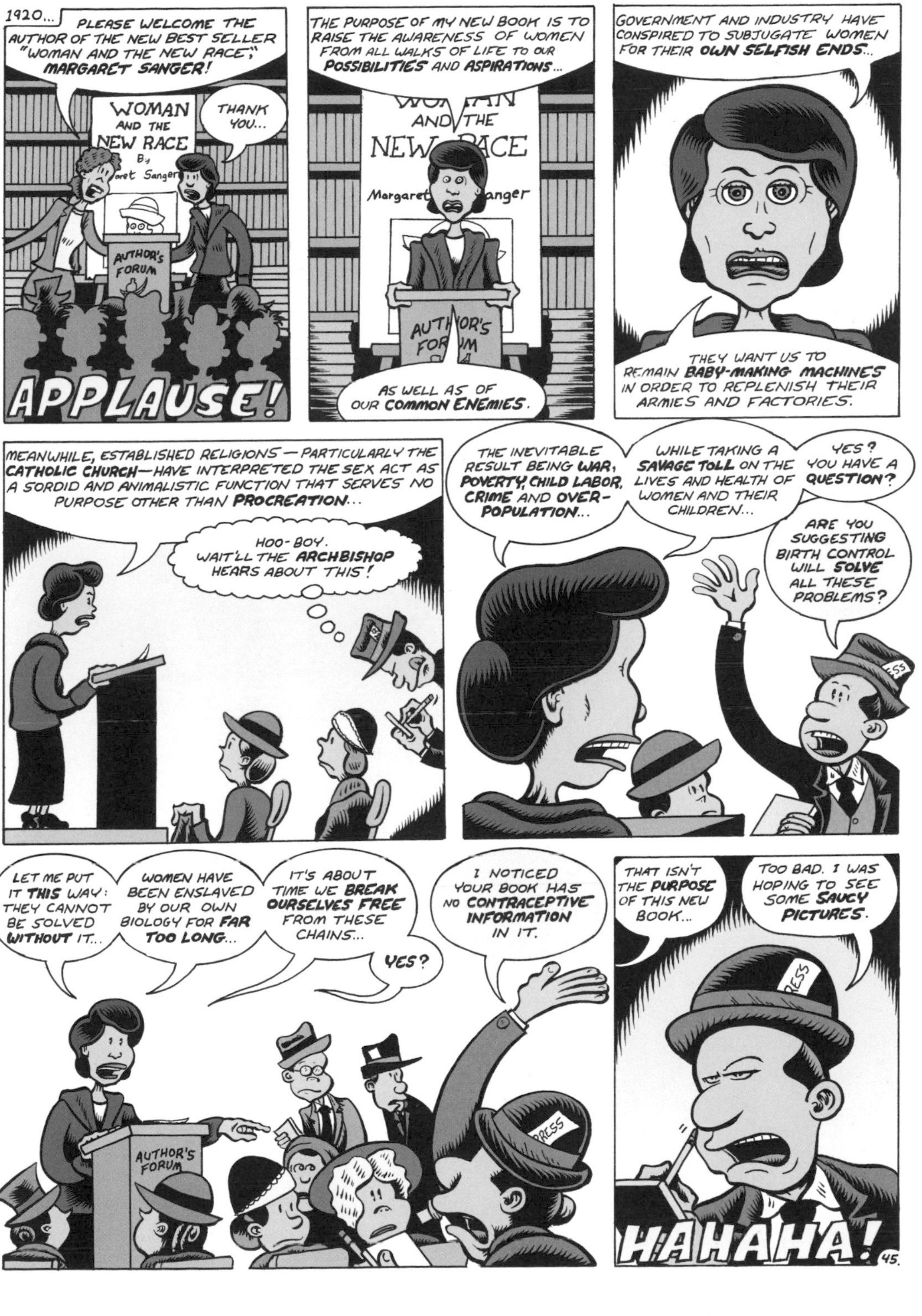

1920...
PLEASE WELCOME THE AUTHOR OF THE NEW BEST SELLER "WOMAN AND THE NEW RACE," MARGARET SANGER!
WOMAN AND THE NEW RACE By aret Sanger
THANK YOU...
AUTHOR'S FORUM
APPLAUSE!
THE PURPOSE OF MY NEW BOOK IS TO RAISE THE AWARENESS OF WOMEN FROM ALL WALKS OF LIFE TO OUR POSSIBILITIES AND ASPIRATIONS...
AND THE NEW RACE Margaret anger
AUTHOR'S FOR M
AS WELL AS OF OUR COMMON ENEMIES.
GOVERNMENT AND INDUSTRY HAVE CONSPIRED TO SUBJUGATE WOMEN FOR THEIR OWN SELFISH ENDS...
THEY WANT US TO REMAIN BABY-MAKING MACHINES IN ORDER TO REPLENISH THEIR ARMIES AND FACTORIES.
MEANWHILE, ESTABLISHED RELIGIONS — PARTICULARLY THE CATHOLIC CHURCH — HAVE INTERPRETED THE SEX ACT AS A SORDID AND ANIMALISTIC FUNCTION THAT SERVES NO PURPOSE OTHER THAN PROCREATION...
HOO-BOY. WAIT'LL THE ARCHBISHOP HEARS ABOUT THIS!
THE INEVITABLE RESULT BEING WAR, POVERTY, CHILD LABOR, CRIME AND OVER-POPULATION...
WHILE TAKING A SAVAGE TOLL ON THE LIVES AND HEALTH OF WOMEN AND THEIR CHILDREN...
YES? YOU HAVE A QUESTION?
ARE YOU SUGGESTING BIRTH CONTROL WILL SOLVE ALL THESE PROBLEMS?
LET ME PUT IT THIS WAY: THEY CANNOT BE SOLVED WITHOUT IT...
WOMEN HAVE BEEN ENSLAVED BY OUR OWN BIOLOGY FOR FAR TOO LONG...
IT'S ABOUT TIME WE BREAK OURSELVES FREE FROM THESE CHAINS...
YES?
I NOTICED YOUR BOOK HAS NO CONTRACEPTIVE INFORMATION IN IT.
AUTHOR'S FORUM
PRESS
THAT ISN'T THE PURPOSE OF THIS NEW BOOK...
TOO BAD. I WAS HOPING TO SEE SOME SAUCY PICTURES.
HAHAHA!

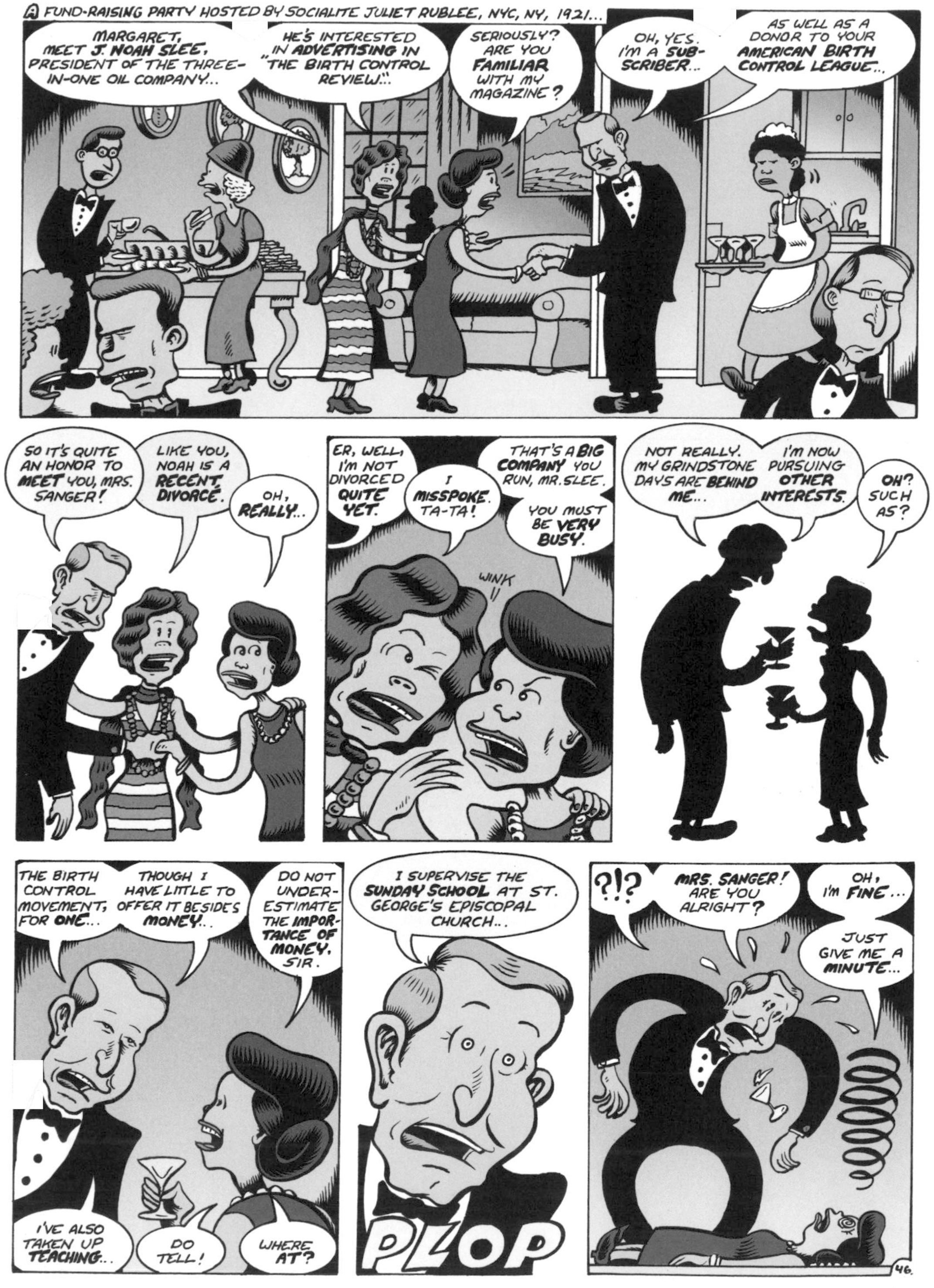
A FUND-RAISING PARTY HOSTED BY SOCIALITE JULIET RUBLEE, NYC, NY, 1921...
MARGARET, MEET J. NOAH SLEE, PRESIDENT OF THE THREE-IN-ONE OIL COMPANY...
HE'S INTERESTED IN ADVERTISING IN "THE BIRTH CONTROL REVIEW"...
SERIOUSLY? ARE YOU FAMILIAR WITH MY MAGAZINE?
OH, YES. I'M A SUB-SCRIBER...
AS WELL AS A DONOR TO YOUR AMERICAN BIRTH CONTROL LEAGUE...
SO IT'S QUITE AN HONOR TO MEET YOU, MRS. SANGER!
LIKE YOU, NOAH IS A RECENT DIVORCÉ.
OH, REALLY...
ER, WELL, I'M NOT DIVORCED QUITE YET.
I MISSPOKE. TA-TA!
WINK
THAT'S A BIG COMPANY YOU RUN, MR. SLEE.
YOU MUST BE VERY BUSY.
NOT REALLY. MY GRINDSTONE DAYS ARE BEHIND ME...
I'M NOW PURSUING OTHER INTERESTS.
OH? SUCH AS?
THE BIRTH CONTROL MOVEMENT, FOR ONE...
THOUGH I HAVE LITTLE TO OFFER IT BESIDES MONEY...
DO NOT UNDER-ESTIMATE THE IMPOR-TANCE OF MONEY, SIR.
I'VE ALSO TAKEN UP TEACHING...
DO TELL!
WHERE AT?
I SUPERVISE THE SUNDAY SCHOOL AT ST. GEORGE'S EPISCOPAL CHURCH...
PLOP
?!?
MRS. SANGER! ARE YOU ALRIGHT?
OH, I'M FINE...
JUST GIVE ME A MINUTE...

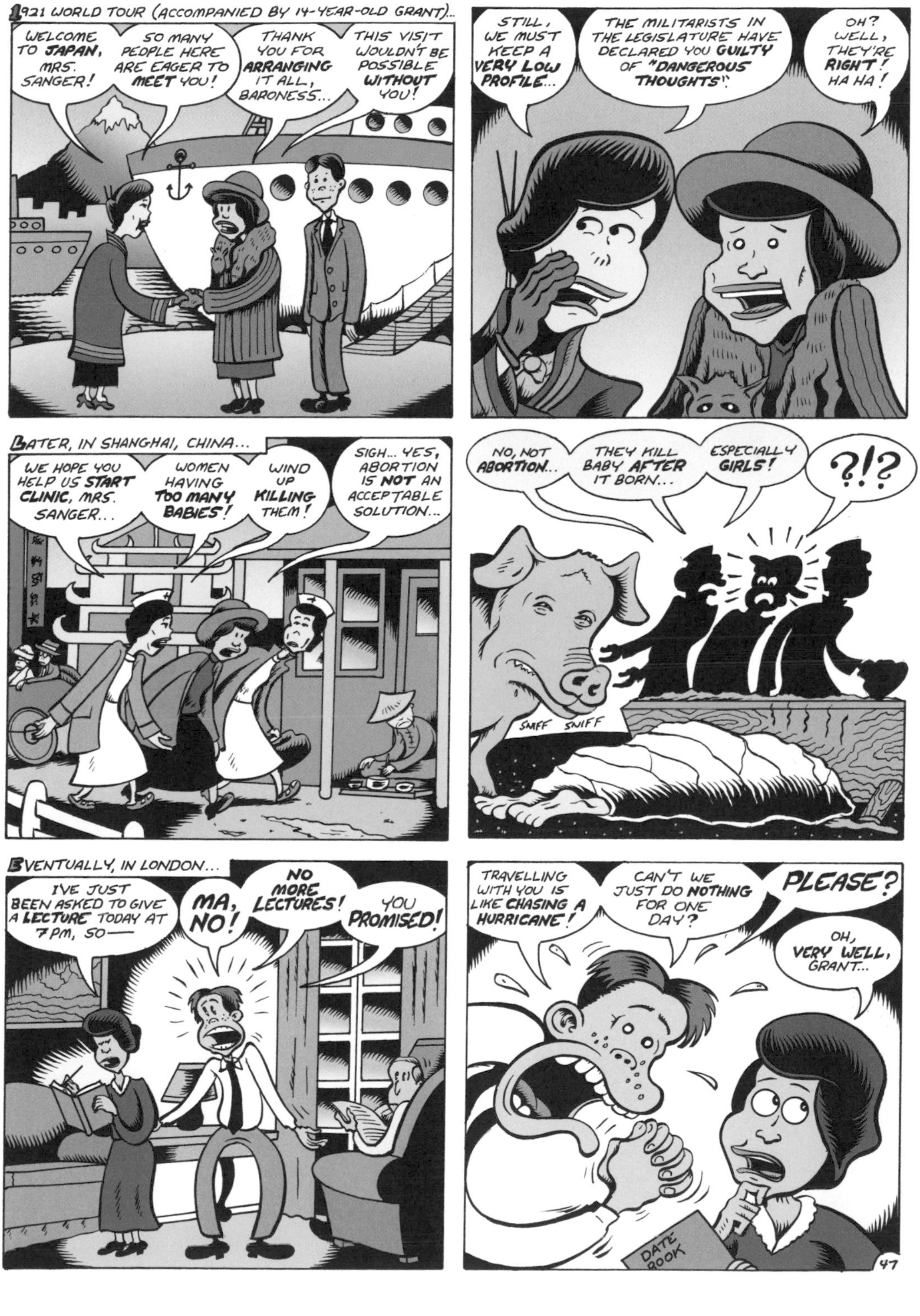
1921 WORLD TOUR (ACCOMPANIED BY 14-YEAR-OLD GRANT)...
WELCOME TO JAPAN, MRS. SANGER!
SO MANY PEOPLE HERE ARE EAGER TO MEET YOU!
THANK YOU FOR ARRANGING IT ALL, BARONESS...
THIS VISIT WOULDN'T BE POSSIBLE WITHOUT YOU!
STILL, WE MUST KEEP A VERY LOW PROFILE...
THE MILITARISTS IN THE LEGISLATURE HAVE DECLARED YOU GUILTY OF "DANGEROUS THOUGHTS".
OH? WELL, THEY'RE RIGHT! HA HA!
LATER, IN SHANGHAI, CHINA...
WE HOPE YOU HELP US START CLINIC, MRS. SANGER...
WOMEN HAVING TOO MANY BABIES!
WIND UP KILLING THEM!
SIGH... YES, ABORTION IS NOT AN ACCEPTABLE SOLUTION...
NO, NOT ABORTION...
THEY KILL BABY AFTER IT BORN...
ESPECIALLY GIRLS!
?!?
SNIFF SNIFF
EVENTUALLY, IN LONDON...
I'VE JUST BEEN ASKED TO GIVE A LECTURE TODAY AT 7 PM, SO—
MA, NO!
NO MORE LECTURES!
YOU PROMISED!
TRAVELLING WITH YOU IS LIKE CHASING A HURRICANE!
CAN'T WE JUST DO NOTHING FOR ONE DAY?
PLEASE?
OH, VERY WELL, GRANT...
DATE BOOK

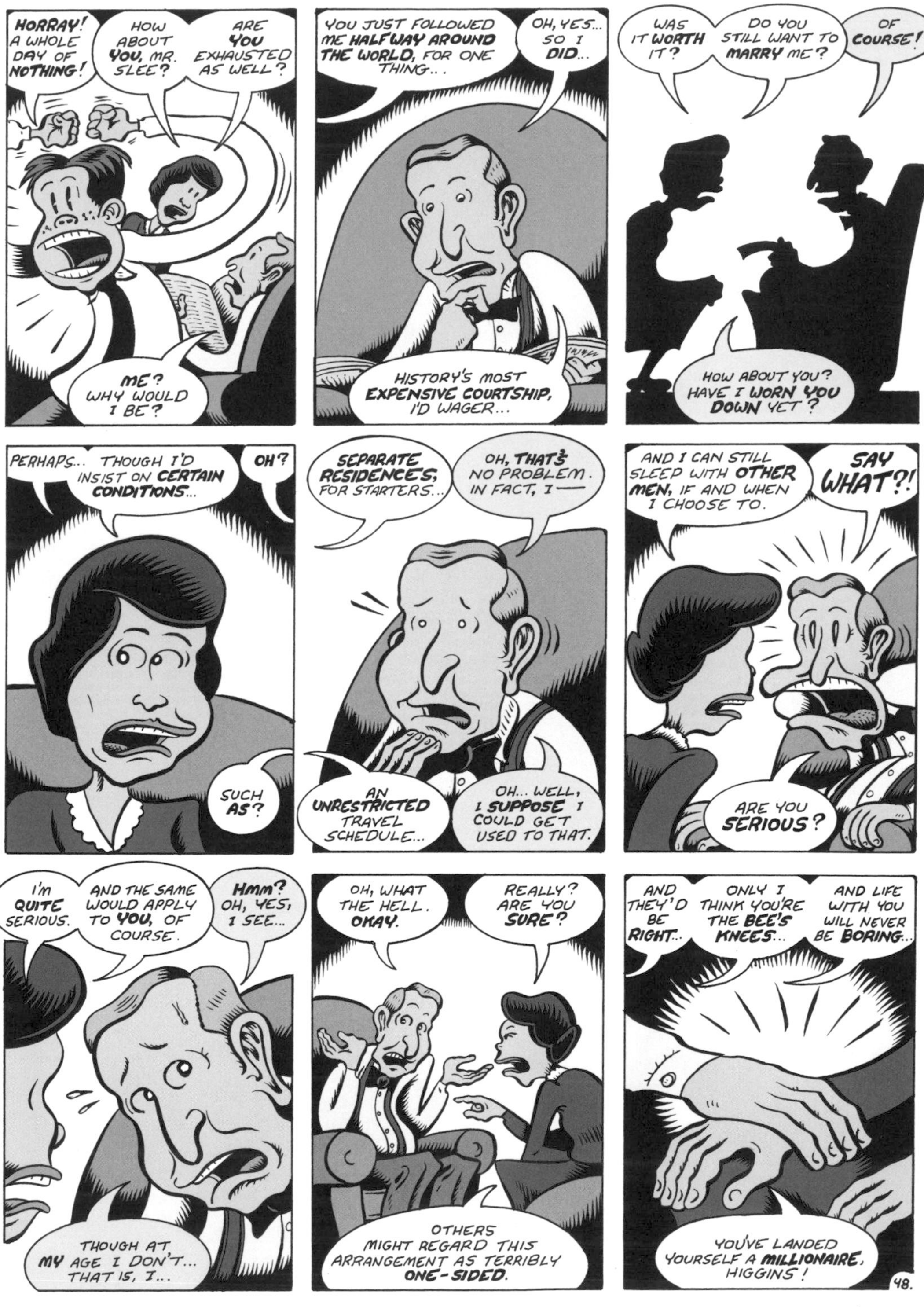
HORRAY! A WHOLE DAY OF NOTHING!
HOW ABOUT YOU, MR. SLEE?
ARE YOU EXHAUSTED AS WELL?
ME? WHY WOULD I BE?
YOU JUST FOLLOWED ME HALFWAY AROUND THE WORLD, FOR ONE THING...
OH, YES... SO I DID...
HISTORY'S MOST EXPENSIVE COURTSHIP, I'D WAGER...
WAS IT WORTH IT?
DO YOU STILL WANT TO MARRY ME?
OF COURSE!
HOW ABOUT YOU? HAVE I WORN YOU DOWN YET?
PERHAPS... THOUGH I'D INSIST ON CERTAIN CONDITIONS...
OH?
SUCH AS?
SEPARATE RESIDENCES, FOR STARTERS...
OH, THAT'S NO PROBLEM. IN FACT, I—
AN UNRESTRICTED TRAVEL SCHEDULE...
OH... WELL, I SUPPOSE I COULD GET USED TO THAT.
AND I CAN STILL SLEEP WITH OTHER MEN, IF AND WHEN I CHOOSE TO.
SAY WHAT?!
ARE YOU SERIOUS?
I'M QUITE SERIOUS.
AND THE SAME WOULD APPLY TO YOU, OF COURSE.
HMM? OH, YES, I SEE...
THOUGH AT MY AGE I DON'T... THAT IS, I...
OH, WHAT THE HELL. OKAY.
REALLY? ARE YOU SURE?
OTHERS MIGHT REGARD THIS ARRANGEMENT AS TERRIBLY ONE-SIDED.
AND THEY'D BE RIGHT...
ONLY I THINK YOU'RE THE BEE'S KNEES...
AND LIFE WITH YOU WILL NEVER BE BORING...
YOU'VE LANDED YOURSELF A MILLIONAIRE, HIGGINS!

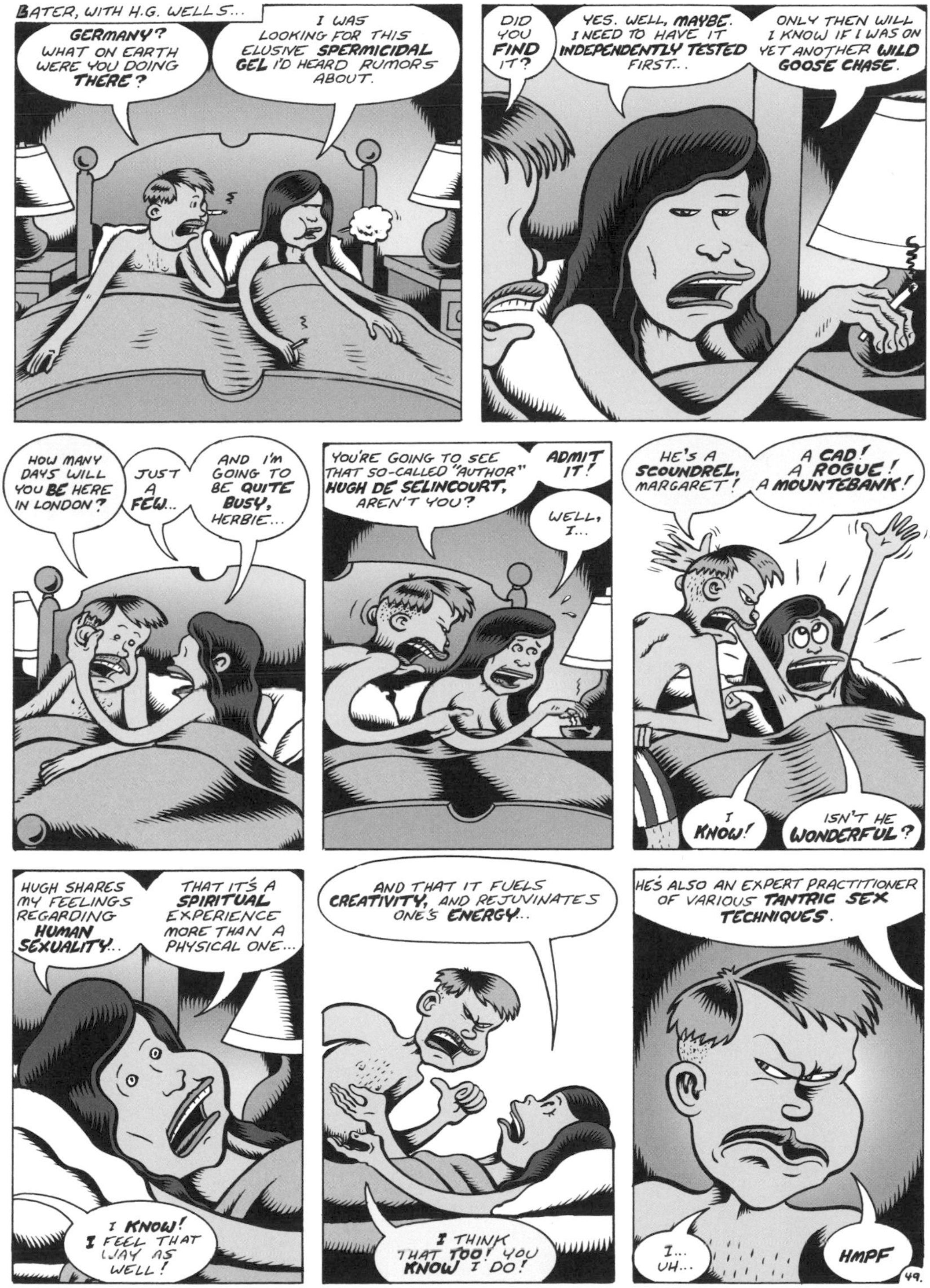
LATER, WITH H.G. WELLS...
GERMANY? WHAT ON EARTH WERE YOU DOING THERE?
I WAS LOOKING FOR THIS ELUSIVE SPERMICIDAL GEL I'D HEARD RUMORS ABOUT.
DID YOU FIND IT?
YES. WELL, MAYBE. I NEED TO HAVE IT INDEPENDENTLY TESTED FIRST...
ONLY THEN WILL I KNOW IF I WAS ON YET ANOTHER WILD GOOSE CHASE.
HOW MANY DAYS WILL YOU BE HERE IN LONDON?
JUST A FEW...
AND I'M GOING TO BE QUITE BUSY, HERBIE...
YOU'RE GOING TO SEE THAT SO-CALLED "AUTHOR" HUGH DE SELINCOURT, AREN'T YOU?
ADMIT IT!
WELL, I...
HE'S A SCOUNDREL, MARGARET!
A CAD! A ROGUE! A MOUNTEBANK!
I KNOW!
ISN'T HE WONDERFUL?
HUGH SHARES MY FEELINGS REGARDING HUMAN SEXUALITY...
THAT IT'S A SPIRITUAL EXPERIENCE MORE THAN A PHYSICAL ONE...
I KNOW! I FEEL THAT WAY AS WELL!
AND THAT IT FUELS CREATIVITY, AND REJUVINATES ONE'S ENERGY...
I THINK THAT TOO! YOU KNOW I DO!
HE'S ALSO AN EXPERT PRACTITIONER OF VARIOUS TANTRIC SEX TECHNIQUES.
I... UH...
HMPF
49.

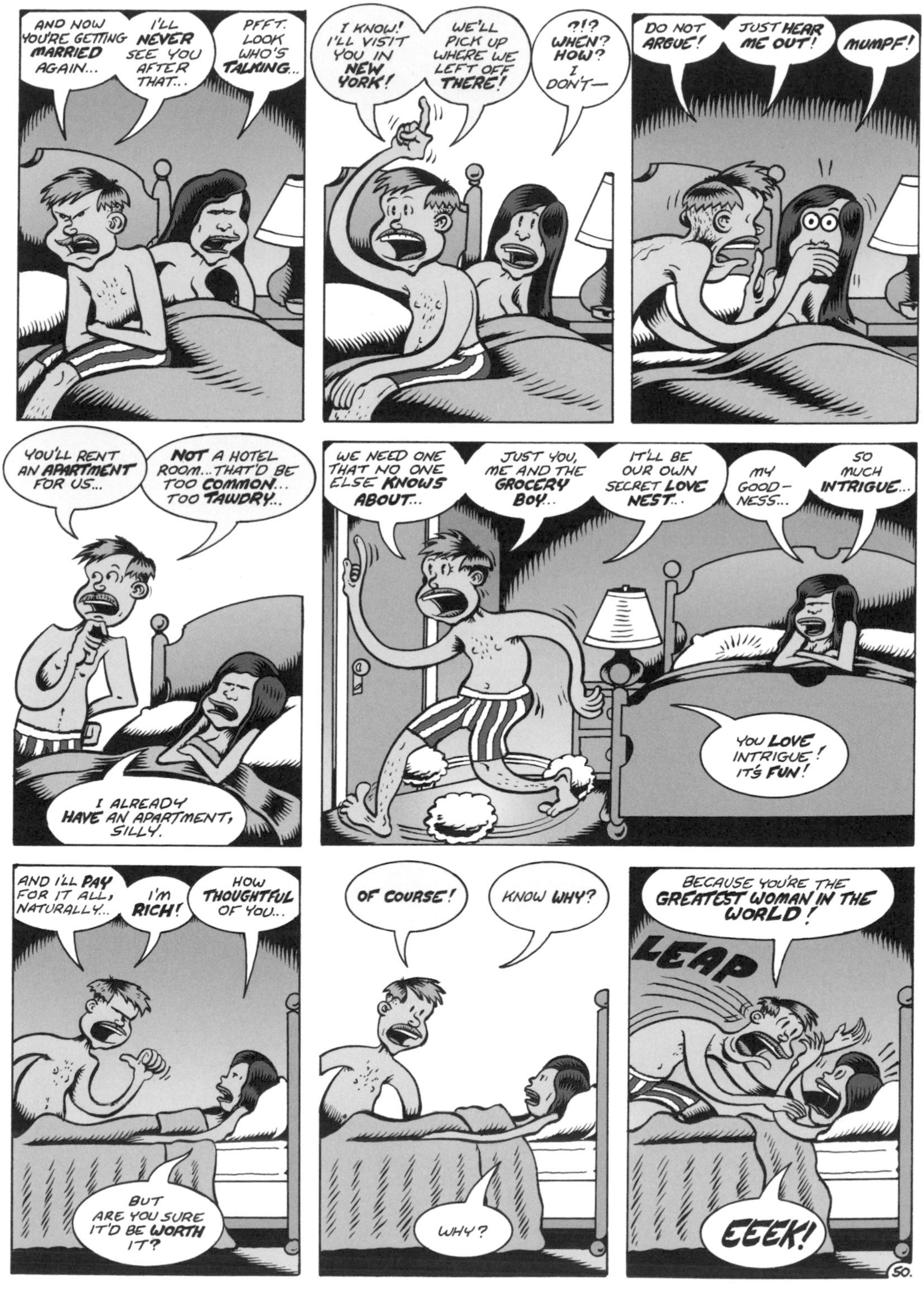
AND NOW YOU'RE GETTING MARRIED AGAIN...
I'LL NEVER SEE YOU AFTER THAT...
PFFT. LOOK WHO'S TALKING...
I KNOW! I'LL VISIT YOU IN NEW YORK!
WE'LL PICK UP WHERE WE LEFT OFF THERE!
?!? WHEN? HOW? I DON'T—
DO NOT ARGUE!
JUST HEAR ME OUT!
MUMPF!
YOU'LL RENT AN APARTMENT FOR US...
NOT A HOTEL ROOM... THAT'D BE TOO COMMON... TOO TAWDRY...
I ALREADY HAVE AN APARTMENT, SILLY.
WE NEED ONE THAT NO ONE ELSE KNOWS ABOUT...
JUST YOU, ME AND THE GROCERY BOY...
IT'LL BE OUR OWN SECRET LOVE NEST...
MY GOOD-NESS...
SO MUCH INTRIGUE...
YOU LOVE INTRIGUE! IT'S FUN!
AND I'LL PAY FOR IT ALL, NATURALLY...
I'M RICH!
HOW THOUGHTFUL OF YOU...
BUT ARE YOU SURE IT'D BE WORTH IT?
OF COURSE!
KNOW WHY?
WHY?
BECAUSE YOU'RE THE GREATEST WOMAN IN THE WORLD!
LEAP
EEEK!

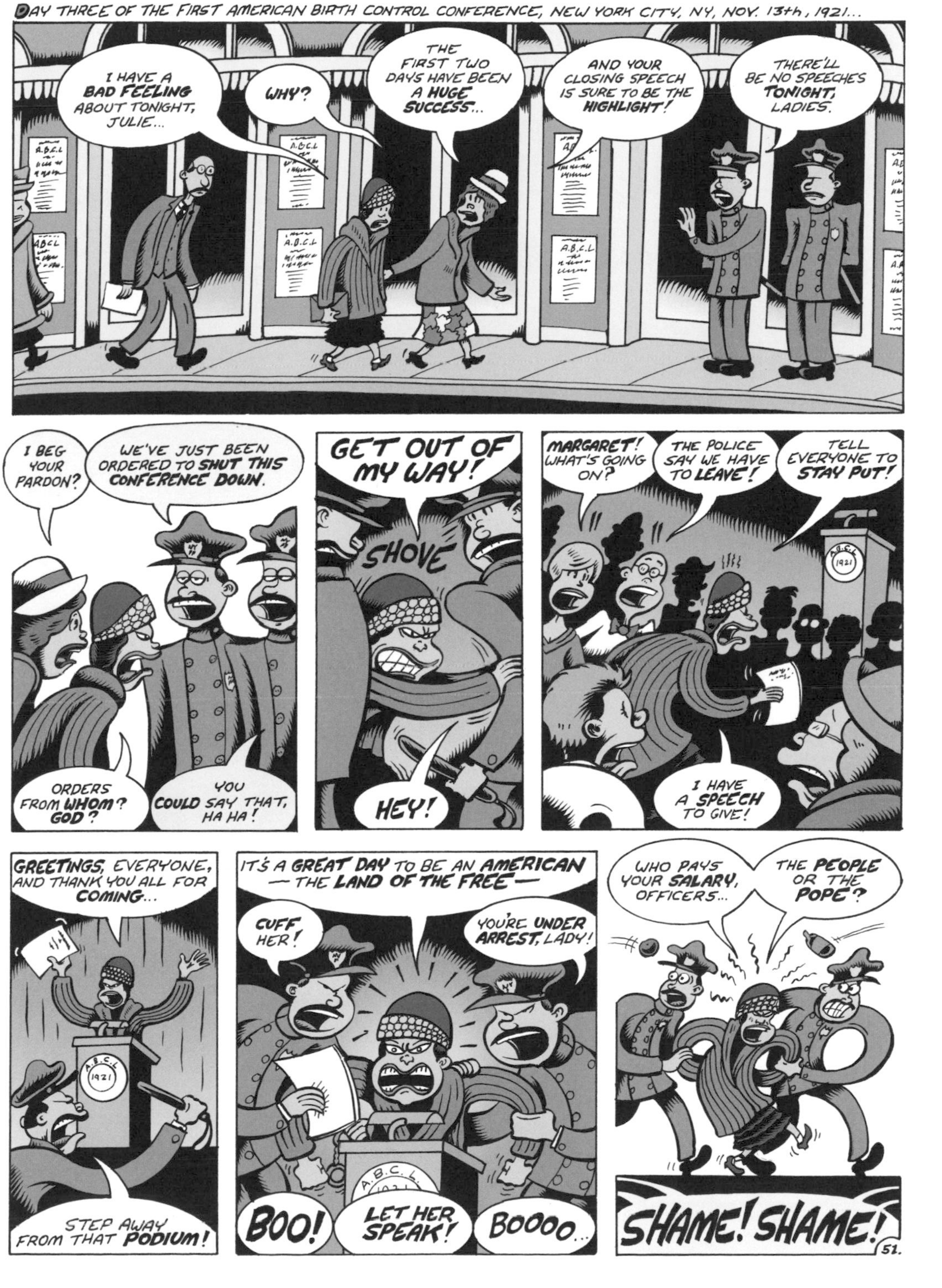
DAY THREE OF THE FIRST AMERICAN BIRTH CONTROL CONFERENCE, NEW YORK CITY, NY, NOV. 13th, 1921...
I HAVE A BAD FEELING ABOUT TONIGHT, JULIE...
WHY?
THE FIRST TWO DAYS HAVE BEEN A HUGE SUCCESS...
AND YOUR CLOSING SPEECH IS SURE TO BE THE HIGHLIGHT!
THERE'LL BE NO SPEECHES TONIGHT, LADIES.
I BEG YOUR PARDON?
WE'VE JUST BEEN ORDERED TO SHUT THIS CONFERENCE DOWN.
ORDERS FROM WHOM? GOD?
YOU COULD SAY THAT, HA HA!
GET OUT OF MY WAY!
SHOVE
HEY!
MARGARET! WHAT'S GOING ON?
THE POLICE SAY WE HAVE TO LEAVE!
TELL EVERYONE TO STAY PUT!
I HAVE A SPEECH TO GIVE!
GREETINGS, EVERYONE, AND THANK YOU ALL FOR COMING...
STEP AWAY FROM THAT PODIUM!
IT'S A GREAT DAY TO BE AN AMERICAN — THE LAND OF THE FREE —
CUFF HER!
YOU'RE UNDER ARREST, LADY!
BOO!
LET HER SPEAK!
BOOOO...
WHO PAYS YOUR SALARY, OFFICERS...
THE PEOPLE OR THE POPE?
SHAME! SHAME!

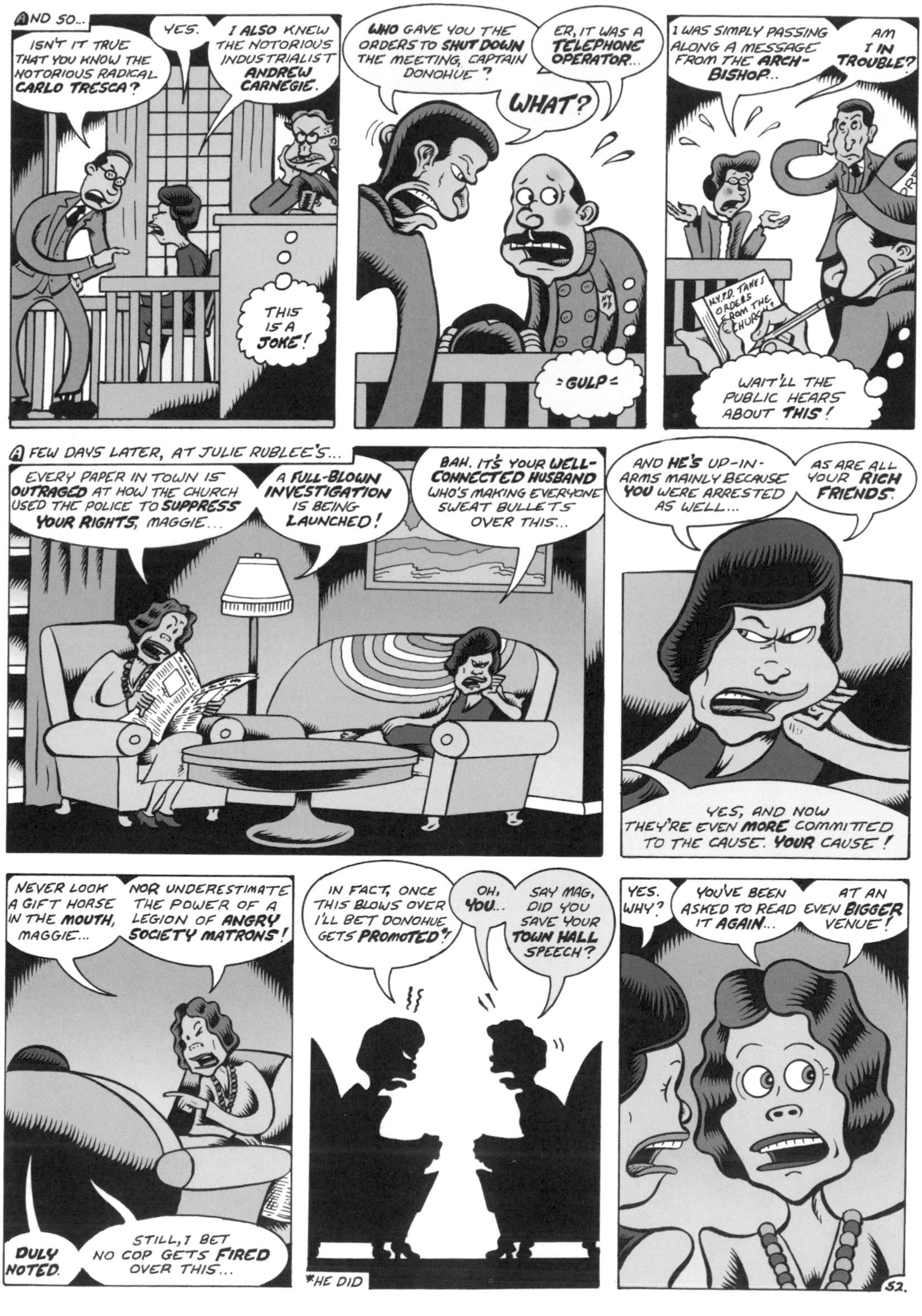
AND SO...
ISN'T IT TRUE THAT YOU KNOW THE NOTORIOUS RADICAL CARLO TRESCA?
YES.
I ALSO KNEW THE NOTORIOUS INDUSTRIALIST ANDREW CARNEGIE.
THIS IS A JOKE!
WHO GAVE YOU THE ORDERS TO SHUT DOWN THE MEETING, CAPTAIN DONOHUE?
ER, IT WAS A TELEPHONE OPERATOR...
WHAT?
=GULP=
I WAS SIMPLY PASSING ALONG A MESSAGE FROM THE ARCH-BISHOP...
AM I IN TROUBLE?
N.Y.P.D. TAKES ORDERS FROM THE CHURCH!
WAIT'LL THE PUBLIC HEARS ABOUT THIS!
A FEW DAYS LATER, AT JULIE RUBLEE'S...
EVERY PAPER IN TOWN IS OUTRAGED AT HOW THE CHURCH USED THE POLICE TO SUPPRESS YOUR RIGHTS, MAGGIE...
A FULL-BLOWN INVESTIGATION IS BEING LAUNCHED!
BAH. IT'S YOUR WELL-CONNECTED HUSBAND WHO'S MAKING EVERYONE SWEAT BULLETS OVER THIS...
AND HE'S UP-IN-ARMS MAINLY BECAUSE YOU WERE ARRESTED AS WELL...
AS ARE ALL YOUR RICH FRIENDS.
YES, AND NOW THEY'RE EVEN MORE COMMITTED TO THE CAUSE. YOUR CAUSE!
NEVER LOOK A GIFT HORSE IN THE MOUTH, MAGGIE...
NOR UNDERESTIMATE THE POWER OF A LEGION OF ANGRY SOCIETY MATRONS!
DULY NOTED.
STILL, I BET NO COP GETS FIRED OVER THIS...
IN FACT, ONCE THIS BLOWS OVER I'LL BET DONOHUE GETS PROMOTED*!
OH, YOU...
SAY MAG, DID YOU SAVE YOUR TOWN HALL SPEECH?
*HE DID
YES. WHY?
YOU'VE BEEN ASKED TO READ IT AGAIN...
AT AN EVEN BIGGER VENUE!

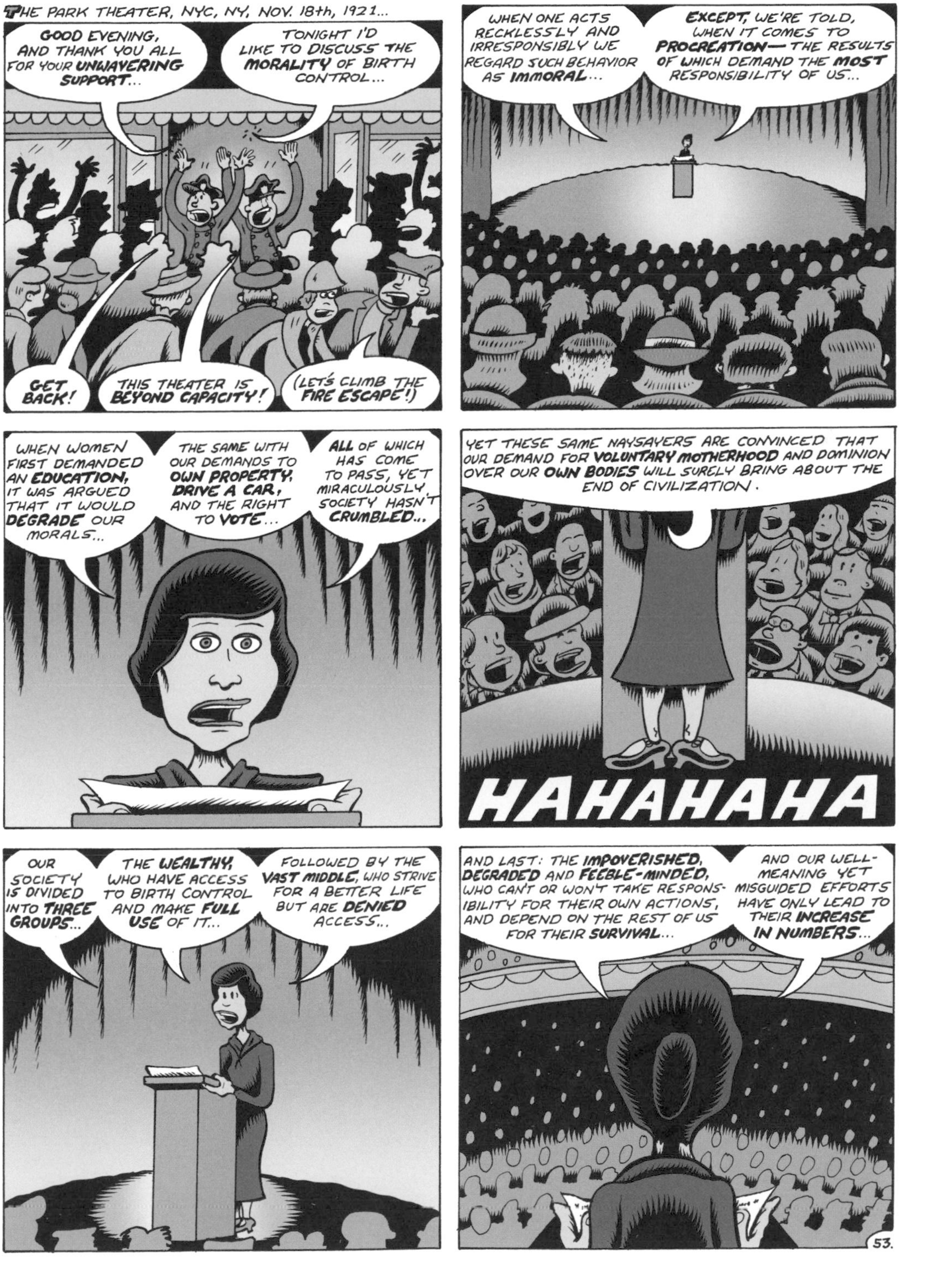

THE PARK THEATER, NYC, NY, NOV. 18th, 1921...
GOOD EVENING, AND THANK YOU ALL FOR YOUR UNWAVERING SUPPORT...
TONIGHT I'D LIKE TO DISCUSS THE MORALITY OF BIRTH CONTROL...
GET BACK!
THIS THEATER IS BEYOND CAPACITY!
(LET'S CLIMB THE FIRE ESCAPE!)
WHEN ONE ACTS RECKLESSLY AND IRRESPONSIBLY WE REGARD SUCH BEHAVIOR AS IMMORAL...
EXCEPT, WE'RE TOLD, WHEN IT COMES TO PROCREATION— THE RESULTS OF WHICH DEMAND THE MOST RESPONSIBILITY OF US...
WHEN WOMEN FIRST DEMANDED AN EDUCATION, IT WAS ARGUED THAT IT WOULD DEGRADE OUR MORALS...
THE SAME WITH OUR DEMANDS TO OWN PROPERTY, DRIVE A CAR, AND THE RIGHT TO VOTE...
ALL OF WHICH HAS COME TO PASS, YET MIRACULOUSLY SOCIETY HASN'T CRUMBLED...
YET THESE SAME NAYSAYERS ARE CONVINCED THAT OUR DEMAND FOR VOLUNTARY MOTHERHOOD AND DOMINION OVER OUR OWN BODIES WILL SURELY BRING ABOUT THE END OF CIVILIZATION.
HAHAHAHA
OUR SOCIETY IS DIVIDED INTO THREE GROUPS...
THE WEALTHY, WHO HAVE ACCESS TO BIRTH CONTROL AND MAKE FULL USE OF IT...
FOLLOWED BY THE VAST MIDDLE, WHO STRIVE FOR A BETTER LIFE BUT ARE DENIED ACCESS...
AND LAST: THE IMPOVERISHED, DEGRADED AND FEEBLE-MINDED, WHO CAN'T OR WON'T TAKE RESPONSIBILITY FOR THEIR OWN ACTIONS, AND DEPEND ON THE REST OF US FOR THEIR SURVIVAL...
AND OUR WELL-MEANING YET MISGUIDED EFFORTS HAVE ONLY LEAD TO THEIR INCREASE IN NUMBERS...

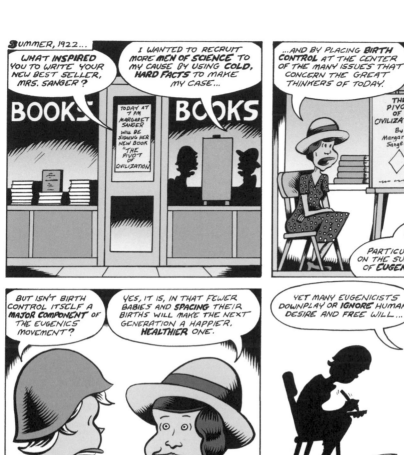

Summer, 1922...

WHAT *INSPIRED* YOU TO WRITE YOUR NEW BEST SELLER, MRS. SANGER?

I WANTED TO RECRUIT MORE *MEN OF SCIENCE* TO MY CAUSE BY USING *COLD, HARD FACTS* TO MAKE MY CASE...

BOOKS

BOOKS

TODAY AT 7 PM MARGARET SANGER WILL BE SIGNING HER NEW BOOK "THE PIVOT OF CIVILIZATION

...AND BY PLACING *BIRTH CONTROL* AT THE CENTER OF THE MANY ISSUES THAT CONCERN THE GREAT THINKERS OF TODAY.

YET YOU'RE ALSO *HIGHLY CRITICAL* OF THE SCIENTIFIC COMMUNITY IN YOUR BOOK...

THE PIVOT OF CIVILIZATION By Margaret Sanger

PARTICULARLY ON THE SUBJECT OF *EUGENICS*...

BUT ISN'T BIRTH CONTROL ITSELF A *MAJOR COMPONENT* OF THE EUGENICS MOVEMENT?

YES, IT IS, IN THAT FEWER BABIES AND *SPACING* THEIR BIRTHS WILL MAKE THE NEXT GENERATION A HAPPIER, *HEALTHIER* ONE.

YET MANY EUGENICISTS DOWNPLAY OR *IGNORE* HUMAN DESIRE AND FREE WILL...

ESPECIALLY REGARDING *SEXUAL BEHAVIOR*...

FOR EXAMPLE, THEY ADVOCATE THE *POSTPONEMENT* OF MARRIAGE...

AS IF *MARRIAGE ALONE* DICTATES HOW MANY BABIES WILL BE BORN IN THE WORLD.

YOU ARGUE THAT THE POOR AND FEEBLE-MINDED ARE THE *LEAST* ABLE TO CONTROL AND LIMIT THEIR *REPRODUCTION*...

AND WHO *SUFFER* THE MOST AS A RESULT, YES.

THAT'S NOT AN OPINION. IT'S A *FACT*!

AS A NURSE I SAW PEOPLE LIVING IN THE MOST *DEPLORABLE, DEHUMAN-IZING* CONDITIONS...

IT'S A *MIRACLE* ANYONE COULD SURVIVE THAT ENVIRONMENT WITH A *SOUND MIND AND BODY*.

ARE YOU SUGGESTING THAT POOR MENTAL FACULTIES ARE MORE THE RESULT OF *NURTURE* THAN OF *NATURE*?

54.

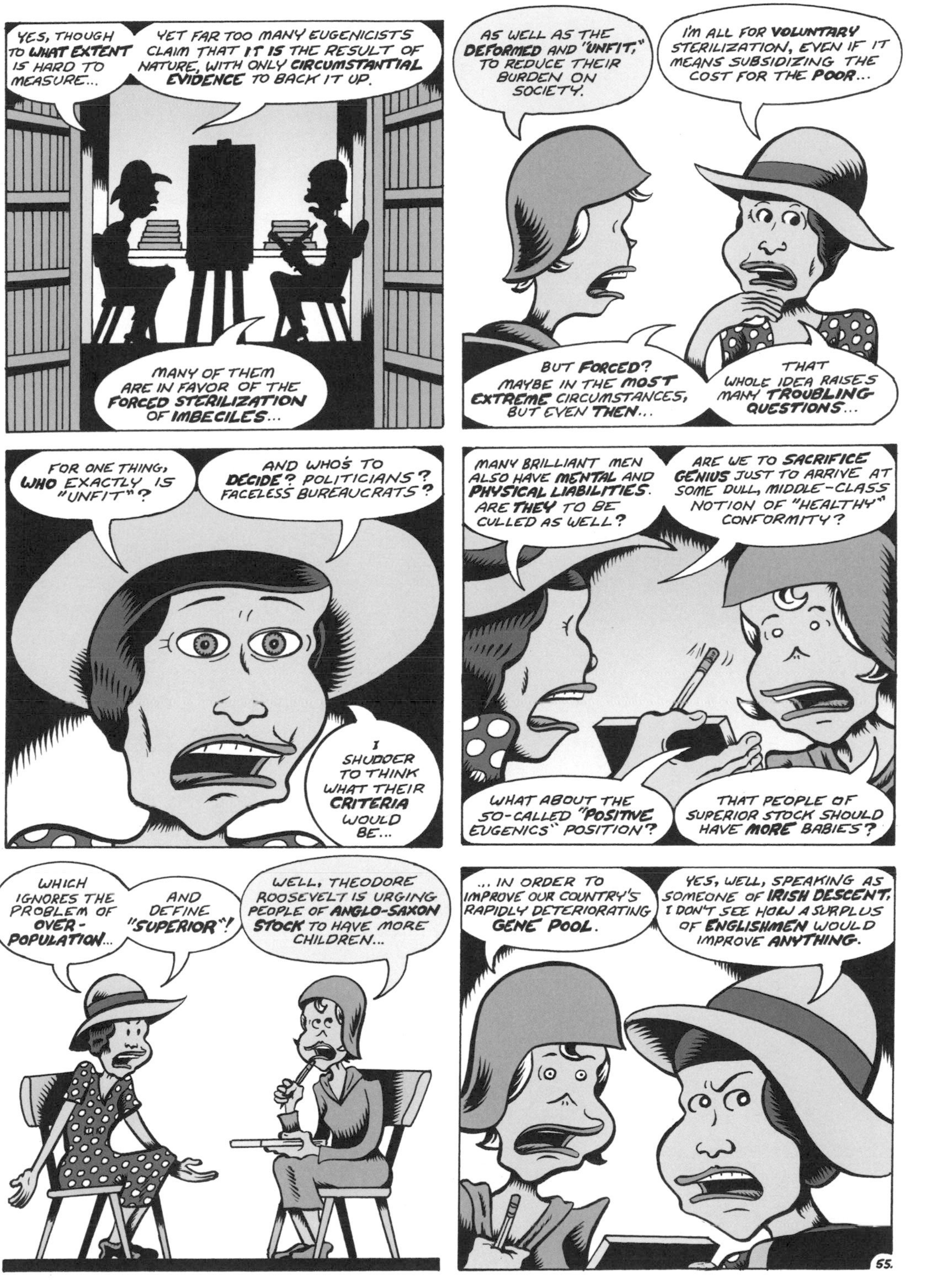
YES, THOUGH TO WHAT EXTENT IS HARD TO MEASURE...
YET FAR TOO MANY EUGENICISTS CLAIM THAT IT IS THE RESULT OF NATURE, WITH ONLY CIRCUMSTANTIAL EVIDENCE TO BACK IT UP.
MANY OF THEM ARE IN FAVOR OF THE FORCED STERILIZATION OF IMBECILES...
AS WELL AS THE DEFORMED AND "UNFIT," TO REDUCE THEIR BURDEN ON SOCIETY.
I'M ALL FOR VOLUNTARY STERILIZATION, EVEN IF IT MEANS SUBSIDIZING THE COST FOR THE POOR...
BUT FORCED? MAYBE IN THE MOST EXTREME CIRCUMSTANCES, BUT EVEN THEN...
THAT WHOLE IDEA RAISES MANY TROUBLING QUESTIONS...
FOR ONE THING, WHO EXACTLY IS "UNFIT"?
AND WHO'S TO DECIDE? POLITICIANS? FACELESS BUREAUCRATS?
I SHUDDER TO THINK WHAT THEIR CRITERIA WOULD BE...
MANY BRILLIANT MEN ALSO HAVE MENTAL AND PHYSICAL LIABILITIES. ARE THEY TO BE CULLED AS WELL?
ARE WE TO SACRIFICE GENIUS JUST TO ARRIVE AT SOME DULL, MIDDLE-CLASS NOTION OF "HEALTHY" CONFORMITY?
WHAT ABOUT THE SO-CALLED "POSITIVE EUGENICS" POSITION?
THAT PEOPLE OF SUPERIOR STOCK SHOULD HAVE MORE BABIES?
WHICH IGNORES THE PROBLEM OF OVER-POPULATION...
AND DEFINE "SUPERIOR"!
WELL, THEODORE ROOSEVELT IS URGING PEOPLE OF ANGLO-SAXON STOCK TO HAVE MORE CHILDREN...
... IN ORDER TO IMPROVE OUR COUNTRY'S RAPIDLY DETERIORATING GENE POOL.
YES, WELL, SPEAKING AS SOMEONE OF IRISH DESCENT, I DON'T SEE HOW A SURPLUS OF ENGLISHMEN WOULD IMPROVE ANYTHING.

1926...

KU KLUX KLAN
WOMEN'S AUXILIARY
SILVER LAKE, NEW JERSEY

GOOD EVENING, LADIES, AND THANK YOU FOR INVITING ME TO SPEAK TO YOU ABOUT THE VERY PERSONAL YET **VERY IMPORTANT** TOPIC OF CONTRACEPTIVES...

NOW, IN SPITE OF YOUR ORANIZATION'S CURRENT POPU-LARITY, IT REMAINS QUITE... **CONTROVERSIAL** IN SOME SOCIAL CIRCLES, INCLUDING THE ONES I MOVE IN...

SO IT SHOULD COME AS NO SURPRISE THAT I WAS UNDER CONSIDERABLE PRESSURE **NOT** TO ACCEPT YOUR GRACIOUS INVITATION...

HOWEVER, I BELIEVE THAT **ALL** WOMEN SHOULD HAVE ACCESS TO THIS INFORMATION, TO DO WITH AS THEY **CHOOSE TO**...

AND IF PROPERLY FOLLOWED, COULD **GREATLY IMPROVE** THE LIVES OF YOU AND YOUR FAMILIES.

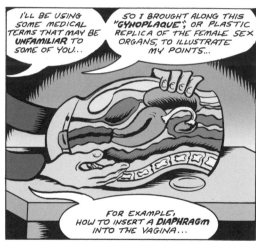

I'LL BE USING SOME MEDICAL TERMS THAT MAY BE **UNFAMILIAR** TO SOME OF YOU...

SO I BROUGHT ALONG THIS "GYNOPLAQUE", OR PLASTIC REPLICA OF THE FEMALE SEX ORGANS, TO ILLUSTRATE MY POINTS...

FOR EXAMPLE, HOW TO INSERT A **DIAPHRAGM** INTO THE VAGINA...

NOW, BEFORE I **START**, I WONDER IF—

OH! SOMEONE HAS A QUESTION **ALREADY**...

YES? WHAT IS IT?

WHAT'S A "VAGINA"?

56.

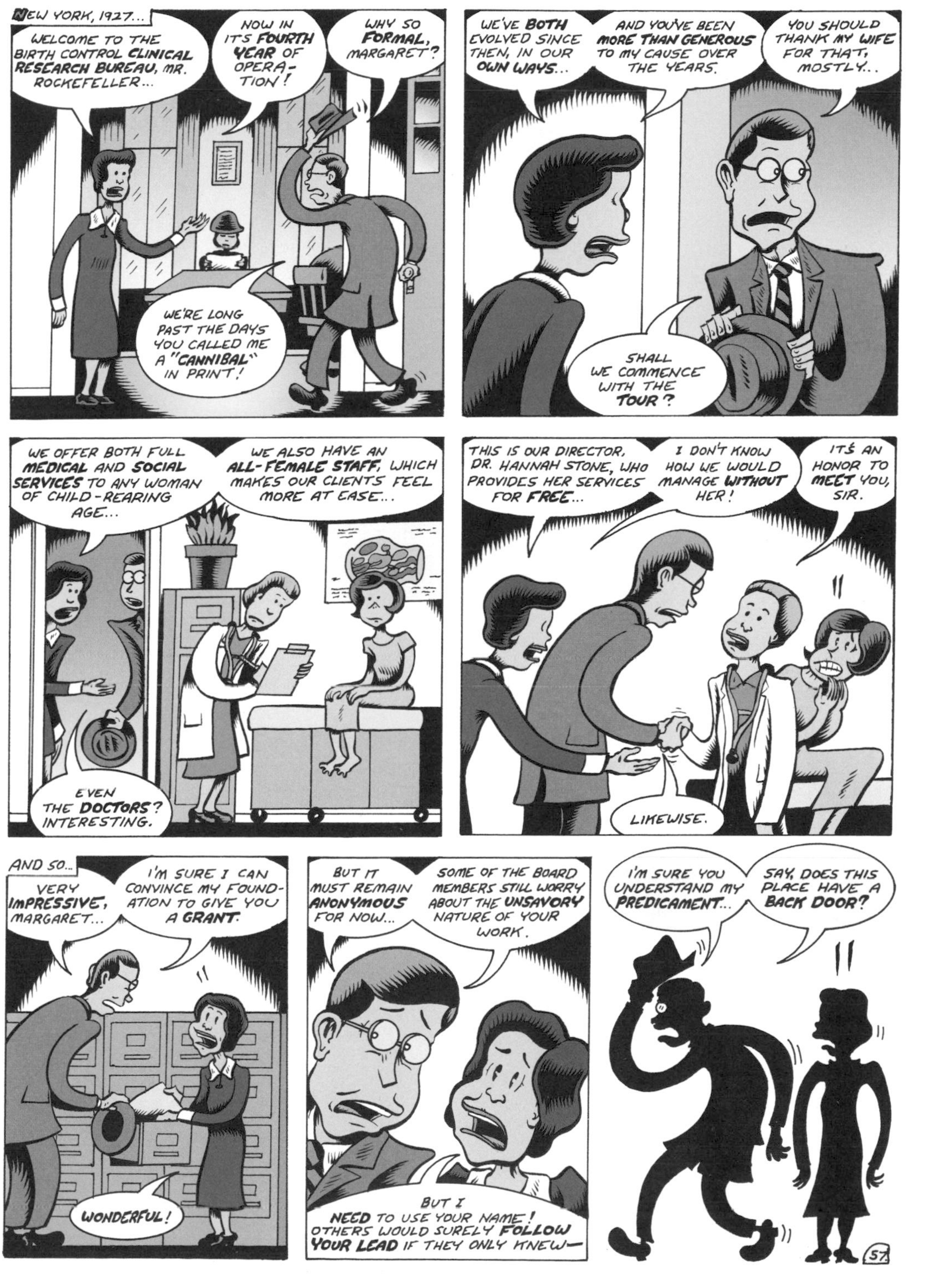
NEW YORK, 1927...
WELCOME TO THE BIRTH CONTROL CLINICAL RESEARCH BUREAU, MR. ROCKEFELLER...
NOW IN ITS FOURTH YEAR OF OPERATION!
WHY SO FORMAL, MARGARET?
WE'RE LONG PAST THE DAYS YOU CALLED ME A "CANNIBAL" IN PRINT!
WE'VE BOTH EVOLVED SINCE THEN, IN OUR OWN WAYS...
AND YOU'VE BEEN MORE THAN GENEROUS TO MY CAUSE OVER THE YEARS.
YOU SHOULD THANK MY WIFE FOR THAT, MOSTLY...
SHALL WE COMMENCE WITH THE TOUR?
WE OFFER BOTH FULL MEDICAL AND SOCIAL SERVICES TO ANY WOMAN OF CHILD-REARING AGE...
WE ALSO HAVE AN ALL-FEMALE STAFF, WHICH MAKES OUR CLIENTS FEEL MORE AT EASE...
EVEN THE DOCTORS? INTERESTING.
THIS IS OUR DIRECTOR, DR. HANNAH STONE, WHO PROVIDES HER SERVICES FOR FREE...
I DON'T KNOW HOW WE WOULD MANAGE WITHOUT HER!
IT'S AN HONOR TO MEET YOU, SIR.
LIKEWISE.
AND SO...
VERY IMPRESSIVE, MARGARET...
I'M SURE I CAN CONVINCE MY FOUNDATION TO GIVE YOU A GRANT.
WONDERFUL!
BUT IT MUST REMAIN ANONYMOUS FOR NOW...
SOME OF THE BOARD MEMBERS STILL WORRY ABOUT THE UNSAVORY NATURE OF YOUR WORK.
BUT I NEED TO USE YOUR NAME! OTHERS WOULD SURELY FOLLOW YOUR LEAD IF THEY ONLY KNEW—
I'M SURE YOU UNDERSTAND MY PREDICAMENT...
SAY, DOES THIS PLACE HAVE A BACK DOOR?

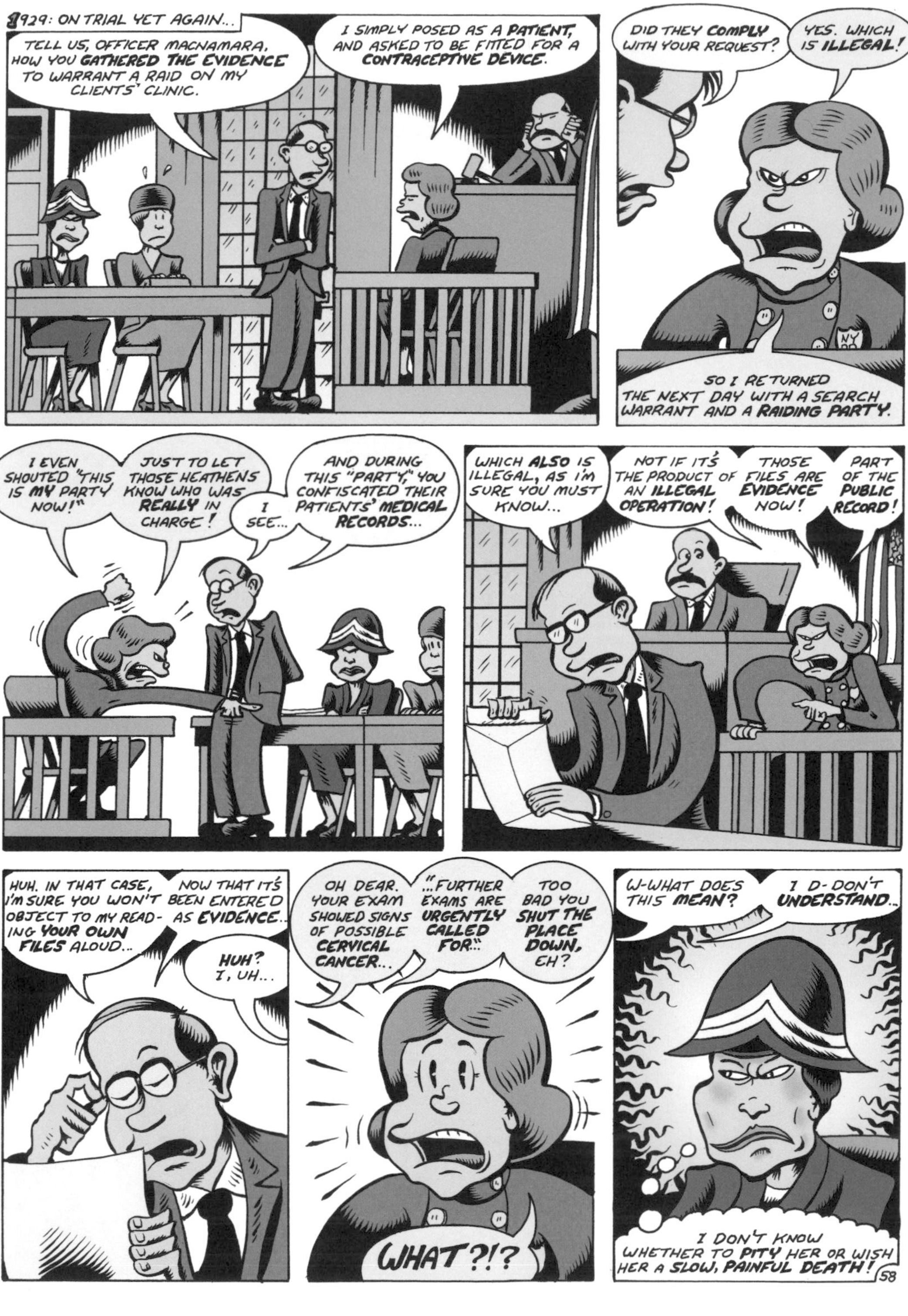
1929: ON TRIAL YET AGAIN...
TELL US, OFFICER MACNAMARA, HOW YOU GATHERED THE EVIDENCE TO WARRANT A RAID ON MY CLIENTS' CLINIC.
I SIMPLY POSED AS A PATIENT, AND ASKED TO BE FITTED FOR A CONTRACEPTIVE DEVICE.
DID THEY COMPLY WITH YOUR REQUEST?
YES. WHICH IS ILLEGAL!
SO I RETURNED THE NEXT DAY WITH A SEARCH WARRANT AND A RAIDING PARTY.
I EVEN SHOUTED "THIS IS MY PARTY NOW!"
JUST TO LET THOSE HEATHENS KNOW WHO WAS REALLY IN CHARGE!
I SEE...
AND DURING THIS "PARTY," YOU CONFISCATED THEIR PATIENTS' MEDICAL RECORDS...
WHICH ALSO IS ILLEGAL, AS I'M SURE YOU MUST KNOW...
NOT IF IT'S THE PRODUCT OF AN ILLEGAL OPERATION!
THOSE FILES ARE EVIDENCE NOW!
PART OF THE PUBLIC RECORD!
HUH. IN THAT CASE, I'M SURE YOU WON'T OBJECT TO MY READING YOUR OWN FILES ALOUD...
NOW THAT IT'S BEEN ENTERED AS EVIDENCE...
HUH? I, UH...
OH DEAR. YOUR EXAM SHOWED SIGNS OF POSSIBLE CERVICAL CANCER...
"...FURTHER EXAMS ARE URGENTLY CALLED FOR."
TOO BAD YOU SHUT THE PLACE DOWN, EH?
WHAT?!?
W-WHAT DOES THIS MEAN?
I D-DON'T UNDERSTAND...
I DON'T KNOW WHETHER TO PITY HER OR WISH HER A SLOW, PAINFUL DEATH!

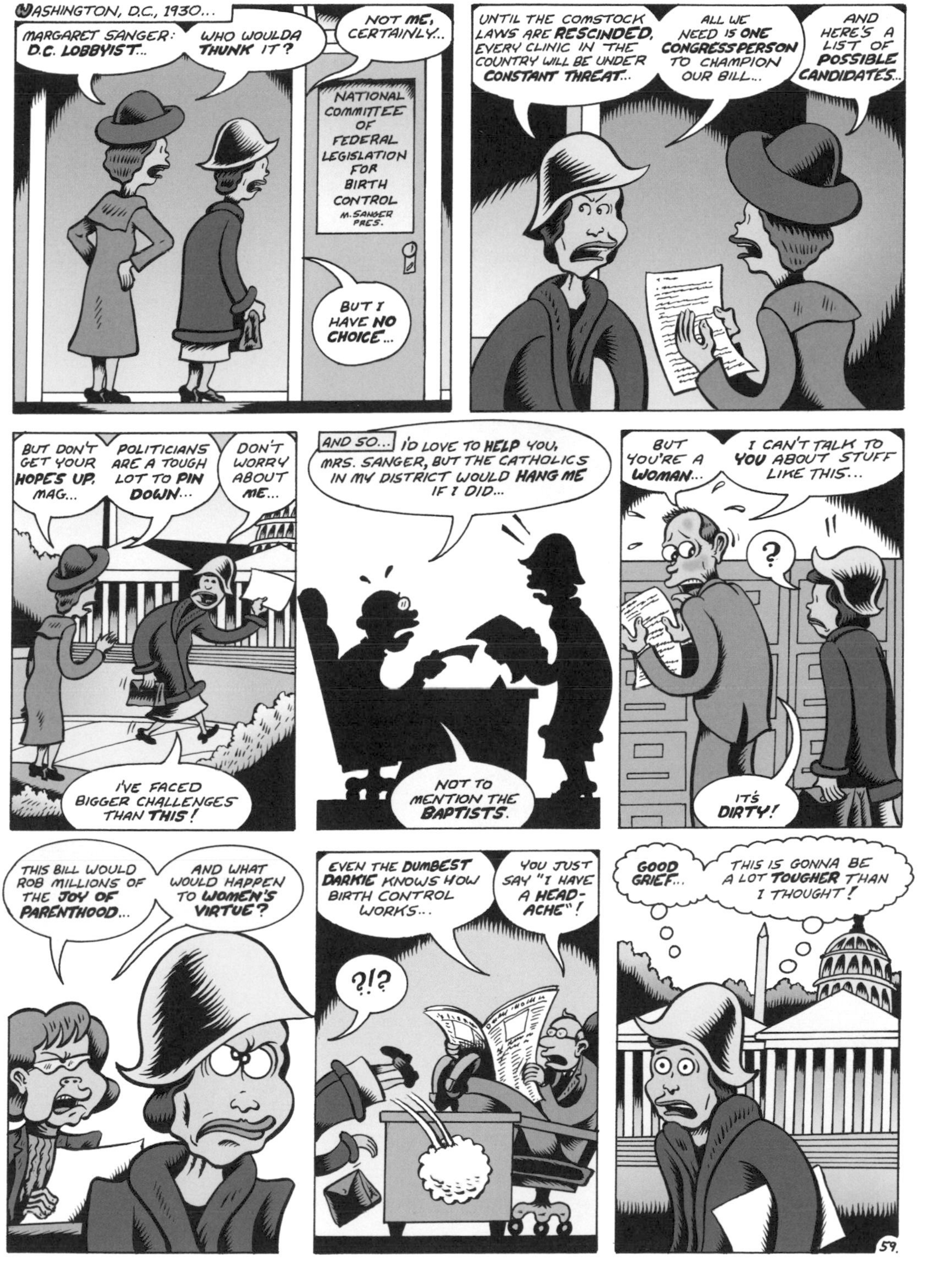
WASHINGTON, D.C., 1930...
MARGARET SANGER: D.C. LOBBYIST...
WHO WOULDA THUNK IT?
NOT ME, CERTAINLY...
NATIONAL COMMITTEE OF FEDERAL LEGISLATION FOR BIRTH CONTROL M. SANGER PRES.
BUT I HAVE NO CHOICE...
UNTIL THE COMSTOCK LAWS ARE RESCINDED, EVERY CLINIC IN THE COUNTRY WILL BE UNDER CONSTANT THREAT...
ALL WE NEED IS ONE CONGRESSPERSON TO CHAMPION OUR BILL...
AND HERE'S A LIST OF POSSIBLE CANDIDATES...
BUT DON'T GET YOUR HOPE'S UP, MAG...
POLITICIANS ARE A TOUGH LOT TO PIN DOWN...
DON'T WORRY ABOUT ME...
I'VE FACED BIGGER CHALLENGES THAN THIS!
AND SO...
I'D LOVE TO HELP YOU, MRS. SANGER, BUT THE CATHOLICS IN MY DISTRICT WOULD HANG ME IF I DID...
NOT TO MENTION THE BAPTISTS.
BUT YOU'RE A WOMAN...
I CAN'T TALK TO YOU ABOUT STUFF LIKE THIS...
?
IT'S DIRTY!
THIS BILL WOULD ROB MILLIONS OF THE JOY OF PARENTHOOD...
AND WHAT WOULD HAPPEN TO WOMEN'S VIRTUE?
EVEN THE DUMBEST DARKIE KNOWS HOW BIRTH CONTROL WORKS...
YOU JUST SAY "I HAVE A HEAD-ACHE"!
?!?
GOOD GRIEF...
THIS IS GONNA BE A LOT TOUGHER THAN I THOUGHT!

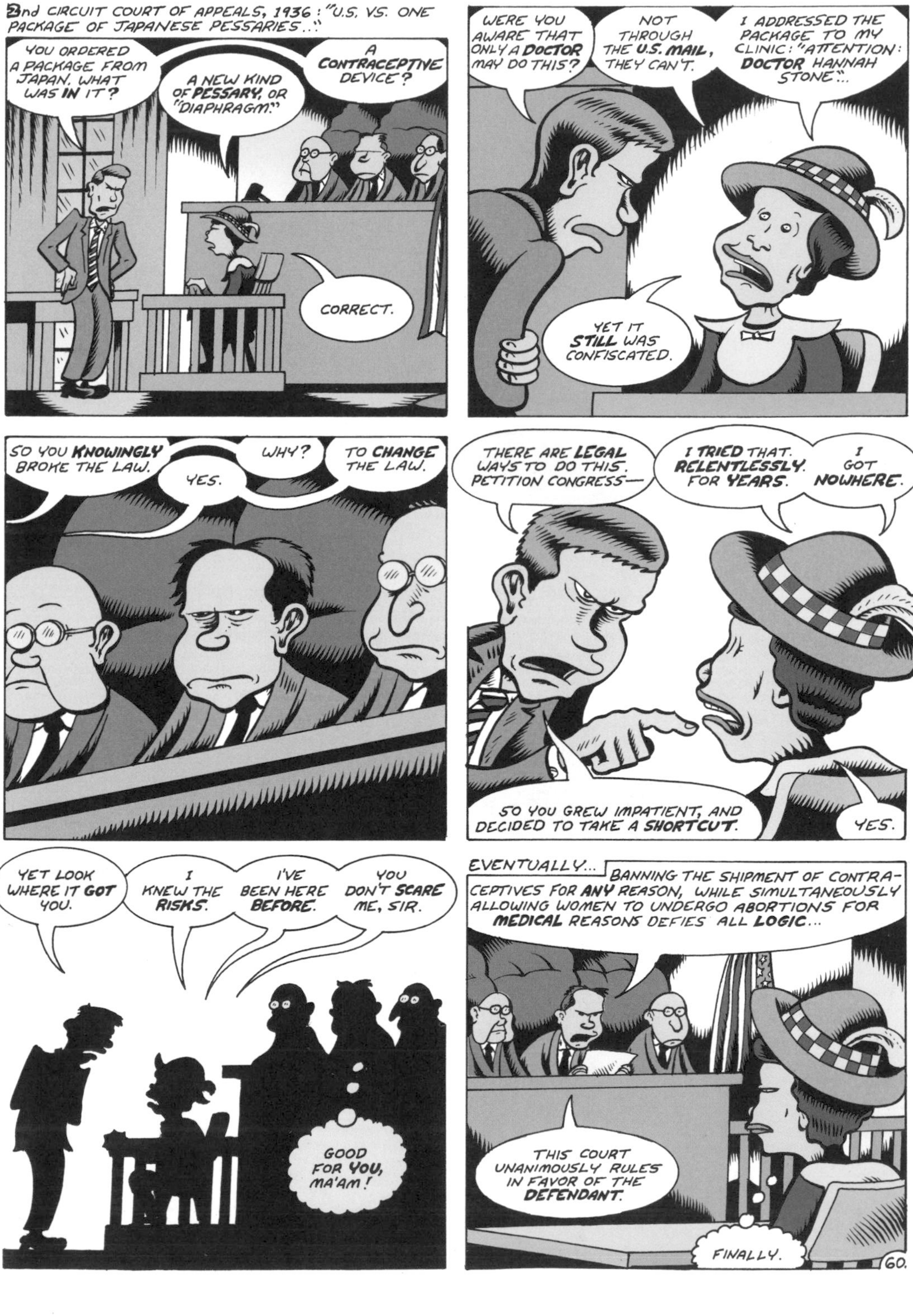
2nd CIRCUIT COURT OF APPEALS, 1936: "U.S. VS. ONE PACKAGE OF JAPANESE PESSARIES..."
YOU ORDERED A PACKAGE FROM JAPAN. WHAT WAS IN IT?
A NEW KIND OF PESSARY, OR "DIAPHRAGM."
A CONTRACEPTIVE DEVICE?
CORRECT.
WERE YOU AWARE THAT ONLY A DOCTOR MAY DO THIS?
NOT THROUGH THE U.S. MAIL, THEY CAN'T.
I ADDRESSED THE PACKAGE TO MY CLINIC: "ATTENTION: DOCTOR HANNAH STONE"...
YET IT STILL WAS CONFISCATED.
SO YOU KNOWINGLY BROKE THE LAW.
YES.
WHY?
TO CHANGE THE LAW.
THERE ARE LEGAL WAYS TO DO THIS. PETITION CONGRESS—
I TRIED THAT. RELENTLESSLY. FOR YEARS.
I GOT NOWHERE.
SO YOU GREW IMPATIENT, AND DECIDED TO TAKE A SHORTCUT.
YES.
YET LOOK WHERE IT GOT YOU.
I KNEW THE RISKS.
I'VE BEEN HERE BEFORE.
YOU DON'T SCARE ME, SIR.
GOOD FOR YOU, MA'AM!
EVENTUALLY...
BANNING THE SHIPMENT OF CONTRACEPTIVES FOR ANY REASON, WHILE SIMULTANEOUSLY ALLOWING WOMEN TO UNDERGO ABORTIONS FOR MEDICAL REASONS DEFIES ALL LOGIC...
THIS COURT UNANIMOUSLY RULES IN FAVOR OF THE DEFENDANT.
FINALLY.

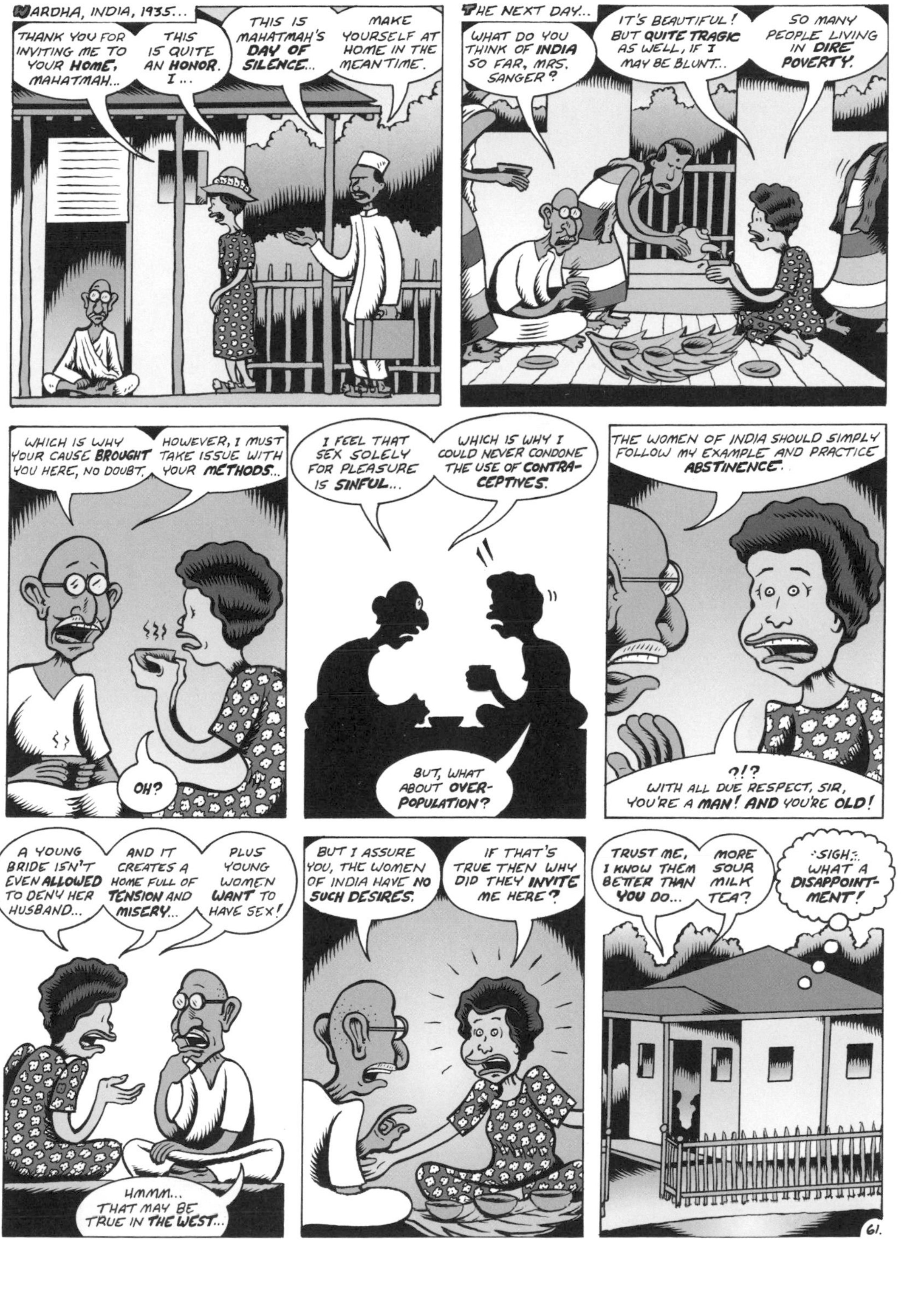
WARDHA, INDIA, 1935...
THANK YOU FOR INVITING ME TO YOUR HOME, MAHATMAH...
THIS IS QUITE AN HONOR. I...
THIS IS MAHATMAH'S DAY OF SILENCE...
MAKE YOURSELF AT HOME IN THE MEANTIME.
THE NEXT DAY...
WHAT DO YOU THINK OF INDIA SO FAR, MRS. SANGER?
IT'S BEAUTIFUL! BUT QUITE TRAGIC AS WELL, IF I MAY BE BLUNT...
SO MANY PEOPLE LIVING IN DIRE POVERTY.
WHICH IS WHY YOUR CAUSE BROUGHT YOU HERE, NO DOUBT.
HOWEVER, I MUST TAKE ISSUE WITH YOUR METHODS...
OH?
I FEEL THAT SEX SOLELY FOR PLEASURE IS SINFUL...
WHICH IS WHY I COULD NEVER CONDONE THE USE OF CONTRA-CEPTIVES.
BUT, WHAT ABOUT OVER-POPULATION?
THE WOMEN OF INDIA SHOULD SIMPLY FOLLOW MY EXAMPLE AND PRACTICE ABSTINENCE.
?!? WITH ALL DUE RESPECT, SIR, YOU'RE A MAN! AND YOU'RE OLD!
A YOUNG BRIDE ISN'T EVEN ALLOWED TO DENY HER HUSBAND...
AND IT CREATES A HOME FULL OF TENSION AND MISERY...
PLUS YOUNG WOMEN WANT TO HAVE SEX!
HMMM... THAT MAY BE TRUE IN THE WEST...
BUT I ASSURE YOU, THE WOMEN OF INDIA HAVE NO SUCH DESIRES.
IF THAT'S TRUE THEN WHY DID THEY INVITE ME HERE?
TRUST ME, I KNOW THEM BETTER THAN YOU DO...
MORE SOUR MILK TEA?
SIGH... WHAT A DISAPPOINT-MENT!

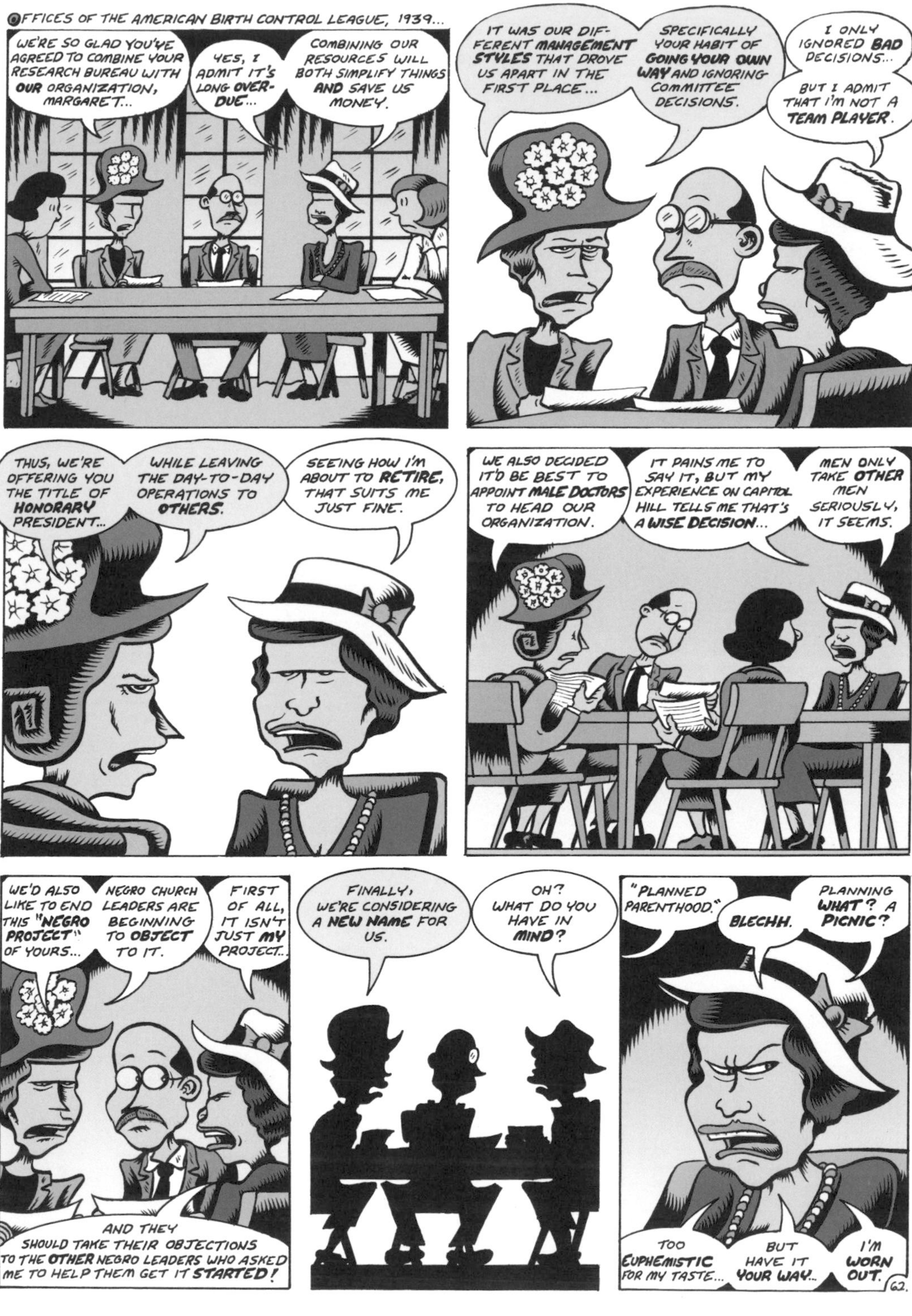
OFFICES OF THE AMERICAN BIRTH CONTROL LEAGUE, 1939...
WE'RE SO GLAD YOU'VE AGREED TO COMBINE YOUR RESEARCH BUREAU WITH OUR ORGANIZATION, MARGARET...
YES, I ADMIT IT'S LONG OVER-DUE...
COMBINING OUR RESOURCES WILL BOTH SIMPLIFY THINGS AND SAVE US MONEY.
IT WAS OUR DIF-FERENT MANAGEMENT STYLES THAT DROVE US APART IN THE FIRST PLACE...
SPECIFICALLY YOUR HABIT OF GOING YOUR OWN WAY AND IGNORING COMMITTEE DECISIONS.
I ONLY IGNORED BAD DECISIONS...
BUT I ADMIT THAT I'M NOT A TEAM PLAYER.
THUS, WE'RE OFFERING YOU THE TITLE OF HONORARY PRESIDENT...
WHILE LEAVING THE DAY-TO-DAY OPERATIONS TO OTHERS.
SEEING HOW I'M ABOUT TO RETIRE, THAT SUITS ME JUST FINE.
WE ALSO DECIDED IT'D BE BEST TO APPOINT MALE DOCTORS TO HEAD OUR ORGANIZATION.
IT PAINS ME TO SAY IT, BUT MY EXPERIENCE ON CAPITOL HILL TELLS ME THAT'S A WISE DECISION...
MEN ONLY TAKE OTHER MEN SERIOUSLY, IT SEEMS.
WE'D ALSO LIKE TO END THIS "NEGRO PROJECT" OF YOURS...
NEGRO CHURCH LEADERS ARE BEGINNING TO OBJECT TO IT.
FIRST OF ALL, IT ISN'T JUST MY PROJECT...
AND THEY SHOULD TAKE THEIR OBJECTIONS TO THE OTHER NEGRO LEADERS WHO ASKED ME TO HELP THEM GET IT STARTED!
FINALLY, WE'RE CONSIDERING A NEW NAME FOR US.
OH? WHAT DO YOU HAVE IN MIND?
"PLANNED PARENTHOOD."
BLECHH.
PLANNING WHAT? A PICNIC?
TOO EUPHEMISTIC FOR MY TASTE...
BUT HAVE IT YOUR WAY...
I'M WORN OUT.

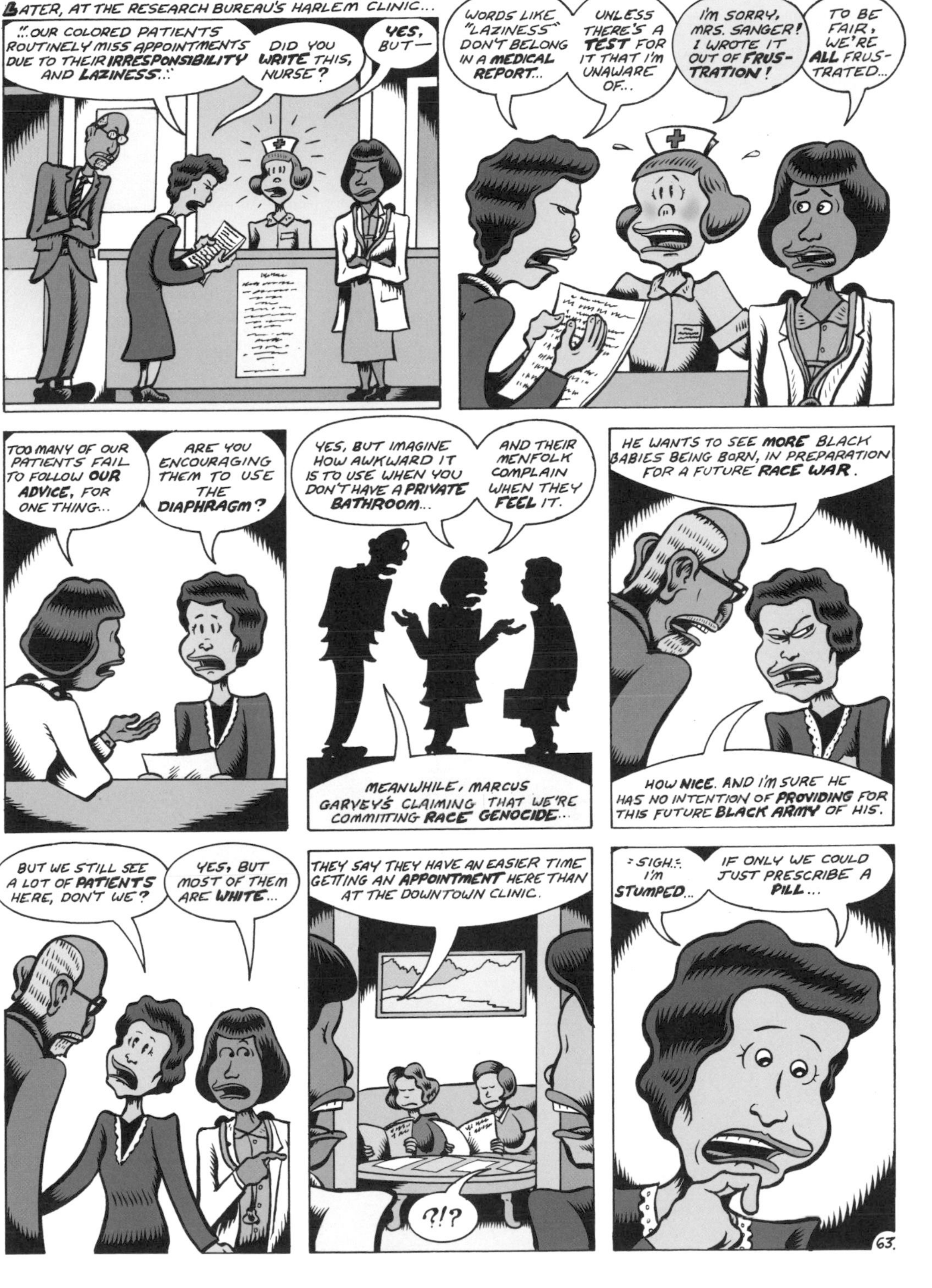

LATER, AT THE RESEARCH BUREAU'S HARLEM CLINIC...
...OUR COLORED PATIENTS ROUTINELY MISS APPOINTMENTS DUE TO THEIR IRRESPONSIBILITY AND LAZINESS...
DID YOU WRITE THIS, NURSE?
YES, BUT—
WORDS LIKE "LAZINESS" DON'T BELONG IN A MEDICAL REPORT...
UNLESS THERE'S A TEST FOR IT THAT I'M UNAWARE OF...
I'M SORRY, MRS. SANGER! I WROTE IT OUT OF FRUSTRATION!
TO BE FAIR, WE'RE ALL FRUSTRATED...
TOO MANY OF OUR PATIENTS FAIL TO FOLLOW OUR ADVICE, FOR ONE THING...
ARE YOU ENCOURAGING THEM TO USE THE DIAPHRAGM?
YES, BUT IMAGINE HOW AWKWARD IT IS TO USE WHEN YOU DON'T HAVE A PRIVATE BATHROOM...
AND THEIR MENFOLK COMPLAIN WHEN THEY FEEL IT.
MEANWHILE, MARCUS GARVEY'S CLAIMING THAT WE'RE COMMITTING RACE GENOCIDE...
HE WANTS TO SEE MORE BLACK BABIES BEING BORN, IN PREPARATION FOR A FUTURE RACE WAR.
HOW NICE. AND I'M SURE HE HAS NO INTENTION OF PROVIDING FOR THIS FUTURE BLACK ARMY OF HIS.
BUT WE STILL SEE A LOT OF PATIENTS HERE, DON'T WE?
YES, BUT MOST OF THEM ARE WHITE...
THEY SAY THEY HAVE AN EASIER TIME GETTING AN APPOINTMENT HERE THAN AT THE DOWNTOWN CLINIC.
?!?
:SIGH: I'M STUMPED...
IF ONLY WE COULD JUST PRESCRIBE A PILL...

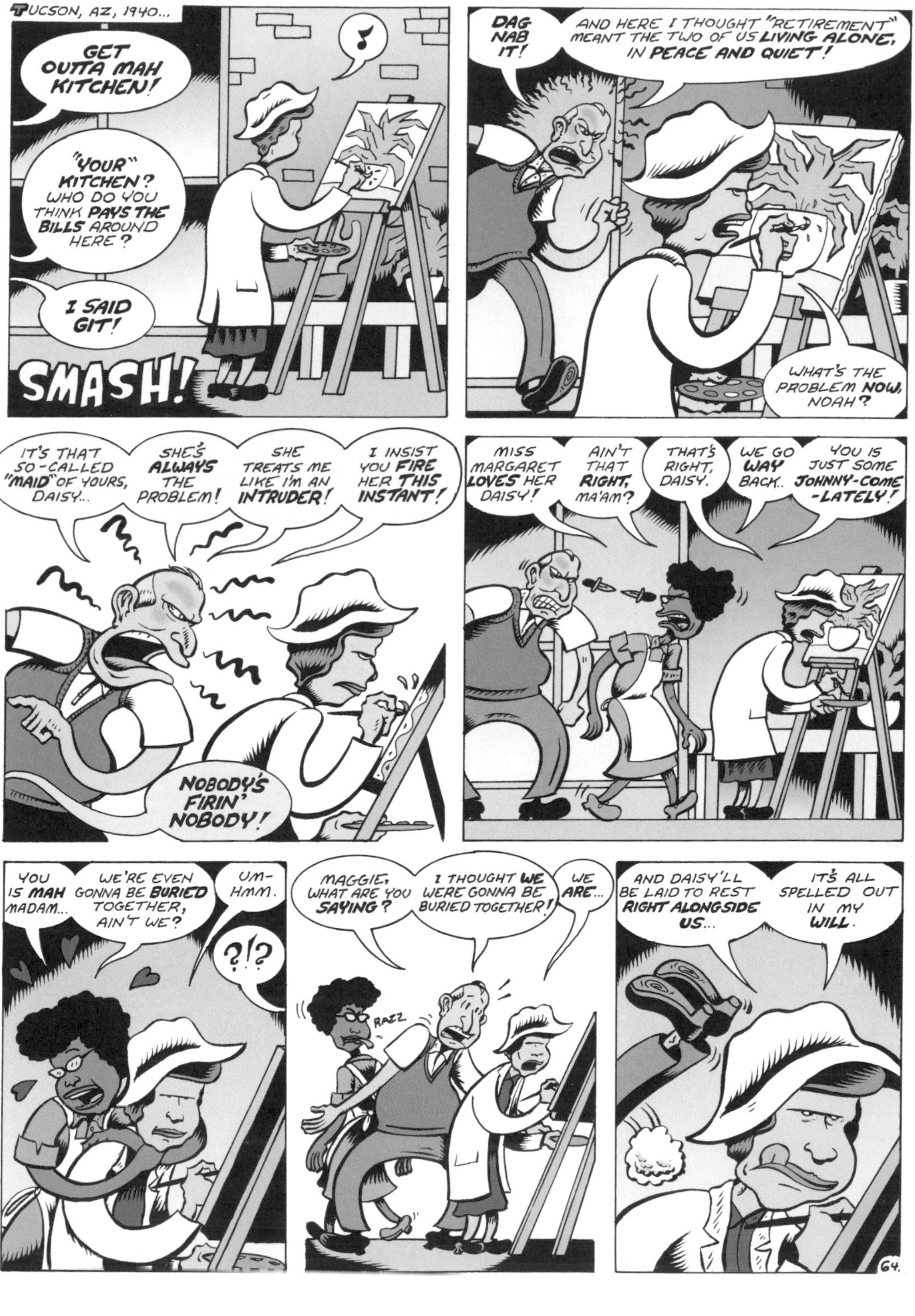
TUCSON, AZ, 1940...
GET OUTTA MAH KITCHEN!
"YOUR" KITCHEN? WHO DO YOU THINK PAYS THE BILLS AROUND HERE?
I SAID GIT!
SMASH!
DAG NAB IT!
AND HERE I THOUGHT "RETIREMENT" MEANT THE TWO OF US LIVING ALONE, IN PEACE AND QUIET!
WHAT'S THE PROBLEM NOW, NOAH?
IT'S THAT SO-CALLED "MAID" OF YOURS, DAISY...
SHE'S ALWAYS THE PROBLEM!
SHE TREATS ME LIKE I'M AN INTRUDER!
I INSIST YOU FIRE HER THIS INSTANT!
NOBODY'S FIRIN' NOBODY!
MISS MARGARET LOVES HER DAISY!
AIN'T THAT RIGHT, MA'AM?
THAT'S RIGHT, DAISY.
WE GO WAY BACK..
YOU IS JUST SOME JOHNNY-COME-LATELY!
YOU IS MAH MADAM...
WE'RE EVEN GONNA BE BURIED TOGETHER, AIN'T WE?
UM-HMM.
?!?
MAGGIE, WHAT ARE YOU SAYING?
I THOUGHT WE WERE GONNA BE BURIED TOGETHER!
WE ARE...
RAZZ
AND DAISY'LL BE LAID TO REST RIGHT ALONGSIDE US...
IT'S ALL SPELLED OUT IN MY WILL.

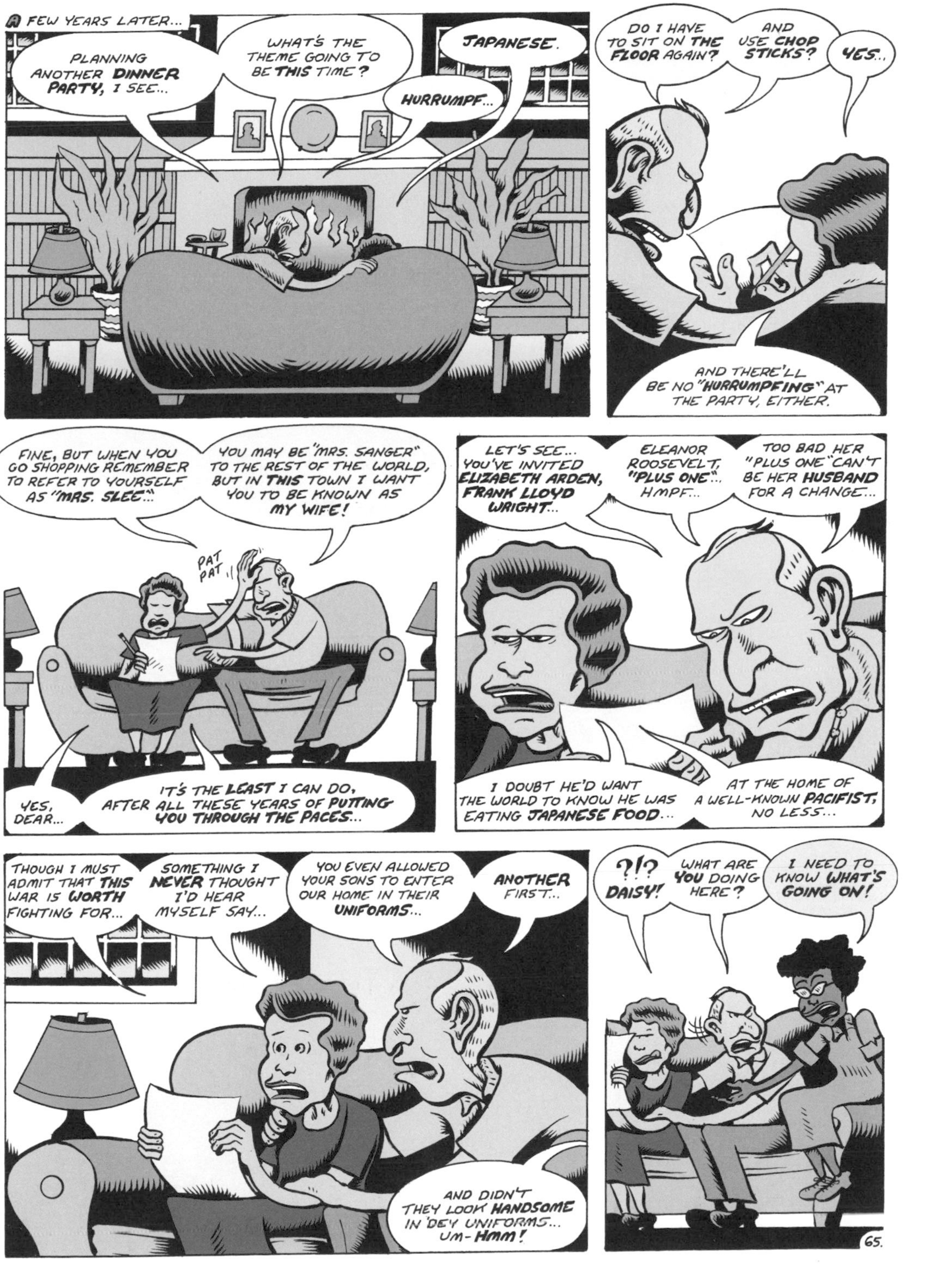
A FEW YEARS LATER...
PLANNING ANOTHER DINNER PARTY, I SEE...
WHAT'S THE THEME GOING TO BE THIS TIME?
JAPANESE.
HURRUMPF...
DO I HAVE TO SIT ON THE FLOOR AGAIN?
AND USE CHOP STICKS?
YES...
AND THERE'LL BE NO "HURRUMPFING" AT THE PARTY, EITHER.
FINE, BUT WHEN YOU GO SHOPPING REMEMBER TO REFER TO YOURSELF AS "MRS. SLEE"...
YOU MAY BE "MRS. SANGER" TO THE REST OF THE WORLD, BUT IN THIS TOWN I WANT YOU TO BE KNOWN AS MY WIFE!
PAT PAT
YES, DEAR...
IT'S THE LEAST I CAN DO, AFTER ALL THESE YEARS OF PUTTING YOU THROUGH THE PACES...
LET'S SEE... YOU'VE INVITED ELIZABETH ARDEN, FRANK LLOYD WRIGHT...
ELEANOR ROOSEVELT, "PLUS ONE"... HMPF...
TOO BAD HER "PLUS ONE" CAN'T BE HER HUSBAND FOR A CHANGE...
I DOUBT HE'D WANT THE WORLD TO KNOW HE WAS EATING JAPANESE FOOD...
AT THE HOME OF A WELL-KNOWN PACIFIST, NO LESS...
THOUGH I MUST ADMIT THAT THIS WAR IS WORTH FIGHTING FOR...
SOMETHING I NEVER THOUGHT I'D HEAR MYSELF SAY...
YOU EVEN ALLOWED YOUR SONS TO ENTER OUR HOME IN THEIR UNIFORMS...
ANOTHER FIRST...
AND DIDN'T THEY LOOK HANDSOME IN 'DEY UNIFORMS... UM-HMM!
?!? DAISY!
WHAT ARE YOU DOING HERE?
I NEED TO KNOW WHAT'S GOING ON!

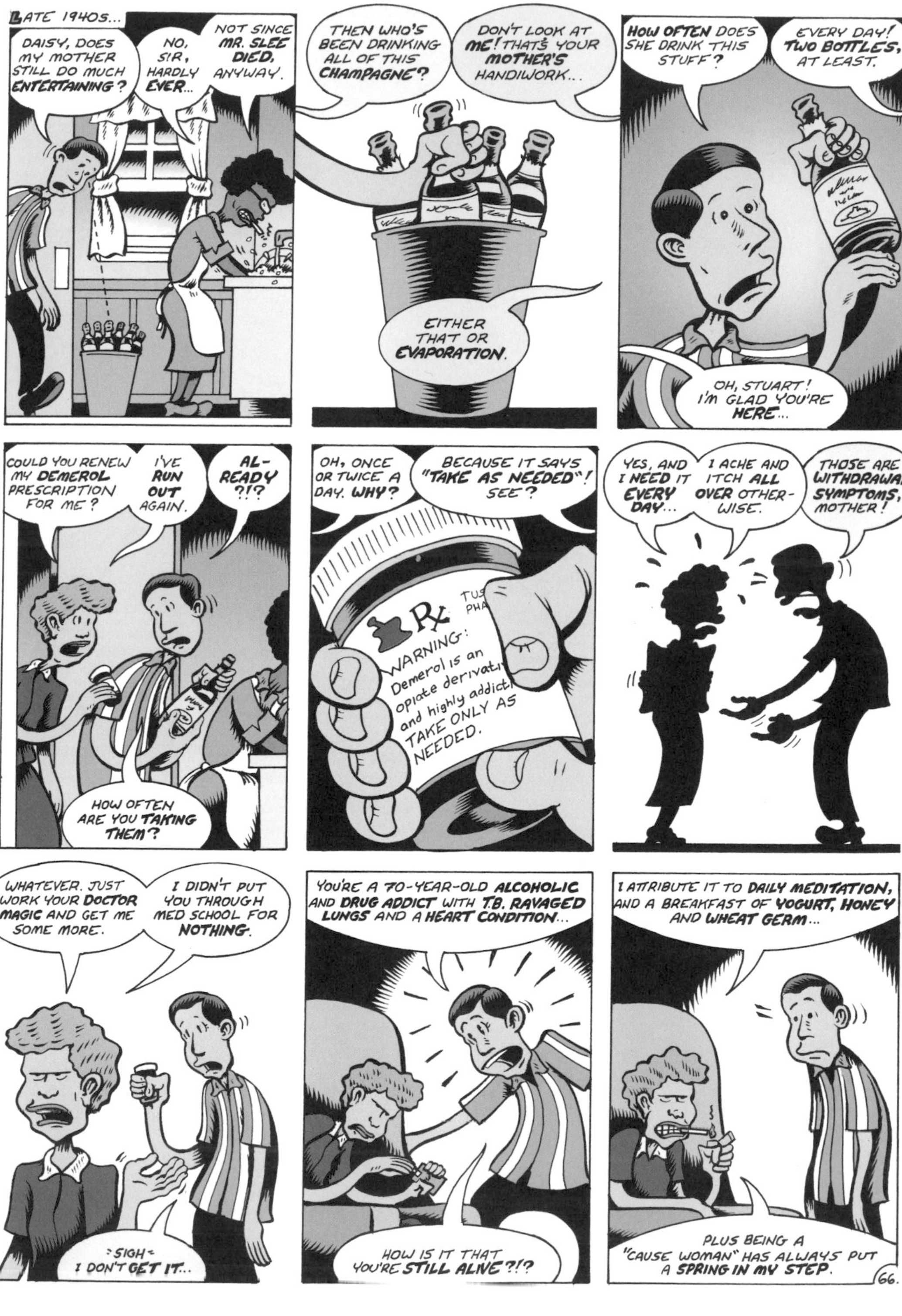
LATE 1940s...
DAISY, DOES MY MOTHER STILL DO MUCH ENTERTAINING?
NO, SIR, HARDLY EVER...
NOT SINCE MR. SLEE DIED, ANYWAY.
THEN WHO'S BEEN DRINKING ALL OF THIS CHAMPAGNE?
DON'T LOOK AT ME! THAT'S YOUR MOTHER'S HANDIWORK...
EITHER THAT OR EVAPORATION.
HOW OFTEN DOES SHE DRINK THIS STUFF?
EVERY DAY! TWO BOTTLES, AT LEAST.
OH, STUART! I'M GLAD YOU'RE HERE...
COULD YOU RENEW MY DEMEROL PRESCRIPTION FOR ME?
I'VE RUN OUT AGAIN.
AL-READY ?!?
HOW OFTEN ARE YOU TAKING THEM?
OH, ONCE OR TWICE A DAY. WHY?
BECAUSE IT SAYS "TAKE AS NEEDED"! SEE?
WARNING: Demerol is an opiate derivati and highly addicti TAKE ONLY AS NEEDED.
YES, AND I NEED IT EVERY DAY...
I ACHE AND ITCH ALL OVER OTHER-WISE.
THOSE ARE WITHDRAWAL SYMPTOMS, MOTHER!
WHATEVER. JUST WORK YOUR DOCTOR MAGIC AND GET ME SOME MORE.
I DIDN'T PUT YOU THROUGH MED SCHOOL FOR NOTHING.
=SIGH= I DON'T GET IT...
YOU'RE A 70-YEAR-OLD ALCOHOLIC AND DRUG ADDICT WITH T.B. RAVAGED LUNGS AND A HEART CONDITION...
HOW IS IT THAT YOU'RE STILL ALIVE?!?
I ATTRIBUTE IT TO DAILY MEDITATION, AND A BREAKFAST OF YOGURT, HONEY AND WHEAT GERM...
PLUS BEING A "CAUSE WOMAN" HAS ALWAYS PUT A SPRING IN MY STEP.

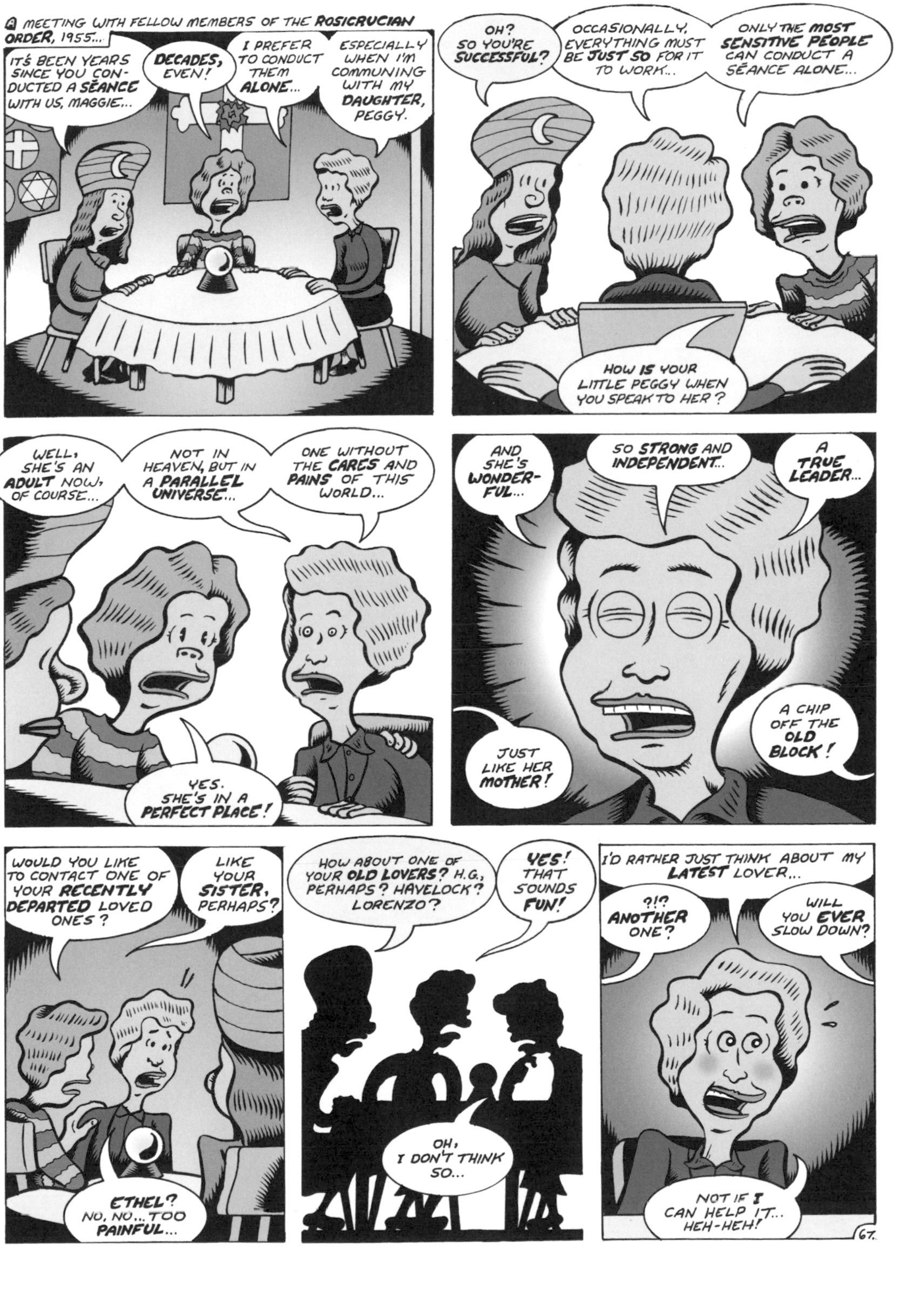

A MEETING WITH FELLOW MEMBERS OF THE ROSICRUCIAN ORDER, 1955...
IT'S BEEN YEARS SINCE YOU CONDUCTED A SÉANCE WITH US, MAGGIE...
DECADES, EVEN!
I PREFER TO CONDUCT THEM ALONE...
ESPECIALLY WHEN I'M COMMUNING WITH MY DAUGHTER, PEGGY.
OH? SO YOU'RE SUCCESSFUL?
OCCASIONALLY. EVERYTHING MUST BE JUST SO FOR IT TO WORK...
ONLY THE MOST SENSITIVE PEOPLE CAN CONDUCT A SÉANCE ALONE...
HOW IS YOUR LITTLE PEGGY WHEN YOU SPEAK TO HER?
WELL, SHE'S AN ADULT NOW, OF COURSE...
NOT IN HEAVEN, BUT IN A PARALLEL UNIVERSE...
ONE WITHOUT THE CARES AND PAINS OF THIS WORLD...
YES. SHE'S IN A PERFECT PLACE!
AND SHE'S WONDERFUL...
SO STRONG AND INDEPENDENT...
A TRUE LEADER...
JUST LIKE HER MOTHER!
A CHIP OFF THE OLD BLOCK!
WOULD YOU LIKE TO CONTACT ONE OF YOUR RECENTLY DEPARTED LOVED ONES?
LIKE YOUR SISTER, PERHAPS?
ETHEL? NO, NO... TOO PAINFUL...
HOW ABOUT ONE OF YOUR OLD LOVERS? H.G., PERHAPS? HAVELOCK? LORENZO?
YES! THAT SOUNDS FUN!
OH, I DON'T THINK SO...
I'D RATHER JUST THINK ABOUT MY LATEST LOVER...
?!? ANOTHER ONE?
WILL YOU EVER SLOW DOWN?
NOT IF I CAN HELP IT... HEH-HEH!

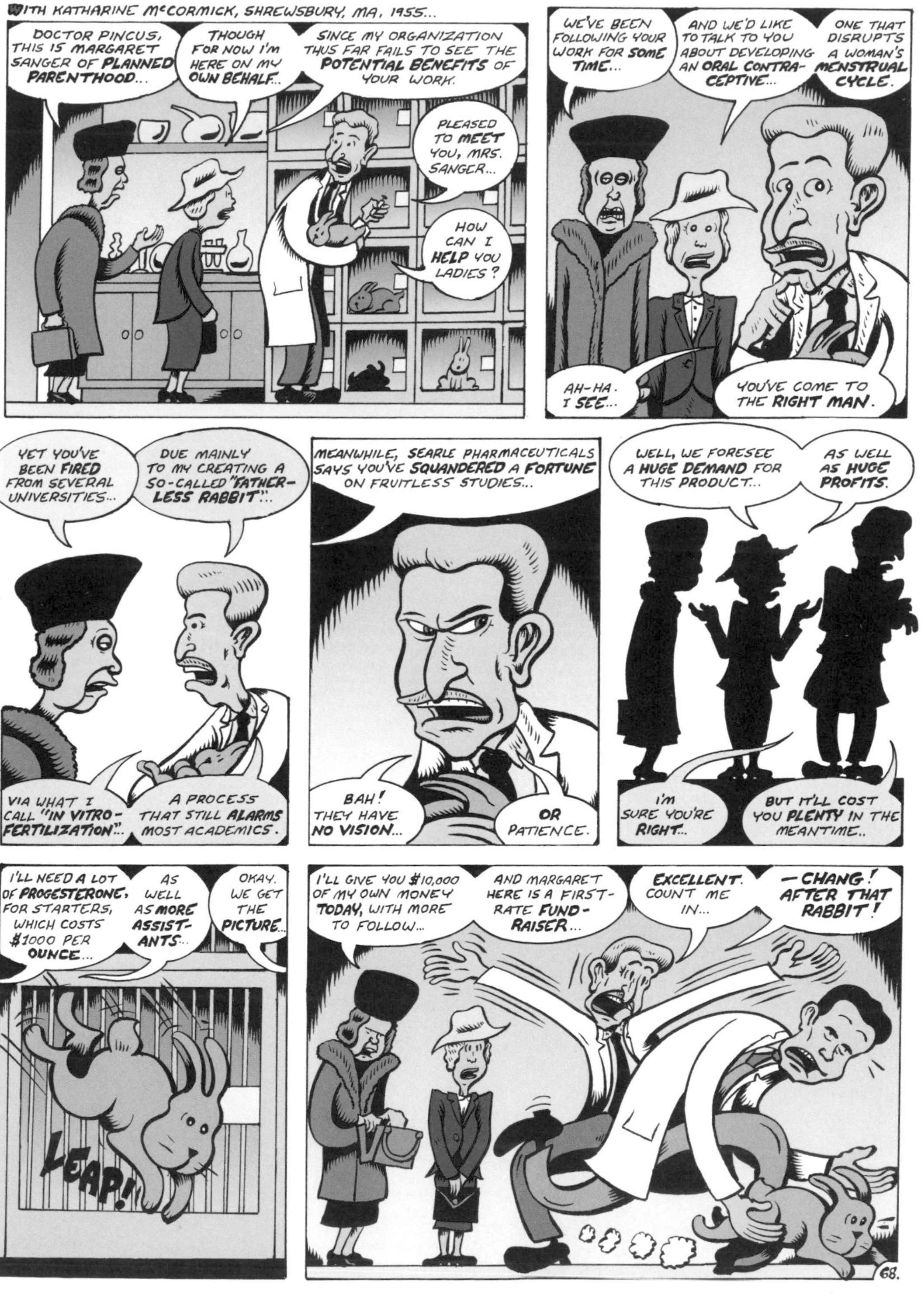
WITH KATHARINE McCORMICK, SHREWSBURY, MA, 1955...
DOCTOR PINCUS, THIS IS MARGARET SANGER OF PLANNED PARENTHOOD...
THOUGH FOR NOW I'M HERE ON MY OWN BEHALF...
SINCE MY ORGANIZATION THUS FAR FAILS TO SEE THE POTENTIAL BENEFITS OF YOUR WORK.
PLEASED TO MEET YOU, MRS. SANGER...
HOW CAN I HELP YOU LADIES?
WE'VE BEEN FOLLOWING YOUR WORK FOR SOME TIME...
AND WE'D LIKE TO TALK TO YOU ABOUT DEVELOPING AN ORAL CONTRA-CEPTIVE...
ONE THAT DISRUPTS A WOMAN'S MENSTRUAL CYCLE.
AH-HA. I SEE...
YOU'VE COME TO THE RIGHT MAN.
YET YOU'VE BEEN FIRED FROM SEVERAL UNIVERSITIES...
DUE MAINLY TO MY CREATING A SO-CALLED "FATHER-LESS RABBIT"...
VIA WHAT I CALL "IN VITRO-FERTILIZATION"...
A PROCESS THAT STILL ALARMS MOST ACADEMICS.
MEANWHILE, SEARLE PHARMACEUTICALS SAYS YOU'VE SQUANDERED A FORTUNE ON FRUITLESS STUDIES...
BAH! THEY HAVE NO VISION...
OR PATIENCE.
WELL, WE FORESEE A HUGE DEMAND FOR THIS PRODUCT...
AS WELL AS HUGE PROFITS.
I'M SURE YOU'RE RIGHT...
BUT IT'LL COST YOU PLENTY IN THE MEANTIME...
I'LL NEED A LOT OF PROGESTERONE, FOR STARTERS, WHICH COSTS $1000 PER OUNCE...
AS WELL AS MORE ASSIST-ANTS...
OKAY. WE GET THE PICTURE...
LEAP!
I'LL GIVE YOU $10,000 OF MY OWN MONEY TODAY, WITH MORE TO FOLLOW...
AND MARGARET HERE IS A FIRST-RATE FUND-RAISER...
EXCELLENT. COUNT ME IN...
—CHANG! AFTER THAT RABBIT!

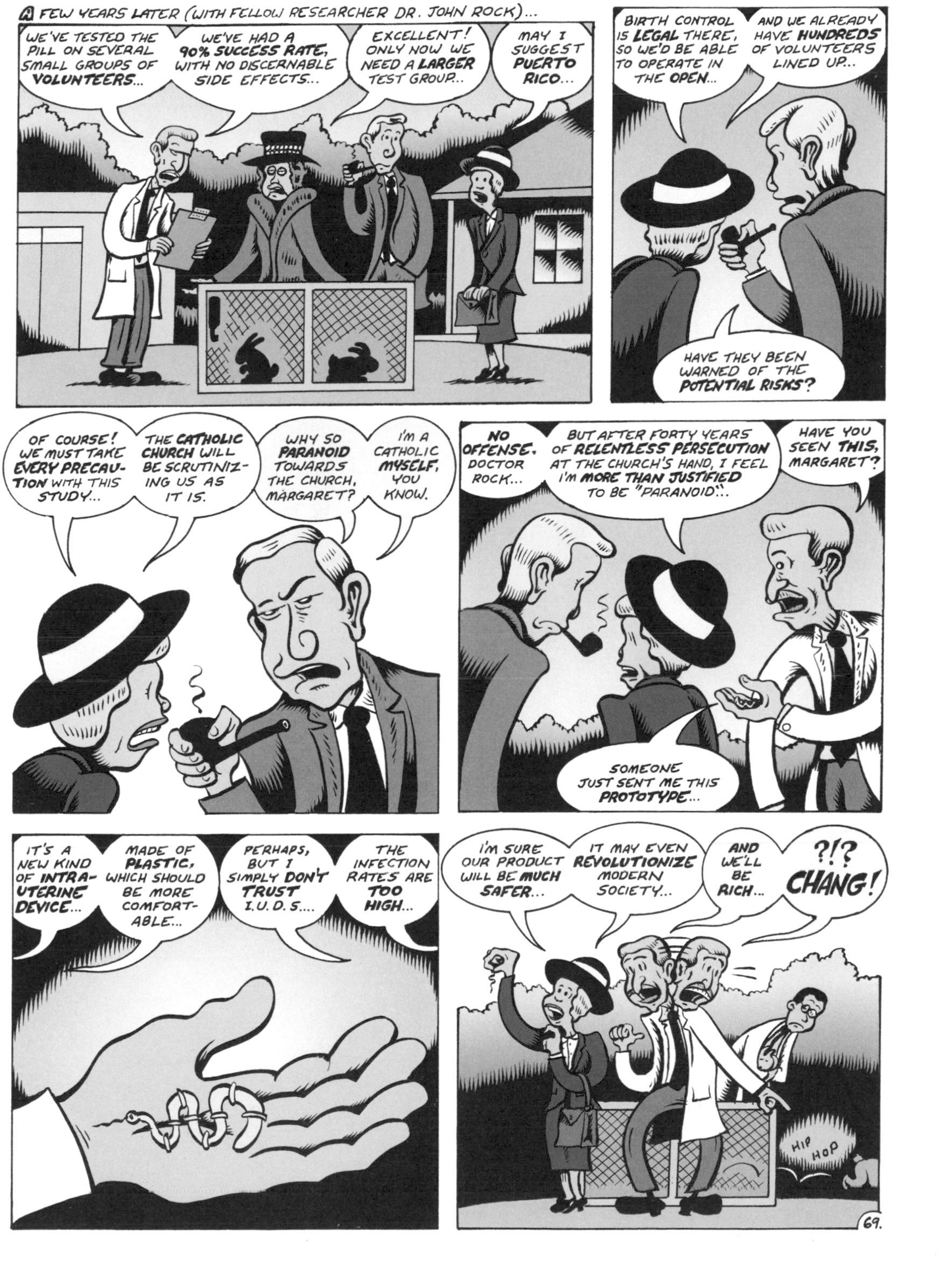
A FEW YEARS LATER (WITH FELLOW RESEARCHER DR. JOHN ROCK)...
WE'VE TESTED THE PILL ON SEVERAL SMALL GROUPS OF VOLUNTEERS...
WE'VE HAD A 90% SUCCESS RATE, WITH NO DISCERNABLE SIDE EFFECTS...
EXCELLENT! ONLY NOW WE NEED A LARGER TEST GROUP...
MAY I SUGGEST PUERTO RICO...
BIRTH CONTROL IS LEGAL THERE, SO WE'D BE ABLE TO OPERATE IN THE OPEN...
AND WE ALREADY HAVE HUNDREDS OF VOLUNTEERS LINED UP...
HAVE THEY BEEN WARNED OF THE POTENTIAL RISKS?
OF COURSE! WE MUST TAKE EVERY PRECAUTION WITH THIS STUDY...
THE CATHOLIC CHURCH WILL BE SCRUTINIZING US AS IT IS.
WHY SO PARANOID TOWARDS THE CHURCH, MARGARET?
I'M A CATHOLIC MYSELF, YOU KNOW.
NO OFFENSE, DOCTOR ROCK...
BUT AFTER FORTY YEARS OF RELENTLESS PERSECUTION AT THE CHURCH'S HAND, I FEEL I'M MORE THAN JUSTIFIED TO BE "PARANOID"...
HAVE YOU SEEN THIS, MARGARET?
SOMEONE JUST SENT ME THIS PROTOTYPE...
IT'S A NEW KIND OF INTRA-UTERINE DEVICE...
MADE OF PLASTIC, WHICH SHOULD BE MORE COMFORTABLE...
PERHAPS, BUT I SIMPLY DON'T TRUST I.U.D.S....
THE INFECTION RATES ARE TOO HIGH...
I'M SURE OUR PRODUCT WILL BE MUCH SAFER...
IT MAY EVEN REVOLUTIONIZE MODERN SOCIETY...
AND WE'LL BE RICH...
?!? CHANG!
HIP HOP

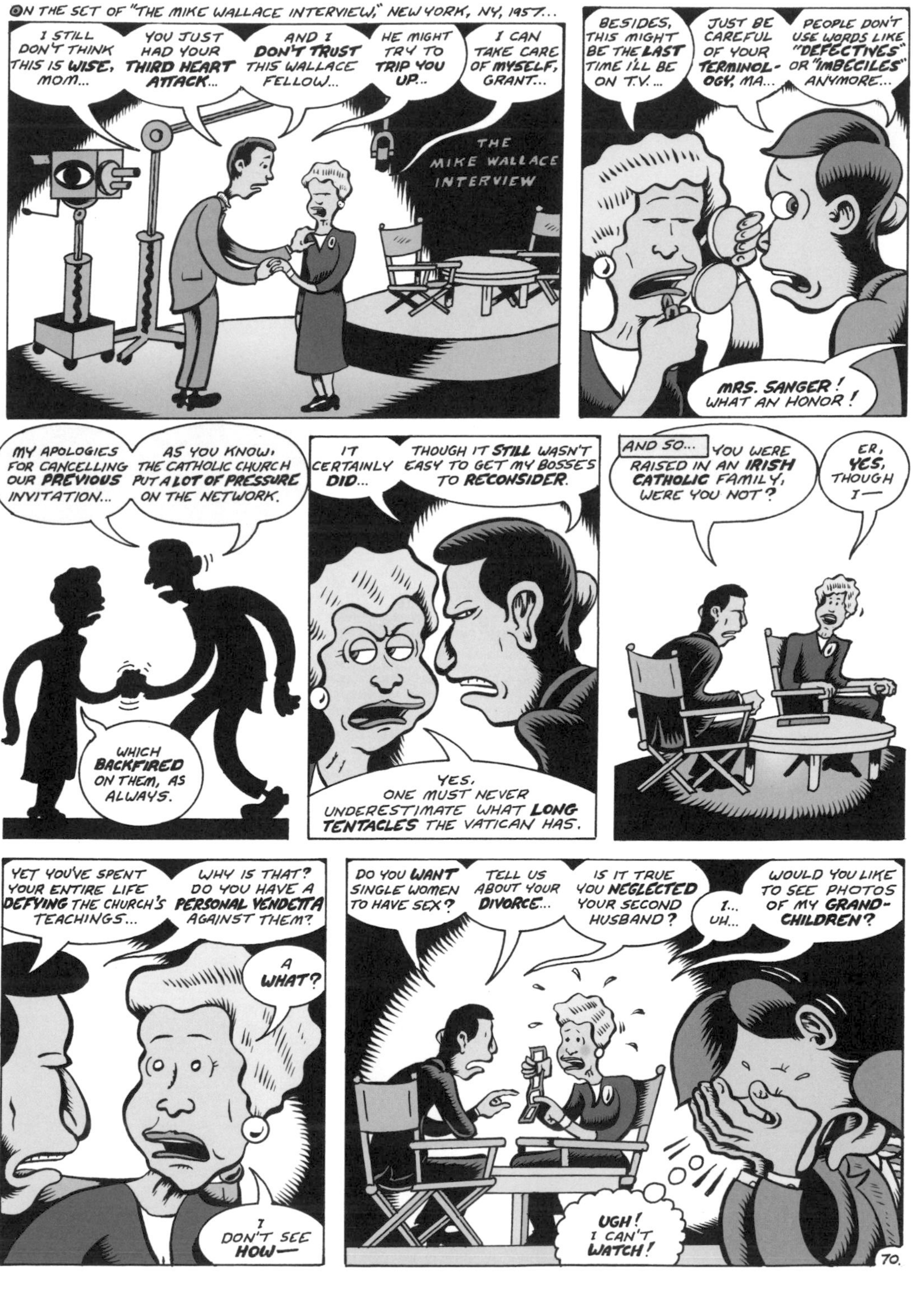

ON THE SET OF "THE MIKE WALLACE INTERVIEW," NEW YORK, NY, 1957...
I STILL DON'T THINK THIS IS WISE, MOM...
YOU JUST HAD YOUR THIRD HEART ATTACK...
AND I DON'T TRUST THIS WALLACE FELLOW...
HE MIGHT TRY TO TRIP YOU UP...
I CAN TAKE CARE OF MYSELF, GRANT...
THE MIKE WALLACE INTERVIEW
BESIDES, THIS MIGHT BE THE LAST TIME I'LL BE ON T.V. ...
JUST BE CAREFUL OF YOUR TERMINOLOGY, MA...
PEOPLE DON'T USE WORDS LIKE "DEFECTIVES" OR "IMBECILES" ANYMORE...
MRS. SANGER! WHAT AN HONOR!
MY APOLOGIES FOR CANCELLING OUR PREVIOUS INVITATION...
AS YOU KNOW, THE CATHOLIC CHURCH PUT A LOT OF PRESSURE ON THE NETWORK.
WHICH BACKFIRED ON THEM, AS ALWAYS.
IT CERTAINLY DID...
THOUGH IT STILL WASN'T EASY TO GET MY BOSSES TO RECONSIDER.
YES. ONE MUST NEVER UNDERESTIMATE WHAT LONG TENTACLES THE VATICAN HAS.
AND SO...
YOU WERE RAISED IN AN IRISH CATHOLIC FAMILY, WERE YOU NOT?
ER, YES, THOUGH I—
YET YOU'VE SPENT YOUR ENTIRE LIFE DEFYING THE CHURCH'S TEACHINGS...
WHY IS THAT? DO YOU HAVE A PERSONAL VENDETTA AGAINST THEM?
A WHAT?
I DON'T SEE HOW—
DO YOU WANT SINGLE WOMEN TO HAVE SEX?
TELL US ABOUT YOUR DIVORCE...
IS IT TRUE YOU NEGLECTED YOUR SECOND HUSBAND?
I... UH...
WOULD YOU LIKE TO SEE PHOTOS OF MY GRAND-CHILDREN?
UGH! I CAN'T WATCH!

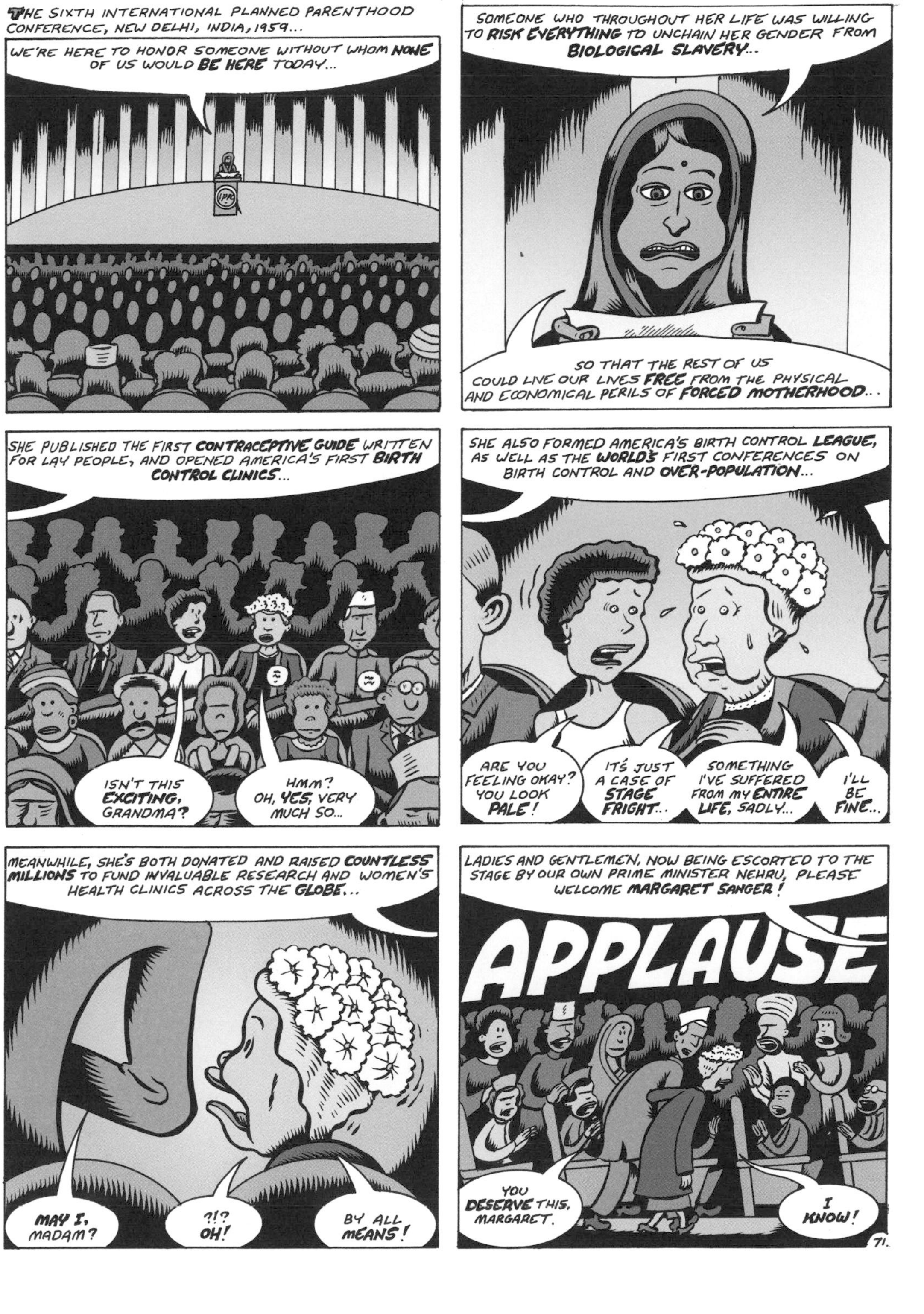
THE SIXTH INTERNATIONAL PLANNED PARENTHOOD CONFERENCE, NEW DELHI, INDIA, 1959...
WE'RE HERE TO HONOR SOMEONE WITHOUT WHOM NONE OF US WOULD BE HERE TODAY...
IPPC
SOMEONE WHO THROUGHOUT HER LIFE WAS WILLING TO RISK EVERYTHING TO UNCHAIN HER GENDER FROM BIOLOGICAL SLAVERY...
SO THAT THE REST OF US COULD LIVE OUR LIVES FREE FROM THE PHYSICAL AND ECONOMICAL PERILS OF FORCED MOTHERHOOD...
SHE PUBLISHED THE FIRST CONTRACEPTIVE GUIDE WRITTEN FOR LAY PEOPLE, AND OPENED AMERICA'S FIRST BIRTH CONTROL CLINICS...
ISN'T THIS EXCITING, GRANDMA?
HMM? OH, YES, VERY MUCH SO...
SHE ALSO FORMED AMERICA'S BIRTH CONTROL LEAGUE, AS WELL AS THE WORLD'S FIRST CONFERENCES ON BIRTH CONTROL AND OVER-POPULATION...
ARE YOU FEELING OKAY? YOU LOOK PALE!
IT'S JUST A CASE OF STAGE FRIGHT...
SOMETHING I'VE SUFFERED FROM MY ENTIRE LIFE, SADLY...
I'LL BE FINE...
MEANWHILE, SHE'S BOTH DONATED AND RAISED COUNTLESS MILLIONS TO FUND INVALUABLE RESEARCH AND WOMEN'S HEALTH CLINICS ACROSS THE GLOBE...
MAY I, MADAM?
?!? OH!
BY ALL MEANS!
LADIES AND GENTLEMEN, NOW BEING ESCORTED TO THE STAGE BY OUR OWN PRIME MINISTER NEHRU, PLEASE WELCOME MARGARET SANGER!
APPLAUSE
YOU DESERVE THIS, MARGARET.
I KNOW!

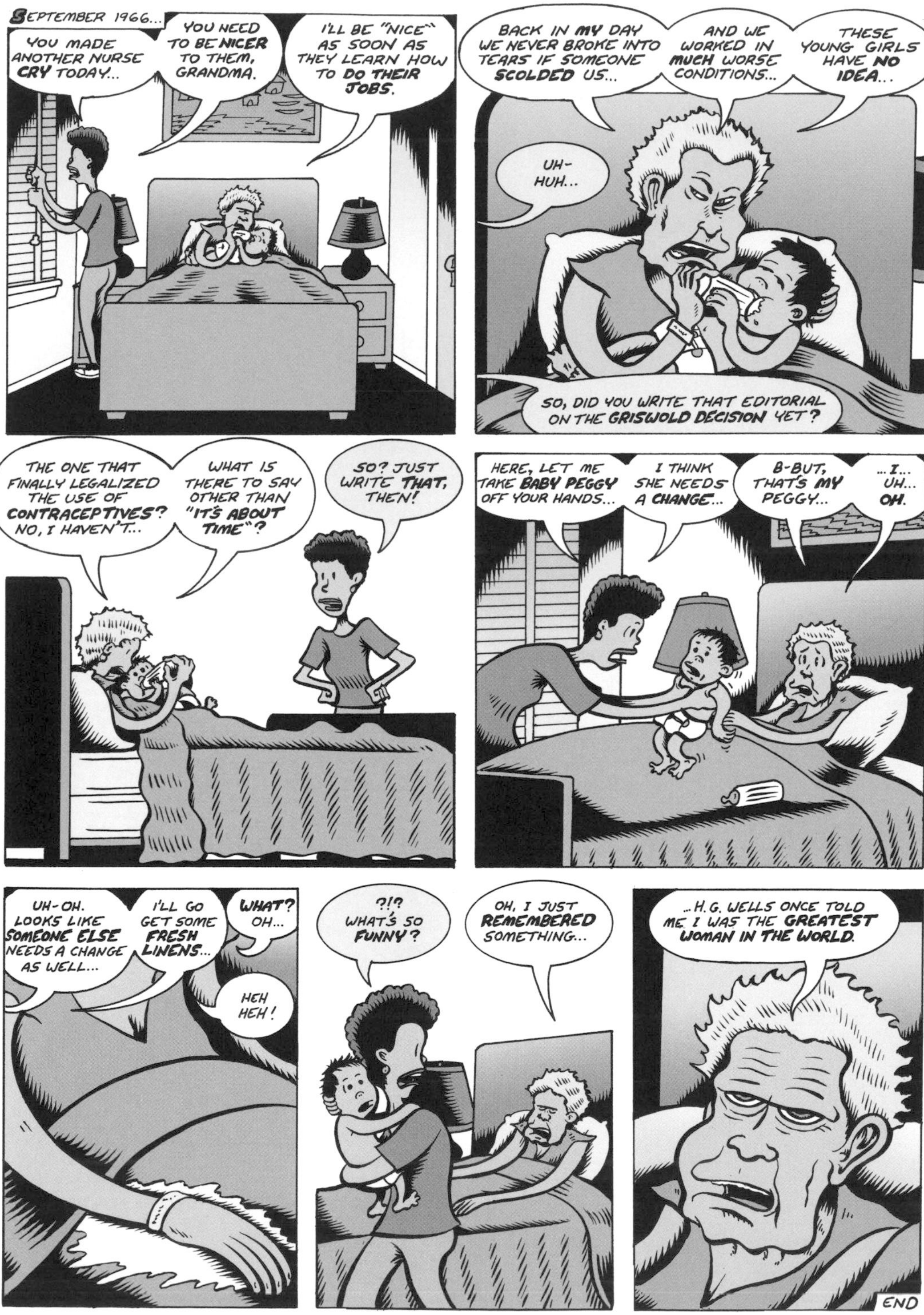
SEPTEMBER 1966...
YOU MADE ANOTHER NURSE CRY TODAY...
YOU NEED TO BE NICER TO THEM, GRANDMA.
I'LL BE "NICE" AS SOON AS THEY LEARN HOW TO DO THEIR JOBS.
BACK IN MY DAY WE NEVER BROKE INTO TEARS IF SOMEONE SCOLDED US...
AND WE WORKED IN MUCH WORSE CONDITIONS...
THESE YOUNG GIRLS HAVE NO IDEA...
UH-HUH...
SO, DID YOU WRITE THAT EDITORIAL ON THE GRISWOLD DECISION YET?
THE ONE THAT FINALLY LEGALIZED THE USE OF CONTRACEPTIVES? NO, I HAVEN'T...
WHAT IS THERE TO SAY OTHER THAN "IT'S ABOUT TIME"?
SO? JUST WRITE THAT, THEN!
HERE, LET ME TAKE BABY PEGGY OFF YOUR HANDS...
I THINK SHE NEEDS A CHANGE...
B-BUT, THAT'S MY PEGGY...
...I... UH... OH.
UH-OH. LOOKS LIKE SOMEONE ELSE NEEDS A CHANGE AS WELL...
I'LL GO GET SOME FRESH LINENS...
WHAT? OH...
HEH HEH!
?!? WHAT'S SO FUNNY?
OH, I JUST REMEMBERED SOMETHING...
...H.G. WELLS ONCE TOLD ME I WAS THE GREATEST WOMAN IN THE WORLD.
END

WHY SANGER?

IF ONE TYPES THE NAME MARGARET SANGER INTO AN internet search engine, most of the results that appear loudly proclaim her guilty of all the worst thought crimes imaginable in our life and times: She's a racist; a genocidal maniac; a member of the KKK; both a fascist *and* a communist (sometimes in the same sentence); and my favorite, the inventor of abortion. None of this is even remotely true, and it is largely the result of a deliberate effort by opponents of abortion to slander the founder of Planned Parenthood through the use of doctored photos, quotes taken out of context, quotes lifted from her old newsletters but not made by her (and which she may have even vehemently disagreed with), or quotes that are simply fabricated.

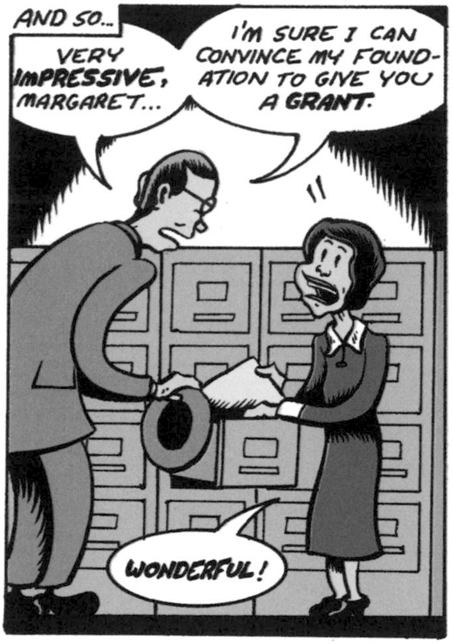
AND SO...
VERY IMPRESSIVE, MARGARET...
I'M SURE I CAN CONVINCE MY FOUNDATION TO GIVE YOU A GRANT.
WONDERFUL!

Sadly, one often has to do one's own digging into original sources to find out the truth, since even people who are pro-choice and support Planned Parenthood often buy into these lies, no questions asked, as they so effectively appeal to liberal guilt. Even a few otherwise sympathetic biographers can't seem to get past her use of outdated phrases like "negro" or "imbecile"—or even her use of the word "race," which for her always referred to the *human* race—without assuming the worst, as if Sanger *knew* these words would fall out of favor one hundred years later and was showing her true colors not to her contemporaries but to the people of the future.

The ironies abound. First and foremost, Margaret Sanger herself was a *lifelong opponent of abortion* (Roe v. Wade happened seven years after her death at the age of eighty-six). Second, when you compare her writings to those of other social commentators of her era, she was probably the *least* bigoted person of the bunch. I myself couldn't find a single instance of her making a negative generalization about a specific race or ethnic group, either publicly or privately (unless one chooses to take something out of context, that is), and she wrote a *lot* in her lifetime.

Yet another irony is her association with the eugenics movement, which her critics often use as evidence that she was an advocate of "ethnic cleansing" and a hero of Hitler's (her books were among the very first to be banned by the Nazis, in fact). One would never know it by the hysterical way the subject is discussed today, but there was no uniform "school" of eugenic thought—rather, it was a catch-all term for a set of practices its proponents believed would improve the human gene pool, including nutrition, hygiene, environmental protection, prenatal care, and, of course, birth control, all now universally acceptable. In fact, most eugenics advocates of the early 1920s (including several US presidents) didn't regard Sanger as a legitimate spokesperson for the movement *at all*, partly due to her refusal to acknowledge ethnicity as any kind of measure of human "fitness." They also accused her of being a poseur, hopping on the eugenics bandwagon simply to give her birth control agenda more scientific, academic, and social acceptability—which was largely true. It's an irony festival!

It's also interesting that her critics will present the fact that Sanger once gave a demonstration on birth control techniques to a meeting of a women's auxiliary of the Ku Klux Klan as proof that she supported the Klan's cause, yet also suggest that her sharing the same information with a black audience is evidence of her intention to wipe out the black race, all the while remaining oblivious to the obvious contradiction built into their argument. One could just as easily argue that she was all about black empowerment while trying to wipe out the *white* race using these same anecdotes. Yet many alleged "scholars" give lectures and write papers based on this backwards logic—including Angela Davis, whose fame and reputation give this garbage instant credibility.

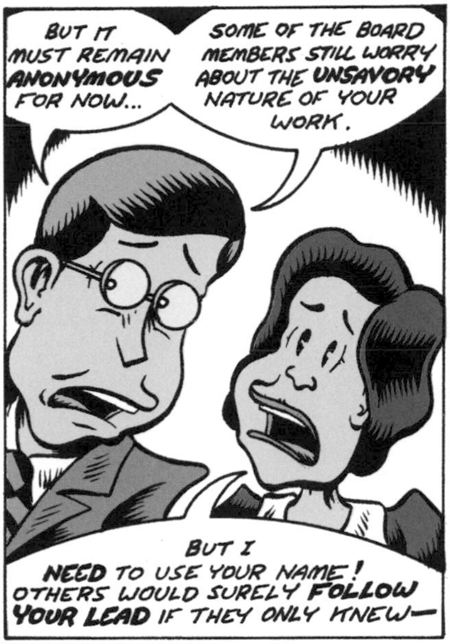
BUT IT MUST REMAIN ANONYMOUS FOR NOW...
SOME OF THE BOARD MEMBERS STILL WORRY ABOUT THE UNSAVORY NATURE OF YOUR WORK.
BUT I NEED TO USE YOUR NAME! OTHERS WOULD SURELY FOLLOW YOUR LEAD IF THEY ONLY KNEW—

So why did I write this book? Because Sanger lived the lives of *ten* people, for one thing. She led such a busy, colorful existence that my hardest task was deciding what parts of her life not to include—and so much of it was literally *action-packed* that all I could think of was "comic book!" whenever I read of her exploits. I also admire—and envy—her ability to multitask while refusing to be distracted by her numerous health issues, the constant threat of arrest and imprisonment, or the death threats she received on a daily basis. What she managed to accomplish in her lifetime is nothing short of astonishing.

I marvel at the fact that, in spite of her steely resolve and intense passionate nature, she never raised a hand to anyone, nor endorsed or justified the use of violence to achieve any end she deemed worthy. She was an effective practitioner of civil disobedience and passive resistance yet never gave her opponents even an ounce of flesh. She was clearly prepared to die for her cause, which made her an even more intimidating opponent. The Catholic Church in particular was obsessed with finding ways to destroy her reputation—and they still are, decades after her death.

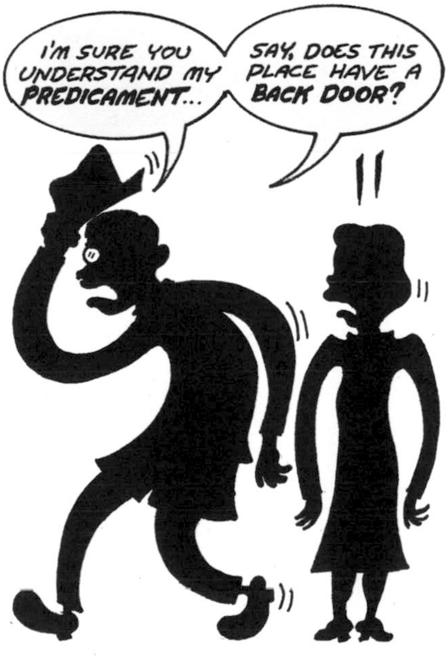
I'M SURE YOU UNDERSTAND MY PREDICAMENT...
SAY, DOES THIS PLACE HAVE A BACK DOOR?

Then there's the fact that she changed the course of human civilization, and all for the better. Legal access to safe and effective methods of birth control (as well as the technological advances that she was instrumental in promoting) made it possible for us to pursue our lives and dreams without being shackled by our own biology. It's amazing the extent to which we now take this fact for granted, but I simply can't imagine a greater gift to humanity.

It will also become obvious by my warts-and-all portrayal that I don't perceive Sanger as some kind of a saint or intend to pass her off as such. While she was incredibly generous and loyal to her friends and family, she also could be amazingly stubborn, impulsive, egotistical, and self-centered. And while her obliviousness to danger is admirable from a distance, it also kept her loved ones in a near-constant state of anxiety. Living and working with her must have felt like being trapped on a runaway train!

I had no choice but to paraphrase Sanger's words to a great extent in order to make them fit into the restrictive confines of comic book panels and word balloons. I also tweaked the timeline here and there, and added and subtracted certain players from certain scenes, Hollywood-style, simply to make the story easier to read and follow. Still, I took great pains to make sure I stayed true to the point she was making in her original texts (though I'm sure some Sanger scholars will take issue with some of my paraphrasing). And lest someone suspects I'm using Sanger as a sock puppet to foist some agenda of my own on my readers, I'd like to point out that there are several instances in this book where I disagree strongly with what she's saying—though I certainly share her opinions on the most important matters, which is another reason I wrote this book.

—PETER BAGGE

WHO'S WHO AND WHAT'S WHAT

I tried to keep the following bios and organization descriptions as brief and as relevant to Margaret Sanger's story as possible. However, many of the people in Sanger's life had amazing lives of their own and are more than worthy of an internet search if you're interested in learning more about them. I certainly couldn't do them justice in the limited space I have here.

I also tried to fill in the gaps and answer any lingering questions I suspect the reader may have in as few words as possible.
— PETER BAGGE

PAGE I

Sanger's parents were both born in Cork, Ireland, and emigrated with their respective families at a young age to escape the potato famine. Her mother's family, the Purcells, settled in New Jersey and became prosperous farmers and landlords. Her father's family, the Higginses, first moved to Montreal. As a teen he enlisted in the Union Army during the Civil War, thus becoming a US citizen.

Anne Purcell Higgins was sober, humble, industrious, thrifty, and a devout Catholic. Michael Hennessy Higgins was an opinionated socialist and atheist who loved to read, debate, drink, and spend money (when he had it). In spite of their temperamental differences, Sanger's parents loved and respected each other, and they rarely argued. After a lot of moving about, they settled in the factory town of Corning, NY, where they mostly remained to raise their family.

Anne Higgins had eighteen pregnancies in twenty-five years. She gave birth to eleven children, ten of whom survived to adulthood (a very good batting average for their time and means). All the children were born at home with just their father assisting in their births.

Anna (AKA "Nan") and Mary were the oldest. Neither married (not uncommon for the oldest girls of large families back then). Nan worked as a secretary before becoming a nurse and spent many of her later years quietly working for her famous sister behind the scenes, both as a nanny for her children and as a nurse at her birth control clinic. Her name rarely comes up in Sanger's biographies, though Margaret relied on her heavily, emotionally and otherwise.

Mary worked for the Abbott family (co-owners of the Corning glassware company) her entire life, both as a maid and as a governess. They treated her well, and she got to see much of the world by accompanying them in their travels. Then came four boys: Joseph, Thomas, John (who left home in 1895, never to be heard from again) and Richard, followed by Margaret herself, born September 14, 1879. After a four-year gap, another girl, Ethel, was born, followed by three more boys. The girls were all shy and studious, while the burly Higgins boys were more interested in hunting and sports (they also all joined the military during WWI, much to Sanger's horror). Only the two youngest boys went straight to college, with their tuitions largely paid for by their sisters: Lawrence became a naval commander, while the youngest (and Sanger's favorite), Bob, became a star college football player and later a college coach. In fact, during his successful nineteen-year run as the head coach at Penn State in the 1930s and '40s, Bob Higgins was as well known nationally as his famous sister.

Barring the occasional feud, the members of the Higgins clan remained close and fiercely loyal to each other throughout their adulthood, particularly the four sisters.

LEFT: *The four Higgins sisters with their father, Truro, MA, 1920s. L – R: Nan, Sanger, Ethel, Mary, and Michael.*

PAGE 2

HENRY GEORGE: An influential political and economic thinker in the late 1800s whose philosophy could be described as an agrarian form of protosocialism. He stayed at the Higginses' home during a failed campaign for a statewide office.

PAGES 3–4
This is one of many remarkable personality-shaping stories from Sanger's childhood. I had a hard time deciding which one to illustrate, though I think this one is a doozy.

PAGE 5
ROBERT INGERSOLL: A controversial orator and politician from the late 1800s. As an unapologetic agnostic, he was greatly reviled by members of established religions. Sanger's father invited Ingersoll to speak in Corning, which led to a full-scale riot and his being barred from speaking at any town venue. In defiance, Michael Higgins led him and his other followers into the woods, and he gave his speech there. This event had a profound impact on a young Sanger and served as a template for her own future activism.

PAGE 6
CLAVERACK COLLEGE: A coed boarding school that closed its doors shortly after Sanger left and was noteworthy in its day for not using corporal punishment. Sanger dated a fellow student while there, to whom she lost her virginity.

LEFT: *A teenage Sanger with her Claverack classmate (and, briefly, fiancé) Corey Albertson, dated late 1890s. There are many existing photos of Sanger, even as a young girl of limited means. She took great pride in her appearance and was particularly proud of her long, reddish-auburn hair, which she would pin up in elaborate (and impossible to draw) buns.*

She was also a stylish dresser, so it should come as no surprise that she loved being photographed!

PAGE 7
Sanger seriously considered pursuing a career in the theater at this time. What dissuaded her was the drama school application, whose requests for her measurements included such minute details as "calf length" and "ankle width," which lead her to conclude that the theater world was run by a bunch of perverts.

PAGE 9
This difficult period was probably the only time that Sanger felt negatively toward her father, who must have

gotten his act together soon afterward. While well aware of his shortcomings, she always spoke fondly of him. Michael Higgins lived to a ripe old age and resided with Ethel in Truro, MA, in his final years.

PAGE 10
Sanger briefly studied and interned at a small nursing hospital in White Plains, NY, before transferring to an eye and ear hospital in New York City, where she met her future husband.

William Sanger was born in Germany to a Jewish family and immigrated to New York with his family at a young age. He was six years older than Sanger and already a successful architectural draftsman, and he was heavily involved in the Socialist Party. Margaret was always ambivalent at best about marriage, but William was so smitten by her and pursued her so relentlessly that she finally agreed to marry him.

RIGHT: *A rare photo of William Sanger, probably dating from around the time he met Margaret.*

Sanger suffered intermittently from TB flare-ups for the rest of her life, which put a huge strain on her heart and lungs. It was long assumed that she contracted it from her mother, though that has since been proven to be impossible—otherwise all of Anne Higgins's children would have been infected. In fact, being born to and weaned by an infected mother most likely meant that the children were *immune* to airborne strains of the disease. However, Sanger often told of how she and her sister Ethel would buy raw milk from a local farmer rather than the more expensive pasteurized milk from a grocery store, and then buy candy with the pennies they saved. Clever! Yet seeing as she and Ethel were the only Higgins children to ever come down with TB, it's now speculated that they may have contracted a food-borne strain in this way.

PAGE 11
It's remarkable to realize that Sanger lived a typically middle-class lifestyle for the first decade of her marriage. Still, she and her husband remained active and unabashed progressives throughout this time, so it wasn't a total shock when they finally decided to surrender the comfort and conformity of the suburbs and move back to the city for less lucrative yet more fulfilling pursuits.

The Sangers' three children were STUART (b. 1903),

GRANT (b. 1907, and weirdly named after U.S. Grant, a hero of Sanger's father) and MARGARET, or "Peggy," born in 1908 (so much for "child spacing"!). Sanger herself was usually referred to as "Peggy" or "Peg" by her close friends and relations, but I chose to reserve that nickname for her daughter in this book to avoid confusion.

PAGE 12

The Sangers' ambivalence toward his family's ethnicity was hardly out of place at a time when assimilation was all-important to ambitious young professionals like them (and in spite of their politics, they still harbored typically middle-class aspirations for their children), and was a recipe for self-marginalization. William Sanger eventually even started to pass himself off as a gentile, a fiction that Margaret weirdly went along with even after they were divorced (her 1938 biography claims he was descended from *Australian sheep ranchers!*). Some sources even claim their sons didn't know they were half-Jewish until they were middle-aged, though other sources insist that's impossible.

That being said, throughout her life, many if not most of Sanger's friends and associates were Jewish, and their Jewishness was never an issue for her. She also went to great effort and personal expense to relocate Jewish colleagues from Nazi Germany prior to WWII, and even succeeded in some cases, in spite of nothing but resistance from the US government. So outdated attitudes aside, Sanger was the farthest thing from an anti-Semite imaginable.

PAGE 13

The abject poverty and horrendous living conditions that Sanger witnessed on a daily basis at this time were far worse than anything we modern Americans could even conceive of. Even her own humble upbringing seemed like heaven in comparison, and it greatly fueled her growing political radicalization.

PAGE 14

The "Sadie Sachs Story" long remained Sanger's number one go-to sob story—one that was sure to elicit tears and open purses. The tale is also impossible to confirm, and most likely was an amalgamation of many similar experiences. The actual story ends with Mrs. Sachs getting pregnant and performing an abortion yet again, only this time she dies as a result. My choosing not to illustrate that last bit isn't meant to suggest I find the tale unbelievable. Indeed, women died horrible deaths from botched abortions every day back then. I skipped it simply because it came off as a bit too melodramatic and over-the-top within the context of this book.

Sanger's experiences as a nurse occurred before the discovery of antibiotics, which may explain not only her lifelong visceral aversion to abortion but to almost any surgical procedure. She even spent years trying to treat

her own defective spleen holistically before she eventually had no choice but to go under the knife. The women who hemorrhaged to death from botched abortions were the "lucky" ones compared with those who died a slow, agonizing death as the result of an infection.

PAGE 15

Not only could doctors and nurses lose their license to practice if word got out that they dispensed contraceptive information, but they could also face imprisonment, and many actually did.

While always considered immoral by many, abortion was technically legal in the US until the mid-nineteenth century. The reasons for banning the practice were twofold: One was the Nativists' (i.e. Protestants') fear of becoming outnumbered by the rapidly reproducing immigrants (i.e. Catholics); the other was the result of lobbying efforts by college-educated, licensed medical practitioners, who exploited concerns for the "safety of the mother" as a way to drive their less-expensive competition (i.e.: midwives and unlicensed doctors) out of business. Many midwives even specialized in abortions, and so the entire practice was demonized and then criminalized—though licensed doctors continued to perform them on friends, relatives, and wealthy clients.

PAGE 16

THE MODERN SCHOOL, or the Ferrer Center, lasted for many years and operated in several NYC locations. Similar schools opened across the country prior to WWI. It was named after Francesc Ferrer I Guàrdia, a Spanish educator, anarchist, and free thinker who was executed by the Spanish government in 1909.

WILL DURANT: An educator and historian who, in collaboration with his wife (and former student) Ariel Durant, wrote the eleven-volume text *The Story of Civilization.* He also helped popularize the subject of philosophy with an earlier work, *The Story of Philosophy.*

ALEXANDER ("SASHA") BERKMAN: Anarchist activist, writer, and editor. Served fourteen years in prison for the failed assassination attempt of businessman Henry Clay Frick in 1892.

EMMA GOLDMAN: Well-known and outspoken anarchist, feminist, editor, and author. Longtime partner of Berkman, both of whom were Jewish immigrants from Lithuania. Started the journal *Mother Earth* with Berkman in 1907.

The term "comrade" was frequently used in those days when addressing anyone with similar views and goals to your own. Considering the wide range of political opinions held by this group alone, Goldman's use of the word was more inclusive than exclusive. Over time people began to resent the word's growing association with indoctrination and enforced groupthink. Thus, we now associate it almost solely with cold war–era caricatures of Eastern European Communists.

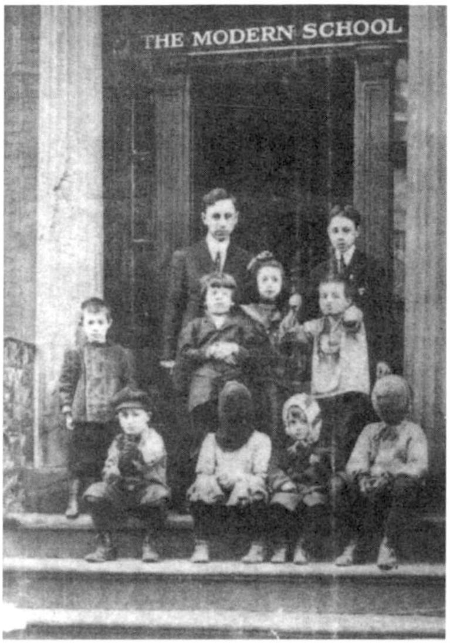
THE MODERN SCHOOL

RIGHT: *Will Durant with a group of poorly disciplined students in 1912. Sanger's oldest son, Stuart, might be one of the scamps with their faces covered.*

PAGE 17
The Ferrer Center's adult courses seem to have been far more stimulating than those designed for children. When asked decades later what he learned while attending the Modern School, Stuart Sanger replied, "Nothing."

While both of the adult Sangers morally approved of the concept of free love, only Margaret practiced it (as far as we know). She probably already had her first of many lovers by this time: a Greek-born editor and publisher named Nicholas Rompapas. She saved several passionate love letters from him (Sanger was a huge sucker for mush), while also preserving letters from a jealous William Sanger urging her to "get rid of the Greek."

PAGE 18
The New York Call was America's most widely read English-language socialist newspaper during the progressive era (though it was still outsold by Yiddish and German language periodicals). It also was allied with the Socialist Party of America. Editor and drama critic Anita Block was a close friend and ally of Sanger prior to WWI, though they seem to have parted ways afterward. I suspect Sanger's later estrangement from the Socialist Party may have had something to do with it. (Note: I couldn't find a single photo of Ms. Block to refer to, so my apologies to her descendants if my guesstimate as to what she looked like is way off base.)

PAGE 19
This is an early example of Sanger's talent for provoking her enemies and then exploiting their inevitable overreactions to her advantage. This became something of a ritual between her and the Catholic Church in later years, when people half-joked that Sanger *needed* to be harassed by the Church in order to make headlines and raise money.

PAGE 20
William Sanger's art, though technically well done, had a sparse, expressionistic gloominess to it that never found an audience. Margaret herself never seemed to care for it, though she reluctantly used some of his illustrations in her later publication *The Birth Control Review*, largely at his insistence.

PAGE 21
THE LAWRENCE TEXTILE STRIKE: A strike organized by the Industrial Workers of the World (or the IWW, AKA "The Wobblies"), to protest shrinking wages and worsening conditions in the many textile mills in Lawrence, MA. The strike was initially surprisingly successful, in that most of the workers were foreign-born women (and thus "unorganizable," according to more established unions like the AFL), though many of their gains were eventually lost. The transporting of the strikers' children to be fed and housed in other cities was such a successful move that the mill owners were determined to stop it, as we see pictured here.

PAGE 23
The brief success and accompanying notoriety of the Lawrence Strike gave Sanger a temporary case of "strike fever," as she was more than willing to assist the Wobblies in any way they asked of her, in spite of the risks involved.

Sanger was charged with attempted assault during the strike in Hazelton, PA, though she claimed she was simply trying to keep her sign from being confiscated. I'm inclined to believe her, since in spite of her passionate nature she was quite the disciplined pacifist, and there's no other known instance of her even *threatening* someone with physical violence. She never even swore!

PAGE 24
Pictured to the right of the Sangers is the wealthy heiress MABEL DODGE, whose Greenwich Village salon (painted and decorated entirely in white) was the scene of frequent radical gatherings. Many political activists regarded Ms. Dodge as something of a poseur and dilettante, though they rarely passed up a chance to gorge themselves at her sumptuous buffet tables.

To the right of Dodge is the communist journalist JOHN REED, who was romantically linked to Dodge at this time. He had just staged the ambitious, elaborate PATTERSON STRIKE PAGEANT in Madison Square Garden, which featured thousands of the Patterson, NJ, mill strikers themselves. Though quite a spectacle, it failed to generate much public support for the strike, which soon ended in failure.

To the right of Reed is ELIZABETH GURLEY FLYNN, a passionate young orator and organizer for the IWW. Flynn worked closely at this time with BIG BILL HAYWOOD, pictured to her right. A product of the Wild West, the one-eyed Haywood was a fearless and innovative labor leader and a major player within the IWW. Sanger had great admiration for him and his organizational skills, and eagerly took instructions from him—behavior otherwise unheard of from the anti-authoritarian Sanger.

Both Haywood and Reed spent their final years in Soviet Russia, where their dreams of a socialist utopia were quickly dashed. Before moving to Russia in 1917, Reed sold his Cape Cod cottage to Sanger.

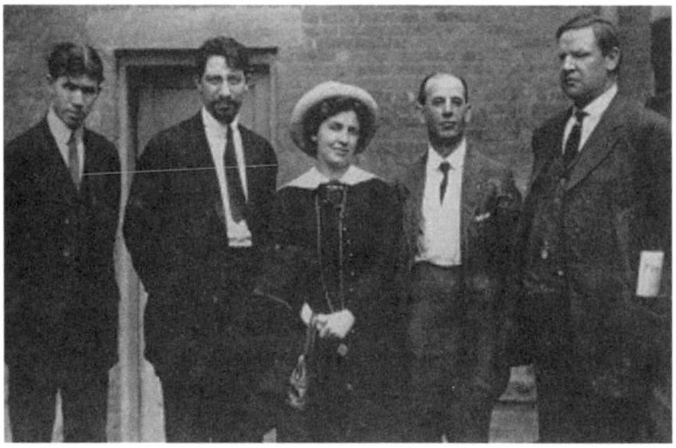

RIGHT: *IWW leaders, Paterson, NJ, 1913. L – R: Pat Quinlan, Carlo Tresca, E.G. Flynn, Adolph Lessig, Bill Haywood.*

PAGE 25
William Sanger remained in Paris through most of 1914. In fact, their Paris trip was the last time the Sangers actually lived together.

BELOW: *The Sanger children in Paris, France, 1913. L – R: Stuart, Peggy, and Grant.*

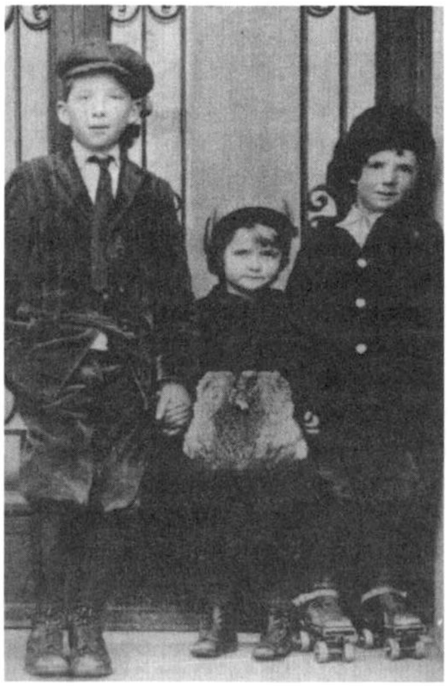

PAGE 26
Sanger's younger sister, Ethel Byrne, had two children with the man she eloped with in Corning, Jack Byrne, who turned out to be a violent drunk. Seemingly unable to obtain a divorce, she left her children temporarily with her in-laws and moved to New York to live and work with Sanger.

The YMCA and YWCA were much despised institutions amongst intellectuals and radicals in the early twentieth century. The "C" stands for "Christian," after all, and their original purpose was mainly an evangelical one. They also were very involved with other moralists and prohibitionists in stamping out "vice," in all that entailed at the time.

PAGE 27
THE HETERODOXY CLUB was an informal all-women's club whose unofficial headquarters was Polly's Restaurant in Greenwich Village. It was a place for progressive-minded women to share their ideals and goals. While the club had an impressive roster of leaders, much of the rank and file included younger lesbians who used the club's tolerant atmosphere to express their sexuality openly, as well as young socialites experimenting in radicalism before eventually getting married and rejoining the status quo.

Sanger had literally *nothing* to say, positive or negative, on the subject of homosexuality, and the nature of her cause may explain why she rarely interacted with people of that persuasion. She also found the young socialites in the club rather silly and annoying, though these same girls would come out in droves whenever Sanger gave one of her lectures on birth control.

Pictured in the first panel are (from left to right): author and feminist CHARLOTTE PERKINS GILMAN; Mabel Dodge; birth control advocate MARY WARE DENNETT; and Sanger. Dennett went on to form the National Birth Control League after this meeting without Sanger's involvement.

The Philadelphia-based Dennett was as fiercely dedicated to the cause of birth control as Sanger was, and did almost as much to further the cause as her better-known contemporary. Unfortunately, differences in style and strategy made it impossible for these two women to successfully work together, while Dennett's personal resentment toward Sanger often led to her deliberately undermining the latter's efforts.

Some of Dennett's beefs with Sanger were legitimate, such as the latter's legislative push for doctors-only access to contraceptives, rather than making them universally available over the counter (an issue that's still being fought to this day). Of course, Sanger was simply being pragmatic, figuring (correctly) that Dennett's over-the-counter strategy was doomed to failure. Yet rather than work out their differences privately, Dennett would routinely air her criticisms publicly, while also accusing Sanger of having an almost fetishistic admiration for the medical profession—not an entirely unfounded accusation, but one obviously fueled by Dennett's petty jealousy toward her more famous and media-savvy rival. In fact, Dennett's reputation would be sterling were it not for this context, in which she's stuck playing Salieri to Sanger's Mozart. While the inability of these two to work together was largely Dennett's fault, this wasn't the last time Sanger would butt heads with another female leader. She had a hard enough time taking orders from anybody, and even being in the *same room* with another alpha-female seemed more than either woman was willing to bear.

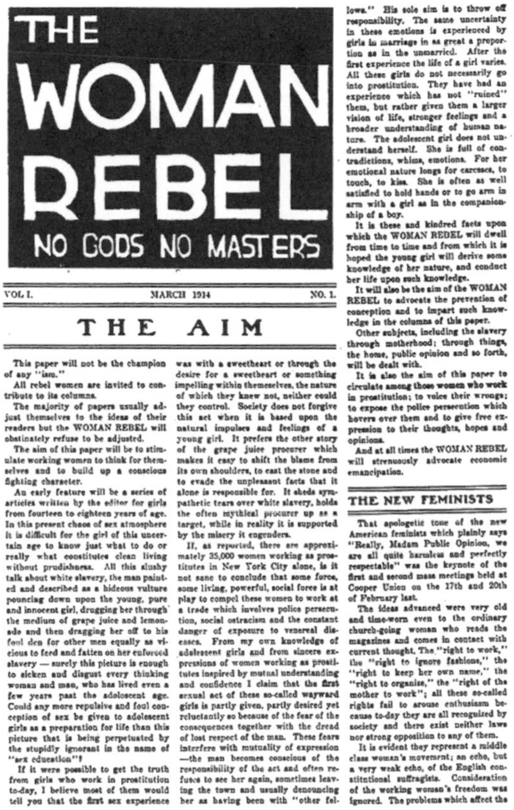
THE WOMAN REBEL

NO GODS NO MASTERS

VOL I. MARCH 1914 NO. 1.

THE AIM

This paper will not be the champion of any "ism."

All rebel women are invited to contribute to its columns.

The majority of papers usually adjust themselves to the ideas of their readers but the WOMAN REBEL will obstinately refuse to be adjusted.

The aim of this paper will be to stimulate working women to think for themselves and to build up a conscious fighting character.

An early feature will be a series of articles written by the editor for girls from fourteen to eighteen years of age. In this present chaos of sex atmosphere it is difficult for the girl of this uncertain age to know just what to do or really what constitutes clean living without prudishness. All this slushy talk about white slavery, the man painted and described as a hideous vulture pouncing down upon the young, pure and innocent girl, drugging her through the medium of grape juice and lemonade and then dragging her off to his foul den for other men equally as vicious to feed and fatten on her enforced slavery — surely this picture is enough to sicken and disgust every thinking woman and man, who has lived even a few years past the adolescent age. Could any more repulsive and foul conception of sex be given to adolescent girls as a preparation for life than this picture that is being perpetuated by the stupidly ignorant in the name of "sex education"?

If it were possible to get the truth from girls who work in prostitution to-day, I believe most of them would tell you that the first sex experience was with a sweetheart or through the desire for a sweetheart or something impelling within themselves, the nature of which they knew not, neither could they control. Society does not forgive this act when it is based upon the natural impulses and feelings of a young girl. It prefers the other story of the grape juice procurer which makes it easy to shift the blame from its own shoulders, to cast the stone and to evade the unpleasant facts that it alone is responsible for. It sheds sympathetic tears over white slavery, holds the often mythical procurer up as a target, while in reality it is supported by the misery it engenders.

If, as reported, there are approximately 35,000 women working as prostitutes in New York City alone, is it not sane to conclude that some force, some living, powerful, social force is at play to compel these women to work at a trade which involves police persecution, social ostracism and the constant danger of exposure to venereal diseases. From my own knowledge of adolescent girls and from sincere expressions of women working as prostitutes inspired by mutual understanding and confidence I claim that the first sexual act of these so-called wayward girls is partly given, partly desired yet reluctantly so because of the fear of the consequences together with the dread of lost respect of the man. These fears interfere with mutuality of expression —the man becomes conscious of the responsibility of the act and often refuses to see her again, sometimes leaving the town and usually denouncing her as having been with "other fellows." His sole aim is to throw off responsibility. The same uncertainty in these emotions is experienced by girls in marriage in as great a proportion as in the unmarried. After the first experience the life of a girl varies. All these girls do not necessarily go into prostitution. They have had an experience which has not "ruined" them, but rather given them a larger vision of life, stronger feelings and a broader understanding of human nature. The adolescent girl does not understand herself. She is full of contradictions, whims, emotions. For her emotional nature longs for carcsses, to touch, to kiss. She is often as well satisfied to hold hands or to go arm in arm with a girl as in the companionship of a boy.

It is these and kindred facts upon which the WOMAN REBEL will dwell from time to time and from which it is hoped the young girl will derive some knowledge of her nature, and conduct her life upon such knowledge.

It will also be the aim of the WOMAN REBEL to advocate the prevention of conception and to impart such knowledge in the columns of this paper.

Other subjects, including the slavery through motherhood; through things, the home, public opinion and so forth, will be dealt with.

It is also the aim of this paper to circulate among those women who work in prostitution; to voice their wrongs; to expose the police persecution which hovers over them and to give free expression to their thoughts, hopes and opinions.

And at all times the WOMAN REBEL will strenuously advocate economic emancipation.

THE NEW FEMINISTS

That apologetic tone of the new American feminists which plainly says "Really, Madam Public Opinion, we are all quite harmless and perfectly respectable" was the keynote of the first and second mass meetings held at Cooper Union on the 17th and 20th of February last.

The ideas advanced were very old and time-worn even to the ordinary church-going woman who reads the magazines and comes in contact with current thought. The "right to work," the "right to ignore fashions," the "right to keep her own name," the "right to organise," the "right of the mother to work"; all these so-called rights fail to arouse enthusiasm because to-day they are all recognized by society and there exist neither laws nor strong opposition to any of them.

It is evident they represent a middle class woman's movement; an echo, but a very weak echo, of the English constitutional suffragists. Consideration of the working woman's freedom was ignored. The problems which affect the

RIGHT: *Issue #1 of Sanger's "zine,"* The Woman Rebel. *This publication shocked the sensibilities of the likes of Anthony Comstock, and even many of Sanger's fellow radicals found it a bit too incendiary—a recipe for trouble. In fact, her own family wondered if it was a "cry for help" and considered having her committed!*

PAGE 28
While frequently the target of overzealous prosecutors, Sanger usually received sympathetic—or at least lenient—treatment from judges, most of whom found the charges against her petty at best, if not completely outrageous.

PAGE 29
This was the beginning of a very lengthy separation between Sanger and her children—one of many separations, in fact, which is something she's always been heavily criticized for. Of course, if she were a man this wouldn't even be a topic for discussion. Still, her kids pined for her terribly during her long absences.

Peggy contracted polio in the summer of 1913. She quickly recovered, though it affected her ability to walk.

Sanger wound up publishing numerous editions and hundreds of thousands of copies of *Family Limitation* over the next ten or so years, all of which were sold and/or distributed illegally—with one ironic exception: The *US Army* wound up handing out copies of it to conscripts during WWI, in response to a rash of unwanted pregnancies and the spread of STDs. So for a brief period this information was legally available to *men*, though still not to women.

PAGE 30
British cleric THOMAS MALTHUS (1766 – 1839) was among the first to take note of the potentially dire effects of overpopulation, as well as to propose possible solutions to the problem. His followers were called Malthusians. Though some of his "negative" solutions proved unworkable—legally prohibiting marriage until the age of twenty-five, for example—his so-called "positive" solutions (i.e.: *promoting* war, famine, and disease) were an even tougher sell. Thus, a later generation of followers dropped the "positive" solutions, revised the "negative" ones and renamed themselves the NEO-MALTHUSIANS.

Almost all the members of this group were also members of the Fabian Society, who could best be described as educated and/or upper-class socialists who advocated social change through gradual, peaceful means and rejected demands for violent upheaval.

For all of the reasons listed above, it was no surprise that this group warmly embraced Sanger upon her arrival in Britain, as she did them, and her life and career became permanently intertwined with many of the people in this circle.

Pictured left to right in panel one:
MARIE STOPES was a university-trained paleobotanist who first came to fame with the publication of

Married Love, a comprehensive sex advice guide (inspired, ironically, by her own loveless first marriage). Unable to find a publisher at first, she asked Sanger (who tried but also failed) to find one in the US. It eventually was self-published by her own doctor (and future husband), and became a bestseller. Stopes went on to become the UK's answer to Margaret Sanger, opening that country's first birth control clinic in 1921 as well as editing her own publication, *Birth Control News*.

Though they were originally staunch allies, the relationship between Sanger and Stopes eventually turned sour, echoing the competitive animosity that existed between Sanger and Mary Ware Dennett in many ways—only in this case, Sanger never really understood where that animosity stemmed from, since she liked Stopes personally (unlike Dennett, whom she truly despised).

Stopes most likely wouldn't have been at this gathering, though the hyperactive Sanger did first meet her around this time.

DR. V.C. DRYSDALE and his wife, BESSIE DRYSDALE, were the nominal leaders of the Neo-Malthusians, an organization started by V.C.'s own father, uncle, and mother, Dr. Alice Drysdale, who was also the UK's first university-trained female physician.

The world-renowned Irish-born playwright GEORGE BERNARD SHAW was a vocal advocate for many progressive causes: women's and children's rights, birth control, pacifism and, perhaps most passionately, vegetarianism. And like almost all intellectuals of his time, he embraced eugenics – including the most extreme (and today, almost universally denounced) aspects of that school of thought, in that he advocated the *humane euthanasia* of mentally and physically handicapped people. Shaw even supported many of the social policies of Nazi Germany early on, though he later criticized that regime for "killing the wrong people" (i.e. killing based on ethnicity, rather than on physical or mental disabilities).

Bestselling novelist, essayist, and historian H.G. WELLS was at the height of his fame at this time. In fact, he was one of the most famous men in the world, and eagerly exploited his celebrity status to promote many radical causes, including feminism and free love (which in his case seemed to be intricately linked).

LORENZO PORTET was a Spanish associate of Francesc Ferrer, and was living in exile in the UK at this time. Sanger met him in Liverpool before arriving in London, where they immediately became lovers. (Note: As was the case with Anita Block, I couldn't find a single photo of Portet, and thus modeled him after Sanger's vague descriptions of him.)

HAVELOCK ELLIS was arguably the world's first sexologist, and is best known for his seven-volume *Studies in the Psychology of Sex* (1897 – 1928). The first volume, *Sexual Inversion*, dealt with homosexuality, and was almost immediately banned. Even other so-called sex experts at the time (including Sigmund Freud) were shocked and offended by his sympathetic and non-judgmental attitude toward gay men and women (psychiatrists used to make a fortune "curing" people of their same-sex urges, so Ellis's take on the matter was a clear threat to their income).

Sanger herself was so shocked by Ellis's first volume when she first read it—what with its frank descriptions of what exactly it is that *gay men do* when behind closed doors—that she almost tossed it into the fire before giving it a second chance. She soon became obsessed with his work, as well as with *him*.

I placed Ellis at this gathering for the sake of convenience, though the painfully shy man (who today would surely be diagnosed with Asperger syndrome, if not high-functioning autism) didn't go to parties at all. Instead, Sanger wrote to him first, practically demanding a meeting with him.

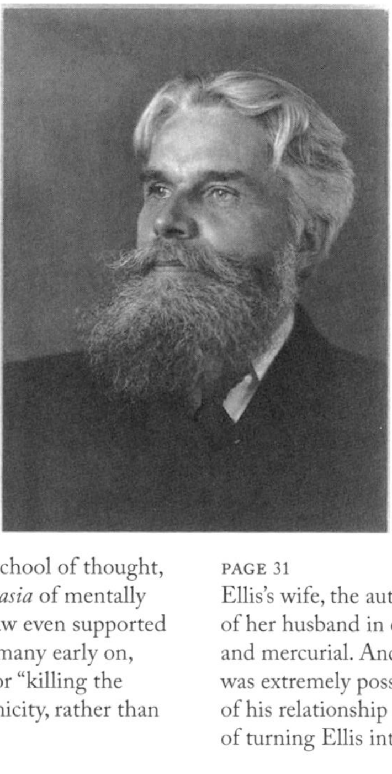

LEFT: *Havelock Ellis, in a photo dating from around the time he first met Sanger.*

PAGE 31

Ellis's wife, the author Edith Lees, was the exact opposite of her husband in every way: short and stout, impulsive and mercurial. And in spite of her own proclivities, she was extremely possessive of her husband and quite jealous of his relationship with Sanger, whom she once accused of turning Ellis into an "egomaniac."

Lees suffered from numerous physical and mental problems, and after years of threats and failed suicide attempts she finally died of diabetes in 1916, leaving Ellis devastated. He later lived with a French woman, Francoise Lafitte, who also seemed to resent Sanger, as Ellis felt obliged to greatly downplay their relationship in his autobiography. Though hurt, Sanger continued to heap praise on Ellis, and even helped financially support him in his final years.

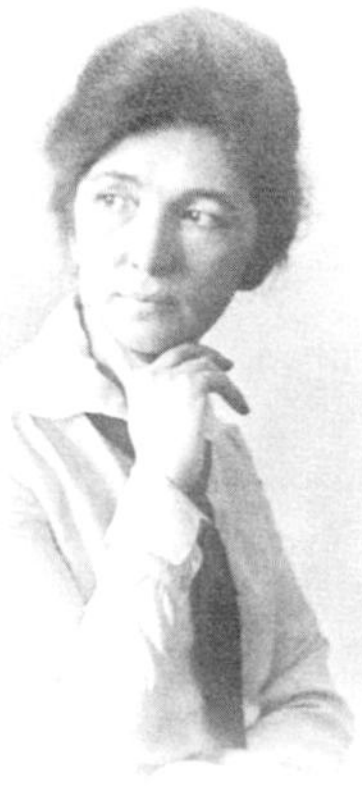

THIS COLUMN:
Two photos Ellis took of Sanger during their first meeting in 1915.

PAGE 32
Sanger was surprisingly conventional in a number of ways: she had little tolerance for pornography or foul language, and was also very much against prostitution (which she naively assumed the widespread availability and use of contraceptives would do away with). Still, she was more than happy to indulge Ellis's urolagnia. She even kept letters from him in which he gleefully reported saving her "golden waters"!

Ellis, in turn, served as a Henry Higgins of sorts to Sanger's Eliza, advising her to dial down her shrill radical rhetoric and to emphasize and exploit her own natural feminine charms—suggesting that she'd attract more flies with honey, basically. He also urged her to focus all of her efforts on the sole cause of birth control. Sanger took all of his advice to heart.

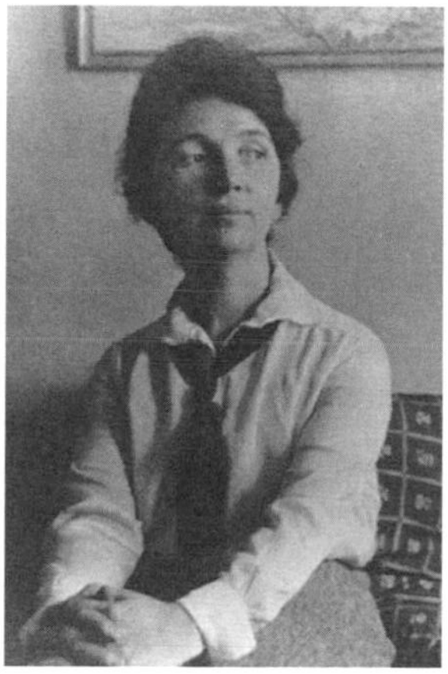

PAGE 33
William Sanger had always battled with depression, and his rambling, emotionally overwrought letters to his wife at this time betrayed an ever-worsening mental state. That the indomitable Sanger never experienced mood swings of any kind might explain why her husband continued to cling to her like a life raft, even years after their marriage was hopelessly doomed. But it was also one more reason she was so eager to be rid of him. He'd simply become much too difficult for her to deal with.

Sanger later had a very happy experience crisscrossing Spain by rail with Lorenzo Portet. In fact, she seemed to have been fonder of Portet than any other man before or since. She greatly enjoyed being in his constant presence, even in close quarters—otherwise unheard-of behavior for the perpetually restless and claustrophobic Sanger.

PAGE 34
The person most responsible for spearheading Holland's first-ever birth control clinics was Dr. Aletta Jacobs, though she refused to meet with Sanger, since the latter was "only" a nurse. This snub didn't seem to phase Sanger at the time, since the social and hierarchical separation between doctors and nurses was much greater back then than it is now—even more so in Europe, where nurses were regarded as little more than maids or orderlies. Using Lysol as a spermicide wasn't as crazy as it sounds. Women had no choice but to douche with common household products back then, with water and vinegar being the most common solution (diluted lemon or lime juice was also commonly used). Yet if properly diluted, Lysol was just as safe and even more effective. Unfortunately, too many women didn't follow the instructions properly—most likely due to getting the information second- or thirdhand, or from barely being able to read in the first place—and seriously injured themselves as a result. Because of this, Sanger dropped this recommendation from later editions of *Family Limitation.*

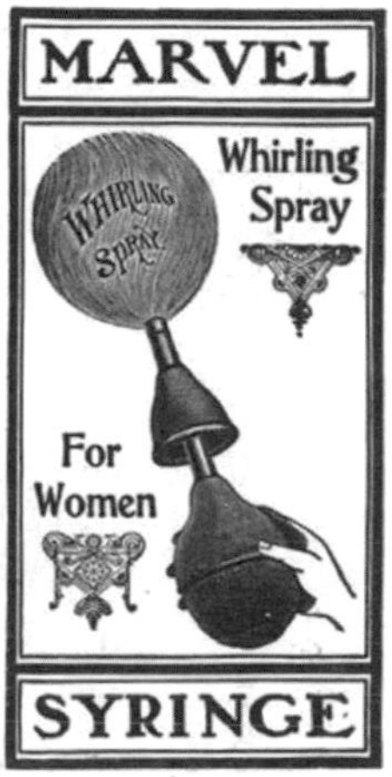
MARVEL
Whirling Spray
WHIRLING SPRAY
For Women
SYRINGE

RIGHT: *New versions and/or hybrids of cervical caps, pessaries, diaphragms, condoms, IUDs, sponges, and douches were constantly being developed and introduced throughout the late nineteenth and early twentieth centuries, though their reliability, safety, and comfort varied wildly. Ads for these products also had to rely on euphemisms like "feminine hygiene"—when they were allowed to appear at all, that is.*

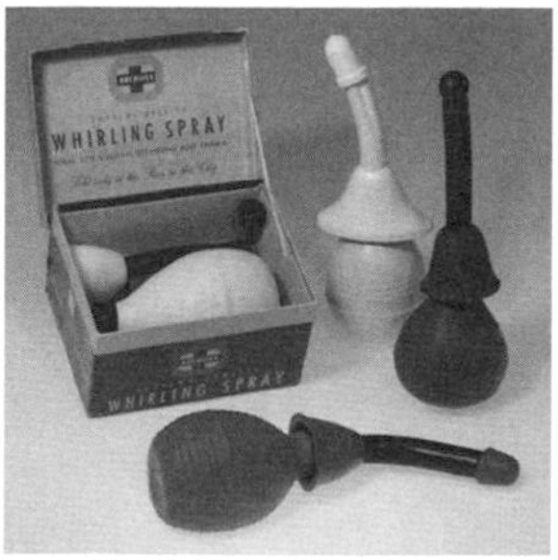
WHIRLING SPRAY

PAGE 35
ANTHONY COMSTOCK (1844 – 1915) was a moral crusader who successfully lobbied an inattentive Congress into passing the so-called "Comstock Laws" of 1873, making it illegal to publish, advertise, mail or transport "lewd and lascivious material," which insanely included information regarding STDs and birth control and even anatomy textbooks. To make matters worse, he was later appointed a "special agent" to the US Postal Service, where he was issued a sidearm that he proudly displayed at all times, while also taking

part in the highly publicized arrests of "pornographers," many of whom were doctors and teachers. He boasted of destroying over fifteen tons of books and of driving at least fifteen people to suicide, all in the name of his "fight for the young."

Sanger was routinely referred to as "the Little Bitch" in Comstock's office's in-house memos. She was his worst nightmare, in almost every way imaginable.

An undercover agent befriended William Sanger, and eventually convinced him to give him copies of Margaret's *Family Limitation*. He also insisted on giving William a "generous donation," something that became routine in future sting operations against Margaret and her cohorts, in order to portray them in court as profiteers.

PAGE 36
Smelling a trap, Sanger didn't return to the US until after her husband was tried and sentenced. Her husband's relatively light sentence, along with a shift in support for her cause among the public, made her conclude that returning was worth the risk.

Although he never wanted a starring role in his wife's cause, William Sanger behaved bravely and admirably throughout his trial, winning widespread admiration in the process. It was his one moment in the spotlight, all while his personal and professional life was unraveling.

Anthony Comstock died from pneumonia shortly after testifying at William Sanger's trial. Both of the Sangers took this as a personal victory of sorts, jokingly claiming that their defiance was what finally did him in. Considering the intense animosity Comstock held for Sanger, that may not have been far from the truth!

PAGE 37
The Sangers enrolled their children in a socialist boarding school in New Jersey with unheated dorms. After Peggy's death, Sanger immediately sent her sons to a more expensive (and more traditional) school.

Goldman's "tough love" speech is actually from a letter she wrote to Sanger a few weeks after Peggy's death.

Peggy's death sent William Sanger spiraling into an even deeper depression. He wound up moving to rural Spain for a few years, living a hermit's life while making paintings that nobody bought. He eventually moved back to NYC, remarried, and had another daughter with his second wife. He worked as an engineer for the city water department until his retirement.

The Sangers' divorce wasn't finalized until 1921, largely due to New York State's tough divorce laws requiring one or both parties to admit to abuse, adultery, and/or neglect, which neither was willing to do. William Sanger also "wanted his name back," yet Margaret was by now well known internationally by the name of Sanger and refused to go back to her maiden name.

The saddest result of their separation and divorce was William Sanger's estrangement from his two sons, whom he didn't see again until they were middle-aged. Apparently he and Margaret couldn't be in the same room without getting into a screaming match, so he must have thought it best for the boys if he kept his distance.

PAGE 38
Exploiting Peggy's death for PR purposes was mostly John Reed's idea, and he also arranged for the haunting publicity portrait of Sanger and her two sons to be taken and distributed. Reed, Goldman and Sanger herself all possessed a remarkable knack for public relations, marketing and fundraising—when needed, that is. One has to wonder what kind of lucrative careers they could have had for themselves if they all weren't such avowed anti-capitalists.

Sanger's dream of starting a multilingual publishing house in Paris with Lorenzo Portet came to a tragic end when he suddenly died from influenza in 1917.

The unavoidably sexual nature of Sanger's lectures made most people squeamish, even amongst her supporters. This remained a problem throughout her public speaking career.

Sanger routinely refused to be fingerprinted, claiming (correctly) that it had nothing to do with the charges against her and was simply meant to serve as an act of public shaming.

PAGE 39
America's first birth control clinic was located at 46 Amboy Street. The building still stands, though it's unmarked, the windows are bricked over, and it appears to be unused.

Sanger and her sister Ethel were greatly assisted by translator FANIA MINDELL, who, like Emma Goldman, was a Jewish immigrant from Lithuania and was very involved in radical causes. Mindell was fluent in both Italian and Yiddish, which were the predominant languages spoken in Brownsville at that time.

Shortly before the raid, an undercover policewoman posing as a patient handed Mindell two dollars and refused the change. Smelling bacon, Mindell pinned the two bills to the wall with a note saying, "This donation made courtesy of the NYC Police Dept."

PAGE 40
Sanger's most virulent critics and enthusiastic tormentors were usually other women—something that never

failed to confound and enrage her. "Don't you have *any idea* what it is I'm trying to do for you?!?" The policewomen who enthusiastically participated in her arrests were also almost always fellow Irish Catholics, which must have made her feel like she was dealing with evil doppelgangers.

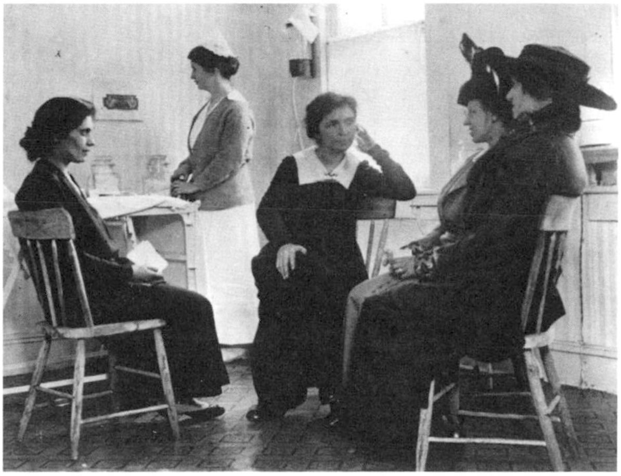

RIGHT: *L – R: Fania Mindell, Ethel Byrne, and Sanger consult with two patients at their Brooklyn clinic, 1916.*

PAGE 41
Upon her arrest, Ethel vowed not to cooperate with her prosecution in any way, refusing a lawyer as well as refusing to speak or eat (and eventually, to drink). She was inspired by the prison hunger strikes of suffragists in the UK, and became the first woman to do so in the US. She also became the first US prisoner to be force-fed, which temporarily made Ethel far more famous than her older sister.

Fania Mindell was ordered to pay a fine rather than serve prison time due to her very poor health. She later successfully sued to have the fine rescinded, as a matter of principle.

JONAH GOLDSTEIN was a highly regarded young attorney (and future judge) who took on Sanger's case gratis. He also became Sanger's lover, and even provided a furnished apartment for her when she came out of prison. Sanger hated feeling like a "kept woman," however, and moved into a cold-water one-room walk-up on West 14th Street soon afterward, where she contentedly remained until she remarried in 1922.

FUN FACT: During the trial, the prosecution claimed not only that the broke Brownsville clinic was a huge "money-making operation," but that its secret aim was *the elimination of the Jewish race*. This ham-fisted attempt at inflaming the jury pool must have come as quite a surprise to Mindell, Goldstein, and Sanger's countless Jewish supporters.

PAGE 42
Sanger gave many informal lectures on the use of contraceptives to her fellow inmates while in prison.

Sanger once saw a group of society matrons taking a tour of the prison. Not recognizing her, they stopped to comment on the deplorable state of her cell, saying they wished there was something they could do to help. At that, Sanger grabbed a filthy towel and threw it at them. "Here! You can wash this!"

PAGE 43
Legally allowing doctors to give contraceptive advice was the first of several legislative victories for Sanger, though in this case it was her and her sister's ordeal that inspired the legislation rather than direct lobbying on her part.

Sanger and Ethel's relationship remained somewhat strained from this point onwards, resulting in Ethel distancing herself from the birth control movement (while simultaneously becoming a lifelong member of the Communist Party, an organization and philosophy that Sanger had a very low opinion of). Ethel also went on to become an anesthesiologist and wound up living in Sanger's Truro summer home to care for their aging father. She entered a long-term relationship with journalist Rob Parker, who also served as a ghostwriter on Sanger's autobiography—a strange arrangement, considering Ethel's resentment of her sister's frequent exploitation of her own prison ordeal.

Sanger's increasingly dismissive attitude toward Emma Goldman is yet another example of her recurring difficulties with other headstrong women, only in this instance the problem seemed to rest entirely at her own feet. Goldman was both a role model for Sanger and a stalwart supporter of her cause. Yet by 1916 the pages of Emma's own *Mother Earth* magazine were filled with letters from Sanger (as well as from her estranged husband William Sanger), making unfounded accusations that Emma was a Johnny-come-lately to the birth control cause, simply riding on her own coattails—all of which Goldman would calmly and correctly refute (Sanger could have *accurately* made the same accusation against Marie Stopes, yet she never did, at least not publicly).

Later, when Emma was arrested and then deported for protesting the draft during WWI, Sanger did next to nothing to defend or support her. And when an ailing and destitute Goldman finally returned to the US years later, Sanger, by then fabulously wealthy, still refused to lend her former cohort a hand, even though she was more than generous with many of her other struggling friends and allies (and yes, Emma did have an overbearing personality, and Sanger had outgrown their student/teacher relationship ages before, but nobody was suggesting she had to *hang out* with her). Perhaps something transpired between these two that no one else knew about, but either way, this was very out-of-character behavior on Sanger's part, and something her biographers still scratch their heads over.

PAGE 44
Sanger put the Cleveland-based socialist and birth control advocate Frederick Blossom in charge of the finances of both her new magazine, *The Birth Control Review,* and her fledgling organization, the American Birth Control League, in 1917 (the ABCL didn't take off for good until 1921). While there's no solid evidence that he defrauded Sanger, his behavior strongly suggests he did—yet the fact the he was a major fundraiser for the Socialist Party would explain why they were so eager to give him a pass.

Complicating things further was the Committee of 100, a group of wealthy and socially prominent supporters of birth control who rallied around Sanger's cause during her trial, and many of whom wished to remain involved with Sanger's efforts afterward. This seems to have created a cultural conflict between Sanger's supporters, with the socialists on the one hand and the socialites on the other.

The Party eventually ruled in Sanger's favor *four years later* (possibly because they were hoping for donations from the newly wealthy Sanger), but by then she was done with the Socialists—and, for the most part, with socialism.

FUN FACT: *Somehow, in the midst of all this madness and activity, Sanger found ~~the time and money to write~~, produce, and star in a full-length silent movie about her life and cause. The film was never shown publicly (the Catholic Church made sure of that), and its only known private screening was for a group of friends—after which all seven reels suddenly disappeared without a trace. Sanger herself never discussed the film or its whereabouts, suggesting that she must not have been happy with the final product. All that remains of its existence is this still photo:*

PAGE 45
Sanger authored six books, not including *What Every Girl Should Know* and *What Every*

Mother Should Know, two collections of her *New York Call* columns.
The others were:

Woman and the New Race (1920)
The Pivot of Civilization (1922)
Happiness in Marriage (1926)
Motherhood in Bondage (1928)
My Fight for Birth Control (1931)
Margaret Sanger: An Autobiography (1938)

The first two books, discussed on this page and on pages 54–55, were both huge bestsellers, earning Sanger quite a bit of money (most of which she reinvested in her organization and newsletter).

Happiness in Marriage, a sex-ed guide for newlyweds, fared less well, largely because many books on this same subject were on the stands by then in the wake of the huge international success of Marie Stopes's *Married Love.* In fact, Sanger's book was considered conservative and tame in comparison.

Motherhood in Bondage is a collection of harrowing letters written to Sanger by desperate women (and some men), accompanied by her own chapter introductions. It also didn't sell very well—probably because it was extremely depressing—though it no doubt served as an effective fundraising tool.

Her last two books were both autobiographies. The latter one outsold the former, most likely due to its warmer, breezier prose style, which in itself was probably the result of more input from the aforementioned ghostwriter, Rob Parker.

Though she was a prolific writer, almost all of Sanger's prose was unadorned and to the point, with only an occasional bit of humor or sarcasm thrown in. She was also hardly the self-reflective type in that she rarely dwelled on the past or second-guessed herself, so all of her autobiographical material existed solely to help promote her cause. Thus, the earnest *My Fight* reads like it was written almost entirely by herself, while *Autobiography* is more personal and anecdotal.

It also has Sanger whitewashing or at least downplaying much of her personal and political past—presumably for pragmatic reasons, but still, it makes one wonder why she decided to go there at all in her last book.

PAGE 46

JULIET RUBLEE was a member of the Committee of 100. Married to a prominent attorney and presidential advisor, she was the "wild child" of the Upper East Side crowd, what with her enthusiasm for radical causes and her multicolored fashion sense. (She also had some wild adventures of her own, including a treasure-hunting expedition off the coast of Italy. She promised her crew a share of the booty, so when no treasure was found they kidnapped her and held her for ransom!) Rublee met Sanger during her Brooklyn clinic trial, and the two of them remained best friends ever after.

JAMES NOAH H. SLEE immigrated to the US from South Africa as a teen, and went on to become a self-made millionaire. All of Sanger's biographical material credits Slee not only as the president of the 3-In-One oil company, but also with founding it and inventing its patented formula. Yet according to 3-In-One's own website the credit for its invention and founding belongs to someone named George W. Cole. Either way, Slee was worth $10 million at the time Sanger met him—$300 million in today's money—and I doubt she cared much *how* he made his dough.

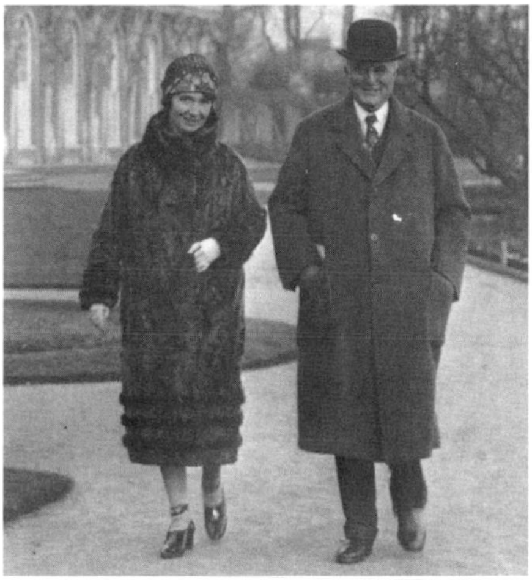

Meanwhile, Sanger was loving everything about the Roaring Twenties: the lighter, looser clothes; the music (she loved to dance, and often improvised her own steps); and especially the more liberated sexual mores. She also loved being single, and was extremely reluctant to surrender that status.

PAGE 47

SHIDZUE KATO (AKA Ishimoto Shizue while still married to the Baron Ishimoto Keikichi) was "the Margaret Sanger of Japan." She later was imprisoned for her birth control advocacy. After WWII she became the first woman elected to the Japanese Diet. A truly remarkable person, and one female leader that Sanger got along with famously (for a change!). Sanger loved the culture and people of Japan, and eventually visited the country a total of six times.

Infanticide was not only a common form of birth control in the most destitute parts of the world—it was often *the* most common.

PAGE 48

Everyone was taken aback by the seemingly one-sided nature of Sanger and Slee's marriage—especially *his* friends, who all thought he'd lost his mind. The union came at other psychic costs as well: it caused an estrangement with Slee's adult children, who (understandably if unfairly) regarded Sanger as a home-wrecker, while her own sons found their new stepdad to be ridiculously strict and conservative (he, in turn, described his stepsons as "feral" when he first met them).

Their marriage, not surprisingly, was a stormy one, though most of the fights were about the huge amount of time she spent traveling. He simply *missed* the dear old gal! Meanwhile, he spent money on her lavishly, and assisted her cause in countless ways. He lost most of his fortune in the crash of '29, which put a huge crimp in their lifestyle—yet they were *still* millionaires, and lived quite comfortably to the end of their days.

LEFT: *Mr. and Mrs. Slee on vacation, circa 1927. Nice mink, Mag!*

PAGES 49 – 50

At this time, the notoriously libidinous H.G. Wells not only had a wife and two sons, but also supported a daughter born to his longtime mistress, the author Amber Reeves. He also had his hands full with countless literary groupies (many of whom were quite insane), and seemed to be loving every minute of it.

Meanwhile, though still a pleasant-looking woman with a carefully maintained waiflike figure (she usually was on one fad diet or another), Sanger was ten to twenty years older than the other women Wells was cavorting with, yet he jumped at every opportunity to be with her. He was plain ol' *crazy* about her, as were many other highly intelligent and accomplished men from that era.

While demure and soft-spoken on the one hand, Sanger could match wits with any of these brainiacs and was able to converse on almost any subject, even sports (the men in her family were all total jocks, including her own sons). She was also very *attentive,* soaking up and retaining everything her man-target had to say—a surefire way to make any fella feel like a million bucks, let alone some egghead who never thought he'd meet a woman who seemed so interested in, say, the warrior rituals of

New Guinea tribesmen. It wasn't an act, either. She *was* interested!

Though they rarely saw each other after this, Sanger and Wells wrote to each other on a regular basis until his death in 1946. In fact, she maintained regular correspondences with almost all of her former lovers right up until the end.

HUGH DE SELINCOURT was a debauched aristocrat and author of several long-out-of-print semi-autobiographical novels detailing his own youthful sexcapades ("The story of an adolescent seduced by his tutor," etc.). His one bestseller was a book about cricket, of all things. He hosted many partner-swapping parties at his massive familial estate, a few of which Sanger herself attended (though she was put off by the jealous tiffs that routinely arose at these gatherings). As with many other former lovers, Sanger kept in constant touch with de Selincourt, who actually served as a reliable and sympathetic sounding board for her.

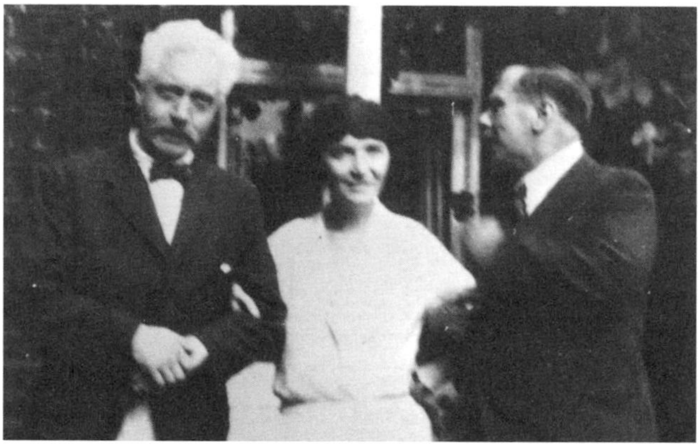

RIGHT: *The only known photo of Sanger and H.G. Wells together, date unknown. Stage actor Otis Skinner is on the left.*

PAGE 51
Sanger was accompanied to Town Hall by both Juliet Rublee and yet another British lover of hers, former MP Harold Cox. He was to give a speech as well. Once again I couldn't find a single photo of him, so I pictured her alone with Rublee instead.

PAGE 52
CARLO TRESCA: An Italian immigrant and longtime leader of the IWW. He fought a long, fruitless battle to keep his union from being infiltrated first by Communists, and later by the Mob (he eventually was killed by the Mafia). The US Government was constantly on his ass as well, the poor guy.

PAGE 53
I paraphrased like crazy from Sanger's Town Hall/Park Theater speech, due to the space restrictions inherent in the use of comic strip panels and word balloons. Still, I did my best to stay true to the thoughts and themes of her famous speech.

PAGES 54 – 55
The Pivot of Civilization is Sanger's best selling and most controversial book. Her critics continue to mine it for evidence of her eugenic thought crimes, yet she spends a large portion of the book criticizing what were then established mainstream eugenic beliefs. Leading eugenicists were equally critical of her and other birth control advocates for their desire to put personal (i.e. female) autonomy over what they considered best for society as a whole (i.e. more white Protestant babies).

The oddest thing about this book from a modern reader's perspective is how Sanger addresses the idea of involuntary sterilization almost as a default position, and then proceeds to raise the problems inherent in that idea. But in 1922, that *was* the default position, at least amongst the intellectuals, academics, and progressives that she was trying so hard to sway. In retrospect, it's hard for us denizens of the twenty-first century to wrap our heads around the fact that they weren't all monsters, either. Instead, they were faced with brand new social problems the likes of which humanity had never dealt with before: exploding population growth, rabid urbanization, and massive waves of immigration—particularly to the US, and from all corners of the globe, cramming people from a wide array of ethnic and cultural backgrounds into the same tight, festering spaces.

All of this lead to increased rates of crime, poverty, and mental illness that overwhelmed major US cities, while placing an enormous financial strain on private charities and government agencies. In the face of all this, the idea of sterilizing violent criminals, drunks, drug addicts, and/or people with mental and physical disabilities seemed like not only a good idea, but the *most humane* one, considering the options available at the time (another popular solution was to *exterminate* some or all of the above). What Sanger was trying to do was *expand* our options, so we wouldn't *have* to resort to such extreme measures.

Interestingly, since we now have more scientifically advanced forms of birth control (thanks largely to Sanger), government agencies impose *temporary* forms of forced sterilization on various wards of the state, such as the "chemical castration" of paroled sex offenders or Norplant devices for "impulsively promiscuous" girls in the foster care system. All things considered, these are not unreasonable solutions—albeit ones that future generations are sure to beat us up over.

PAGE 56
In her biographies, Sanger describes a rather harrowing trip from the train station to the hall where this clandestine meeting was held. The women (and handful of men) involved in her transport were obsessed with maintaining anonymity and secrecy—yet considering the huge popularity and relative social acceptance of the KKK at the time, we have to wonder who and what they were so afraid *of*. No one's ever attempted to answer this, but my own hunch is that the leaders of the Klan would have never approved of a lecture on birth control, both for religious reasons and for maintaining demographic superiority. If that was the case, Sanger's lecture was a risky act of defiance on the part of the people who invited her.

Sanger was invited to speak at other Klan women's meetings, but she was way too freaked out by this one to accept any more offers.

Sanger loved her handy new "gynaplaque," and for the next thirty years took it with her wherever she went.

PAGE 57
JOHN D. ROCKEFELLER JR. wound up donating a lot of money to Sanger's various organizations, both publicly and privately. Sanger also became very close friends with John D.'s wife, the philanthropist and art matron Abby Rockefeller, especially by the late 1930s when they all wintered in Tucson, AZ. Her Arizona posse also included the likes of beauty maven Elizabeth Arden, further illustrating the rarefied social circles Sanger moved in as she got older.

Opening in 1922, the Birth Control Clinical Research Bureau was Sanger's pride and joy, and she soon dedicated most of her efforts toward running it, leaving *The Birth Control Review* and the American Birth Control League largely in the hands of others. It was the research aspect of the BCCRB that was the most important to Sanger. A dearth of reliable data regarding the potential benefits of birth control often left her scrambling for anything that might support her cause, and she even admitted to *making stuff up* at times (in fairness, her opponents also routinely invented their own statistics). The careful screening of information collected at her clinic soon gave her the cold, hard facts she so desperately needed.

After a long struggle trying to find a (preferably female) gynecologist to work with her, Sanger was blessed with the arrival of the highly capable DR. HANNAH STONE. Stone's husband, Abraham, had a successful gynecology practice of his own, thus affording her the ability to work at Sanger's clinic for free. The two women worked well together, and Sanger would be the first to admit that Dr. Stone was the best thing that ever happened to her. Stone died suddenly in 1944, and her husband, by then retired, took her place at the clinic. Sanger and Abraham didn't get along as well, however, since he was far more interested in providing fertility services than in providing contraceptive advice.

PAGE 58
The event described in this scene is 100 percent true. You can't make this stuff up! Though not present herself at the time of this raid, Sanger was enraged that Dr. Stone and other employees had to endure the humiliation of being handcuffed and booked. She and many others were also shocked that the raid even occurred, after six years of the clinic operating openly and with much high-level support. Still, the laws regarding such an establishment were vague and thus easily abused by her enemies.

PAGE 59
Sanger's lobbying committee was chaired by Katharine Houghton Hepburn (mother of the actress Katharine Hepburn), who accompanied Sanger to her many Capitol Hill meetings, including one last big push for a birth control information freedom bill in 1934 (pictured below). Nationally syndicated radio pundit Father Coughlin testified against them at this hearing, declaring, among other things, that condoms were "communistic." Coughlin's paranoid hysterics won the day: the bill went down in defeat.

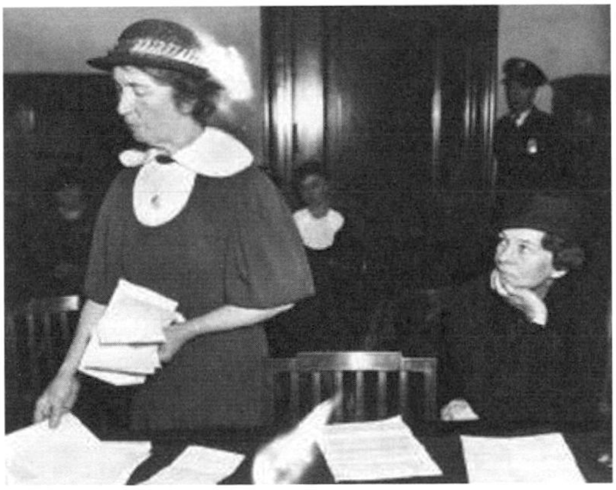

LEFT: *Sanger and Katherine Houghton Hepburn testifying before a congressional committee c. 1934.*

FUN FACT: Both Sanger and Houghton Hepburn grew up in Corning, NY (the Houghtons co-owned the glassware factory). Though the same age, these two women were raised on opposite sides of the tracks, and thus barely knew each other as children. That they wound up working together so closely as adults is yet one more irony in the irony parade that was Sanger's life.

PAGE 60
Sanger won this case in a lower court, but the US Government appealed it and lost again. The three judges on this panel seemingly *couldn't wait* to rule in her favor.

For many years, Sanger illegally imported diaphragms and other contraceptive devices by slipping them into crates of her husband's 3-In-One oil products—with Slee's approval, of course. In fact, it probably was his idea.

PAGE 61
Sanger must have been disgusted, and not merely "disappointed," by Gandhi's self-righteous and unrealistic attitude toward human sexuality, though she bent over backwards to downplay and rationalize it (guessing it had something to do with him learning his father had died while in flagrante or some such Freudian nonsense), simply because she idolized the man in every other respect—including his advocacy for the equal rights of women.

PAGE 62
The woman in the big hat is MRS. F. ROBERTSON JONES, who more or less ran the ABCL after Sanger's resignation. Though the two women shared the same goals—including actively pushing for the legalization of euthanasia, as well as for birth control—they also frequently butted heads (here we go again!), which is a big part of *why* Sanger stepped down as the head of her own organization and severed official ties between the ABCL and her Clinical Research Bureau. But with Sanger's impending retirement, it made sense to everyone to recombine their efforts under one umbrella organization.

Robertson Jones is generally portrayed as a stuffed shirt compared with Sanger in all of the latter's biographies, but then who *wouldn't* come off that way in such a comparison? For one thing, Sanger's freewheeling personal life would be a source of concern and potential scandal for any organization even *today,* let alone eighty years ago. And her lifelong insistence on doing things her own way only became more pronounced as the years went by, alienating even some of her staunch allies. The resistance she was getting on so many fronts is part of why Sanger decided to go into semi-retirement by this time.

PAGE 63
Sanger's Clinical Research Bureau opened a Harlem branch in 1931, but it closed shortly afterward due to many logistical problems. At the urging of NAACP head W.E.B. DUBOIS (pictured on the left in panel one), DR.

DOROTHY FEREBEE (pictured on the right), Abyssinian Church founder Adam Clayton Powell Sr., and black women's civil rights advocate Mary McCloud Bethune (a who's who of 1930s black civil rights leaders, basically), Sanger opened a new Harlem clinic in 1938, which lasted into the early 1940s before succumbing to insurmountable problems, as illustrated here. This clinic is sometimes conflated with a parallel project to disseminate contraceptive information to black communities in the South (both projects were largely funded by businessman and philanthropist Albert Lasker). Sanger was only tangentially involved in this latter project: She refused to personally visit the South in protest of Jim Crow laws, for one thing, which prevented her hands-on involvement. She also wanted to work closely with Southern black clergymen, though those who *were* on the ground claimed (correctly) that they would more likely be the source of resistance due to their susceptibility to genocidal conspiracy theories being actively spread by birth control opponents. However, attempting to work *around* said clergymen only fueled their paranoia. Thus it also came to an end in the usual big racial mess.

Dr. Ferebee didn't actually work at the Harlem clinic, other than in an advisory role, though the clinic was staffed mostly by black doctors and nurses.

The white nurse portrayed on this page was fired by Sanger, in case you were wondering.

PAGE 64
Sanger became an avid watercolorist during her retirement. Her output wasn't very impressive, however, due to her extremely limited drawing abilities.

DAISY MITCHELL worked off and on for Sanger as far back as 1918, when she allegedly "came with" the furnished apartment Sanger's lawyer/lover Jonah Goldstein provided for her. Daisy served as both a housemaid and a caretaker of Sanger's two sons (a rather easy gig, considering the amount of time Sanger spent on the road and the boys spent away at school). Daisy was fiercely loyal to Sanger and her sons but snapped and growled at everyone else, including poor old Slee. Sanger and her sons returned her loyalty (in spite of the fact that she was by all accounts the worst maid in the world), with son Grant taking her in after Sanger died. And she is indeed buried alongside Sanger, at her and Slee's former country estate in Fishkill, NY.

PAGE 65
Noah Slee suffered a debilitating stroke shortly after this scene and remained bedridden for almost a year before passing away in 1943. Rather than hiring full-time nurses, Sanger tended to his needs herself. It's hard to imagine ol' Ramblin' Sanger forgoing travel for such a long stretch, though I guess she felt she owed the guy—which she certainly did!

PAGE 66
Sanger's oldest son, the affable Stuart, was a big man on campus during his undergrad years at Yale: captain of the football team, president of his fraternity, etc. He also liked to party, and constantly hit up his parents for more dough, resulting in endless arguments. After a few years of mucking about, he wound up fulfilling his mother's own thwarted dream of attending Cornell's med school and becoming a doctor (as did his younger brother, Grant—to say Sanger projected herself onto her children would be putting it mildly!).

Sanger first visited the Tucson area with Stuart in 1934 to see if the climate would help her son's chronic asthma. They both fell in love with the area, and Sanger and Slee chose it as their main residence for their retirement years. Soon Stuart (who by then was married and had two daughters) was living right next door, giving him his long-sought-after desire for "quality time" with his mother, which unfortunately also meant having to deal with her intractable stubbornness. He also must have resented the incredible amount of time and attention Sanger showered on his own two daughters.

This is the only period in her life when it was even suggested Sanger had a drinking problem, and that may have been the result of boredom and loneliness. She otherwise always drank moderately. Stuart also eventually weaned his mother off the Demerol.

FUN FACT: One of Stuart's daughters recalled running into her grandma's house early one morning only to discover Sanger and fellow septuagenarians Juliet Rublee and Liz Arden all *standing on their heads* while still in their nightclothes. "It adds color to one's complexion," they informed her.

RIGHT: *Sanger described herself as a non-smoker, though photos from this time suggests she lit up on occasion, TB-ravaged lungs be damned. Though a health nut for the most part, Sanger also took huge risks with her health—especially when it came to traveling in developing nations, which she often undertook against the strenuous objections of her doctors and loved ones.*

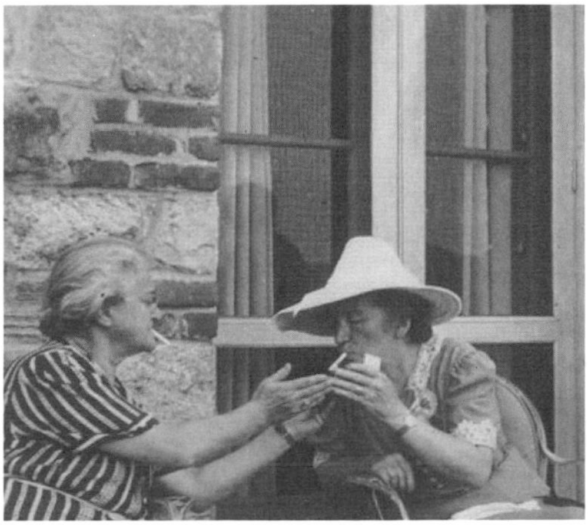

PAGE 67
THE ROSICRUCIAN ORDER is a decentralized, unorthodox, quasi-religious cult that first started among literate Germans in the early 1600s before being violently suppressed by the Church. It was inspired by then-popular tracts promising to reveal "the Mysteries of the Orient," and was—and is—a new-age-y hodgepodge of whatever religious, spiritual or mystical elements might appeal to an individual practitioner.

Rosicrucianism experienced a revival in the late nineteenth century, particularly in Victorian England. It mostly appealed to women, who were mostly drawn to the practice of séances in order to contact deceased loved ones. British friends of Sanger introduced her to it as a way to cope with her young daughter's death in 1915, and she instantly found it comforting and appealing. Though disdainful of established religions, Sanger always was a deeply spiritual person who felt a strong connection to the Great Beyond (her many dreams and premonitions about the fates of close friends and family members tended to be eerily accurate, which only reinforced her rather narcissistic belief that she was a uniquely fine-tuned conduit between here and Out There).

As illustrated on this page, the highly evolved "adult" life Sanger constructed for Peggy reveals the extent to which she projected herself onto her daughter. Even when Peggy was alive, Sanger always described her as if she were describing herself: "willful," "fearless," "a born leader," etc. She clearly had a lot invested in her daughter from a very young age, and had the highest hopes for her.

Twice every year, on both Peggy's birthday and the anniversary of her death, Sanger would shut herself in her room and speak to no one—except, that is, her younger son Grant via telephone. Grant and Peggy were inseparable as children, and he was as haunted and traumatized by his sister's death as his mother was.

Sanger's libido never diminished with age, much to the amazement of her friends (one of Stuart's daughters even jokingly recalled her grandmother being a "nymphomaniac"). This led to some embarrassing situations, however, such as with one of her last known lovers, a landscape painter twenty years her junior. They even (according to her) discussed marriage at one point, but having people constantly ask if she was his *mother* must have got to him, and he soon started to keep his distance. A clueless Sanger didn't get it, though: "Why won't he be seen in public with me?" she'd ask the exasperated Rublee. "I don't understand..."

PAGES 68 – 69

The "Pill Team"

KATHARINE MCCORMICK was the first woman to graduate from MIT with a science degree and was a leader in the women's suffrage movement, becoming the first vice president of the League of Women Voters. Born into a wealthy family herself, Katharine (née Dexter) married into the even wealthier McCormick family (of Harvester Tractor fame). Her husband suffered from schizophrenia (then referred to as "dementia praecox"), of which very little was known at the time. Her search for a way to cure—or at least treat—her husband's condition led to an interest in endocrinology, the study of hormones and their potential medical benefits. This, combined with her dedication to women's rights and birth control, is how she wound up bringing Sanger together with the leading endocrinologists at the time. She wound up paying for most of the research on this project out of her own (admittedly sizable) pocketbook.

LIST NO. 67
TABLETS 50 COMPRIMÉS
SEARLE
Enovid
10 mg.
Each Tablet Contains
norethynodrel... 9.85 mg.
mestranol........0.15 mg.
C-10
G.D. SEARLE & CO.
OF CANADA LTD.
BRAMALEA (BRAMPTON), ONT.

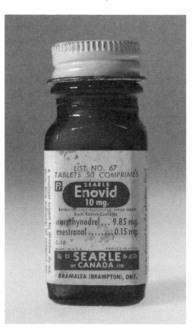

Biologist and researcher DR. GREGORY PINCUS was denied tenure at Harvard when his "fatherless rabbit" made the cover of *Life* magazine in 1937, generating controversy as a result (hormone therapy continues to be a controversial field to this day, what with the high risk of side effects and the overall uneasiness about "playing God" when it comes to reproduction, aging, gender, steroids, etc.). Other stints at other leading universities were also short-lived, so he co-founded his own independent lab in 1944.

Pincus had actually met Sanger earlier through mutual friend Abraham Stone.

Chinese immigrant DR. MIN CHUEH CHANG was Pincus's primary assistant at this time and went on to become a leading figure in his own right in the field of hormone research.

DR. JOHN ROCK was a leading researcher in fertility (he was the first to successfully fertilize a harvested human egg). Though a father of five who attended mass daily, Rock also was very much in favor of birth control—whether that meant helping his patients have more children or fewer of them. Sanger wound up not only admiring Rock but even crushing on him—describing him in one letter to the board of Planned Parenthood as a "Greek God." Someone hose that woman down! Scientists had known of the potential of hormones as a contraceptive as far back as 1921, but this was the first concentrated effort to pursue it as a real and marketable possibility. The FDA approved Enovid (the Pill's first commercial name) in 1957 to help with menstrual disorders only, and it was approved as a contraceptive (after some formula tweaking) in 1960, though was not publicly available until 1961. It was illegal even to married women in some states until *Griswold v. Connecticut* in 1965, and remained illegal in many countries (including Japan) for decades after that.

The Pill was an instant success, though it is not as widely used today as it was in the 1960s and '70s due to continued concerns over its potential long-term side effects, along with an increased preference for both older and newer forms of contraceptives.

PAGE 70

Pictured here with Sanger is her younger and more sensitive son, Grant, who may or may not have accompanied her to the set of *The Mike Wallace Interview*, though he did live in the NYC area. Grant and his wife had six children (much to his mother's chagrin): five boys and, finally, a girl (it's been speculated they kept trying until Grant "replaced" his long-dead sister). Grant seemed to have inherited his biological father's tendency toward depression, which got so bad at one point that he had to give up his practice (which he later resumed) and temporarily stay at a sanatorium.

Sanger's interview with longtime television personality and later *60 Minutes* mainstay MIKE WALLACE is easily accessible on the internet. While she certainly seemed to have all her faculties intact, she was also clearly ill-prepared for Wallace's "gotcha" tactics, and easily thrown off balance as a result—much to the mortification of her old friends, who knew that a younger Sanger would have handed him his head.

PAGE 71

Sanger devoted most of her post-"retirement" efforts to promoting and expanding the International Planned Parenthood Federation and served as its president until 1959, at the age of eighty.

PAGE 72

Margaret Higgins Sanger Slee died of congestive heart failure on September 6, 1966, at the age of 86.

RIGHT: *Sanger and Shidzue Kato at the 5th International Planned Parenthood Conference, Tokyo, 1955.*

The sources of information I relied on the most were first and foremost Sanger's own writings, most of which can be found unabridged on this pro-life website, of all places: http://www.lifedynamics.com/library/#books. I tried not to rely solely on anything from her 1938 autobiography, however, since it was written while she was still actively lobbying congress, and thus is as reliable as any other politician's propagandist campaign literature. While most of its contents are verifiable, she downplays much of her activist past in it ("The Socialists *made* me do it!"), while also including some downright whoppers.

Another great online source is the *Margaret Sanger Papers Project*: http://www.nyu.edu/projects/sanger/index.html. They also have an excellent blog: http://sangerpapers.wordpress.com/

The most helpful biographies, starting with the most recent, were these:

Margaret Sanger: A Life of Passion, by Jean H. Baker (2011, Hill and Wang).

Margaret Sanger: Her Life in Her Words, by Miriam Reed (2003, Barricade Books).

Woman of Valor: Margaret Sanger and the Birth Control Movement in America, by Ellen Chesler (1992, Simon and Schuster).

The Margaret Sanger Story, by Lawrence Lader (1955, Doubleday), long out of print, was also helpful, though its accuracy is somewhat dubious since it was written during Sanger's lifetime and with her heavy involvement.

There are also a few anti-Sanger bios with unambiguous titles like *Killer Angel*, written by raving lunatics in the midst of some theological temper tantrum. They would almost be funny if so many people didn't take them seriously.

Another source to avoid is *Choices of the Heart*, the only film I know of about Sanger, and which in typical Lifetime-channel fashion not only presents her as a martyr and a saint, but unfairly portrays her father and first husband as patriarchal oppressors. In one gratuitously inaccurate scene, Bill Sanger leeringly suggests they practice "free love," while Margaret rolls her eyes in disgust—all of which was the exact opposite of the truth. Like, why even go there?.

Peter Bagge is the Harvey Award-winning author of the acclaimed nineties alternative comic series *Hate*, featuring the semi-autobiographical anti-hero Buddy Bradley (whose adventures have been collected in two volumes: *Buddy Does Seattle* and *Buddy Does Jersey*, both from Fantagraphics). More recently, he has written three graphic novels: *Apocalypse Nerd* (Dark Horse), *Other Lives* (DC/Vertigo), and *Reset* (Dark Horse). Two collections of Bagge's short comic strips have been published: *Everyone is Stupid Except For Me* and *Peter Bagge's Other Stuff* (both from Fantagraphics). A graduate of the School of Visual Arts in New York, he got his start in comics in the R. Crumb-edited magazine *Weirdo*. Bagge lives in Seattle with his wife Joanne, daughter, and two cats.